Poetry Markets
for
Canadians

**The most comprehensive guide to publishing opportunities for
Canadian poets ever assembled.**

Poetry Markets
for
Canadians

SEVENTH EDITION

Edited by Marie Savage

THE MERCURY PRESS
&
THE LEAGUE OF CANADIAN POETS

Toronto

The publishers gratefully acknowledge the financial assistance of the Canada Council for the Arts and the Ontario Arts Council in their ongoing operations.

Cover design & photograph by Orange Griffin
Composition and page design by TASK
Printed and bound in Canada by Metropole Litho

Canadian Cataloguing in Publication Data
The National Library of Canada has catalogued this publication as follows:
Main entry under title:
Poetry markets for Canadians
Biennial.
Continues: Poetry markets in Canada.
Publisher varies.
ISSN 0843-2287
ISBN 1-55128-069-8 (7th ed.)
1. Poetry - Authorship - Periodicals. 2. Publishers and publishing - Canada - Directories. 3. Canadian Periodicals (English) - Directories. I. League of Canadian Poets.
PN155.P6   070.5'2'0971 C89-032442-5

THE MERCURY PRESS
Represented by the Literary Press Group
Distributed by General Distribution Services

ACKNOWLEDGEMENTS

I appreciate the support of League of Canadian Poets' Executive Director, Edita Petrauskaite, of Past-President Linda Rogers and the help of the League of Canadian Poets' staff who made the effort to track down even the most obscure information I requested.

To the many members of the League of Canadian Poets who cheered me on over the months it took to research and compile this book, I thank you. My special thanks to Joe Blades and Stephanie Bolster.

James Deahl, editor of the previous edition of *Poetry Markets for Canadians*, laid an excellent foundation for future editions and continues to support the work of new and established writers.

Thank you to my children, Edward, Graeme and Tatum, who bring to me a passion for language and laughter that makes every day wonderful.

Finally, thank you to my mother and copyeditor, Jean, who, though she believes I can do anything well, doubts me just enough to check my spelling.

CONTENTS

Introduction to the Seventh Edition

This edition of *Poetry Markets for Canadians* is meant to serve well both writers and editors. I encourage you to pursue your publishing goals through a thorough and professional approach to submissions.

Many avenues were explored to provide you with an extensive collection of English-language poetry markets from around the world. Response from publishers was enthusiastic— they want to hear from Canadian writers.

While most of the markets listed have a history of publishing a variety of literary work, some markets are extremely small. *Ellery Queen's Mystery Magazine*, though its circulation is an astounding 500,000 per issue, uses few poems. Those it does use are tempered by both humour and the magazine's subject limits. A caution that will be repeated throughout this book is to KNOW YOUR MARKETS. You've taken a solid step toward this goal by purchasing *Poetry Markets for Canadians*.

Most of the markets listed here have a number of things in common: an interest in Canadian work; at least a two-year publishing record; and in the case of periodicals, a circulation of over 300 per issue. Many expressed interest in considering the work of new writers.

The US Periodicals section in this edition has been broadened to include a wider variety of publishing opportunities. You will also note many new international opportunities. Information on the UK and Ireland was reviewed with the help of Welsh poet, Peter Finch, whose address listing book *Small Presses and Little Magazines of the UK and Ireland* is now in its 14th edition. I am grateful to the writers and editors around the world who responded with speed to my queries.

Read through the information on web publishing carefully. Some e-zines, like the *Alsop Review* (http://alsopreview.com/index.html), are excellent and professionally executed. Others simply offer an opportunity to see your name in "print." As a rule, I do not submit to e-zines which claim they will publish "anything," though you may choose to participate in such ventures.

Copyright and licensing rights are discussed in Chapter One. It is your responsibility to be aware of copyright issues. You should know that e-rights are a contentious issue. It is up to you to get writer's guidelines from publications which interest you and to clarify with editors what rights they are asking for. It is up to you to KNOW THE MARKETS.

Poetry Markets for Canadians is an excellent resource which will help you choose which markets to approach, and offer you basic information on the editors' needs. But take the next logical step: do your best to find a copy of the magazine to which you may submit. Look in your local bookstore, a university or college library or your local public library. If you live near Toronto you can take advantage of the League of Canadian Poets' on-site library. Don't be satisfied with a single issue more than a year old. Look through several recent issues to get a clear picture of the magazine's needs. If you are researching book publishers, request a copy of their current catalogue. Be resourceful in your search for information.

Print magazines, e-zines and book publishers may offer on their websites writer's guidelines, a company history, editor's bio as well as excerpts of recently published works. Many book publishers have their catalogues online. Take advantage of this. If you do not have internet access, it may be available free through your local library.

HTML and Java script have led some poets to stretch themselves in new directions. In recognition of this, the Newfoundland and Labrador Arts Council leads the way in providing a new series of grants, under the NewTel-Arts Council Cultural Innovation Fund, which support the expanding role of technology in the arts.

All publications have a clear interest in Canadian poetry submissions. In some cases, publications or publishers with a particularly narrow editorial slant appeal to my personal interests (*Spitball: The Literary Baseball Magazine*) while others are included to illustrate the complexity of the poetry market place.

Following in the lead of previous editions, this 7th edition of *Poetry Markets for Canadians* covers only English-language or bilingual markets.

Marie Savage
Editor
oraccoon@coastnet.com

ABOUT THE LISTINGS

Completed surveys were returned by every periodical or book publisher listed in this edition. Expanded definitions are provided below to help you clearly understand their responses.

PERIODICAL LISTINGS:

1. Each listing begins with the name of the publisher or publication.

2. Mailing address.

3. Telephone number and fax number. In some cases, the editor requested these numbers NOT be published. NEVER fax work to an editor without prior permission.

4. Editor's name. Where the poetry editor and the main editor are the same person, their name appears only once as "editor."

5. E-mail address. A caution must go out to all readers who intend to submit work via e-mail: many editors have been deluged with unsolicited submissions via e-mail and for that reason have chosen not to list their e-mail addresses. Read a publication's online information carefully BEFORE contacting the editor. Readers should be aware that e-mail addresses can change without notice.

6. Website address. Again, this may change. A brief discussion of how to find a website address or deal with a dead link is found in Chapter Three: Publishing Online.

7. Since. This is the year the publication started publishing. Where a publication stopped and then restarted or began web publishing in addition to print publication, I have used the earliest date.

8. Format. Some publications are available both in print and online. Others may have an online "presence" offering sample work from back issues, etc., without actually having a full online publication. Where the format is listed as Paper/Web, the publication appears regularly in full, both in print and online.

9. Circ. The circulation of any publication varies from issue to issue. I made no effort to differentiate between print-run and actual circulation. These figures are meant as guidelines only.

10. Sample. The cost of a sample copy is generally that of a current issue. Often publications will offer recent back copies at reduced rates. Inquiries should be

made directly to the magazine. All samples and subscriptions for US periodicals should be ordered using US funds unless otherwise noted.

11. Time. This is the average response time from the moment your submission is received to the time you receive a response. This does not include the length of time to actual publication as this varies too widely to report with accuracy. Once your work is accepted, ask when it might appear.

12. Money. All editors were asked if they pay for accepted work. Most who do, pay only on publication. Few offer more than a few dollars per poem.

13. Copies. All writers should receive at least one free copy of any magazine in which their work appears. Many publications offer two or more copies and may offer a special discounted rate if you wish to purchase additional copies of the issue in which your work appears.

14. Subscription. The subscription rates listed here are for one-year individual subscriptions. Some publications have graduated subscription rates for students, seniors and institutions and other rates for foreign or multi-year subscriptions. If these interest you, please contact the publication directly.

15. Authors published. Obviously, we could not list every author published by each magazine or publishing house, nor was there a need to do so. Names which have been provided by the editors are meant to help you get a sense of the kind of work the editors prefer.

16. Associated with a press. This helps you get a better understanding of the scope of work associated with the magazine. It may also provide another publishing opportunity.

17. Send poems. Each editor has a personal preference for how many poems they prefer to receive in any one batch. Most magazine editors prefer three or more to give them a sense of the writer's abilities. Some have stated "any number." Use common sense here and do not send more than ten. Where a limit online length has been stated, respect it.

18. Rights requested. The most common request for rights is "first North American serial rights." However, unless an editor stated their request in those exact words, I did not assume that is what they meant by "first rights," or any of the other versions of same. What is stated in the listings is what was provided by the respective editors. It is up to you to clarify what the editor is really asking for. (An explanation of copyright, licensing rights and e-rights follows in the next section.)

19. Accepts simultaneous submissions if so noted. If you offer material to two or more publications at the same time you MUST advise them of this. Not all publications accept simultaneous submissions and those that do will want to be informed immediately if you sell the piece elsewhere.

20. E-mail submissions. That an editor has agreed to list their e-mail address does NOT imply that you may e-mail them a submission. Check the listing carefully. Check the website if you are unsure. Many editors are accepting e-mail submissions but use your common sense and do not send 45 pages of material.

21. Number of submissions used. Obviously, this number will change from year to year. It will also change with any editorial change or focus. Some magazines listed in the last edition of *Poetry Markets for Canadians* no longer use poetry at all; others have increased their poetry content. Few magazines have a formal tracking system so all numbers can be interpreted as approximations. However, the ratio of rejected to accepted is still good information as you consider where to submit your work.

22. Unless otherwise noted, editors receive and consider work year-round.

23. Do they comment on rejections. Do not be disappointed if you receive a rejection which does not offer any comment. Many editorial positions are voluntary and undertaken in addition to full-time employment elsewhere. Any comment, barring those that may be obnoxious, is a useful learning tool.

24. Please do not send... Editors have been very clear about what they do NOT want you to submit to them. Respect this. Every editor was asked if in addition to poetry they would also be interested in book reviews, translations, fiction, artwork or photography. Most had some interest in at least one of these.

25. Book Reviews. Book reviews are generally sought of new releases, that is, not more than one year old. Book reviews are time-consuming and pay poorly. Review the work of an author with whom you are very familiar and whose book you had intended to buy for yourself in any case. Rare are the instances of receiving a free review copy unless you have established such an arrangement with the magazine.

26. Translations. You MUST have the permission of the original author before offering a translation of their work for publication. Editors will expect you to provide a copy of this permission and a copy of the original version of the work, along with a copy of your translation. Do not attempt translation work unless you have a good understanding of the nuances of the language of the original as well as a strong perspective to bring to the piece.

27. Fiction. Some editors have indicated a word-length limit. Others have not. Where no word-length has been provided, you might assume 2,500 words is a good average. Make the effort to obtain complete writer's guidelines to better target your work.

28. Artwork and photography. It would be unusual to find a writer who is equally dedicated to producing quality artwork or photography. If this is not your forte, it is best left to those who create it with passion. Nonetheless, it may be that you have created a striking image and wish to have it considered for publication. Never send original artwork or photography for consideration unless it is specifically requested by the editor. Many editors will request either excellent photocopies or slides of your work.

29. Theme issues. These come about in two ways. Often there is a series of planned theme issues. Information about these can be found at the back of the magazine or on online writers' bulletin boards. The second way they come about is by the serendipitous gathering of like material over time on the editor's desk. The first you can target your work toward; the second is beyond your control.

30. Writing contests. Many publications run writing contests. Some specify a specific theme. Others, like the League of Canadian Poets' "National Poetry Contest," are open to quality poetry of any form, style or content. Be aware that publicity posters are meant to generate interest in a contest and may not provide complete rules. Always request the complete rules from the contest organizers. Fortunately, many contests now list their rules online. (More information on how to enter poetry contests can be found in Chapter Six.)

BOOK LISTINGS:

1. Each listing begins with the name of the publisher or publication.

2. Mailing address.

3. Telephone number and fax number. In some cases, the editor requested these numbers not be published. NEVER fax work to an editor without prior permission.

4. Editor's name. Where the poetry editor and the main editor are the same person, their name appears only once as "editor."

5. E-mail address. Never submit a manuscript-length submission by e-mail unless the publisher's guidelines specifically state such submissions are welcome. Readers should be aware that e-mail addresses can change without notice.

6. Website address. Again, this may change. A brief discussion of how to find a website address or deal with a dead link is found in Chapter Three: Publishing Online.

7. Since. This is the year the publisher opened for business. Where a publisher closed and then restarted I have used the earliest date.

8. Average length of books. This will vary widely depending on the type of book being published. It is a guideline only.

9. Initial press run. These figures are meant as guidelines only and may vary widely from project to project.

10. TWUC contract. Refers to The Writers' Union of Canada standard contract. Useful as a guide to what to expect from a contract, it can be ordered as part of "The Writers' Union of Canada Contracts Self-Help Package." Information on this can be found in section 5.3, "Building Your Writer's Bookshelf."

11. Royalties. Again, this is only a guideline and the most common response was ten per cent. You need to know if that ten per cent is of gross or net. It is your responsibility as a writer to learn as much as you can about contract terminology and negotiation.

12. How many poetry titles per year. Again, this can only be a guideline as a publisher cannot guess how many manuscripts may be offered which are both excellent and appropriate to their house. However, if a publisher expects to publish only one poetry title per year, you can surmise that the competition may be fierce for that one spot.

13. Interested in publishing other material. Most publishing houses publish much more than just poetry. A brief listing of these opportunities is included for each publisher. Ask for their writers' guidelines and catalogue to better understand their focus and preferences.

14. Many publishers will accept unsolicited manuscripts. However, where possible, initiate contact by querying first. If an editor is interested in seeing more of your work she will ask you to submit a full manuscript. This is not a guarantee of publication but is much better than sitting in a slush pile waiting to be discovered.

15. Response time. As you can appreciate, it takes longer to work through full-length manuscripts than it does to read a few poems. Responses can take many months and even up to a year. In some houses, the manuscript must pass through several editorial levels before being approved for negotiation. Be patient if you really believe you've sent your work to the right publisher(s).

Be aware that most publishers prefer NOT to receive simultaneous submissions due to the amount of time which may be invested in considering your work. If you do offer material to two or more publications at the same time you MUST advise them of this in your cover letter. Editors MUST also to be informed immediately if the work is accepted elsewhere.

16. Chapbooks or full-length manuscripts. Canadian publishers often publish smaller collections of poetry in chapbooks. This is an excellent place to start for any writer, and many well-known writers continue to publish in chapbook form. Most publishers specialize in one form or the other but some do both.

I'll say it again— KNOW YOUR MARKETS.

Website and e-mail information is current at the time of writing. Many publishers plan to develop websites in either 1999 or 2000. Look for them.

THE LEAGUE OF CANADIAN POETS

The League of Canadian Poets (LCP) is a Registered National Arts Service Organization, recognized by all levels of government, and receiving government funding. Founded in 1966 by Raymond Souster, Ralph Gustafson, Ronald G. Everson, Louis Dudek, and Michael Gnarowski the League actively promotes the work of Canadian poets through its many innovative programs.

From the original five, membership has grown to over 450 Canadian poets located across Canada and around the world. The LCP offers a number of different memberships. Full membership is for poets who have published at least one trade book or two chapbooks, or produced poetry tapes, videos or CDs. The annual dues are $175. Associate membership is for those who write poetry and have publishing credits or who do public readings regularly but have not yet met the requirements for full membership. The annual dues are $60. Student membership is for high school or post-secondary students with an interest in writing poetry. The annual dues are $30. Annual dues are $100 for supporting members like publishers, booksellers, librarians, teachers, and other poetry lovers.

Brief descriptions of the League of Canadian Poets' many programs follow. For more detailed information contact:

> **The League of Canadian Poets**
> **54 Wolseley Street, Suite 204**
> **Toronto, Ontario M5T 1A5**
> **Telephone: (416) 504-1657**
> **Fax: (416) 504-0096**
> **E-mail: league@ican.net**
> **Website: www.poets.ca**

LCP SERVICES AND BENEFITS

NEWSLETTER/MUSELETTER

The LCP newsletter, published bimonthly, is sent to all members. Non-members may subscribe for $30 + GST. It contains news of poetry events, calls for submissions, market information, and members' activities.

The Museletter is the LCP's popular newsletter insert. Published irregularly, it contains poems and essays on various aspects of the craft of poetry. Often included are papers presented to the Annual General Meeting.

PUTTING THE SPOTLIGHT ON POETRY

The LCP website, active since 1996 and updated regularly, offers a sampling of members' work as well as the opportunity to send a poetry postcard to a friend. Of special note are the links to various writers' groups as well as a number of national and provincial government resources. (Chapter Five also has information about Government Resources.)

The LCP works to increase awareness and sales of Canadian poetry books. Twice a year 10,000 flyers are sent to libraries, schools, universities, booksellers, interested individuals, other arts organizations, government departments, and Canadian cultural centres abroad. Each flyer features poetry books by members and poetry books that have won major Canadian poetry awards.

The LCP's Poetry Spoken Here network links poetry-friendly bookstores, media and reading venues which carry books from the direct mail flyers and/or promote readings from the Poetry Spoken Here bimonthly calendar of public readings by members across the country. To help promote awareness of poetry in your own community, clear Poetry Spoken Here stickers appropriate for applying to a window surface are available from the LCP for $2 each plus shipping.

The LCP actively promotes and sells members' books at many book festivals and displays across Canada.

PUBLIC READINGS PROGRAM

In cooperation with the Canada Council, The Ontario Arts Council, and the Toronto Arts Council, the LCP organizes hundreds of readings across Canada each year. The variety of reading venues is highlighted in Chapter Four and more venues are opening each year as the surge of renewed interest in poetry grows. To find readings in your area consult the Poetry Spoken Here flyers or the arts section of your local paper.

EDUCATIONAL WORKSHOPS AND SEMINARS

Individual members of the League can be found leading workshops held across Canada at educational institutions, writers' workshops, and writers' retreats. Each year during the LCP Annual General Meeting (AGM) a number of workshops are open to the public. These offer an excellent opportunity to spend time with other writers, as members of the LCP address the concerns of Canadian poets. Held in late spring, the AGM takes place in a different city each year.

POETS IN THE SCHOOLS

In cooperation with the Ontario Arts council, the LCP offers a unique opportunity for Ontario students to meet, hear and talk with published Canadian poets. Through the Poets in the Schools program, poets visit classrooms to read from their work, conduct creative writing workshops, talk about the craft of writing poetry, and discuss related topics. These contacts inspire students and teachers alike to wrestle with the many issues of poetics.

ADMINISTRATION OF LITERARY PRIZES

Each year the LCP sponsors two literary prizes. The Pat Lowther Memorial Award is given for the finest book of poetry by a Canadian woman and published in the preceding year. The award carries a $1,000 prize. The Gerald Lampert Memorial Award is given for the finest first book of poems published by any Canadian in the preceding year. The award carries a prize of $1,000. Winners are announced at the AGM.

POETRY CONTESTS SPONSORED BY THE LCP

The LCP runs the National Poetry Contest annually with cash prizes of $1,000, $750, and $500. The LCP and a literary press publish an anthology, *Vintage*, of the best 50 poems entered in the contest. Sold at bookstores across Canada, *Vintage* highlights diverse writers and styles and for many is the starting point of their careers.

Begun in 1998, the annual Canadian Youth Poetry Competition offers youth in two categories (Junior and Senior) the opportunity to receive prizes of $500, $350, and $250 as well publication in *Vintage*.

The Canadian Poetry Chapbook Competition is the largest competition of its kind in Canada. The first-prize winner is published by the League of Canadian Poets and receives $1,000 plus 10 printed and bound copies.

POETS ABROAD

With the assistance of the Department of Foreign Affairs and the Canada Council, the LCP has sent its members to the UK, China, France, Finland, Mexico, Italy, Chile, Germany, Cuba and many other countries to share their work and to promote cultural exchange. The LCP also organizes poetry book exhibitions abroad, such as the one at Canada House, London, England in June 1999.

PUBLISHING OF EDUCATIONAL MATERIALS

Beyond publishing *Poetry Markets for Canadians*, the LCP publishes a variety of material of use to the literary and educational communities, including *Who's Who in the League of Canadian Poets*, which contains biographical and bibliographical information for easy reference. A separate publication is *Poets in the Classroom* (Pembroke Press, 1995) a guide to the teaching of poetry. Either can be easily ordered through the LCP website.

The Living Archive Series is a project of the Feminist Caucus of the League. Since 1986, the LCP has published in chapbook form papers presented at the LCP's AGM. They include some of the most important documents of feminist thought about poetry in Canada. *Siolence*, edited by Susan McMaster (Quarry Press, 1998) is the first anthology of these essays.

LITERARY ARCHIVES

The LCP has produced a sound archive of readings by senior members, an important step in preserving our cultural heritage. The LCP also maintains a comprehensive library including books by LCP members and a variety of literary magazines. Members of the public are welcome to make an appointment to conduct research at the LCP offices but please note that all materials must remain onsite. LCP papers from before 1985 are held in the National Archives in Ottawa.

ADVOCACY

The LCP represents the interests of Canadian poets to government and other bodies. The LCP is an active member of the Canadian Conference of the Arts, and the Book and Periodical Council (which serves all parties involved in Canadian publishing and deals with issues affecting literature such as copyright, censorship, public lending right, reprography, taxation and literacy). The LCP is also a member of The Electronic Rights Licensing Agency (TERLA) a body brought together by the need to develop guidelines regarding the use of a writer's work in either a primary or secondary electronic form. The League also supports members with issues involving contracts and grievances, copyright, and freedom of expression.

ONE: GETTING PUBLISHED IN PERIODICALS

Today, poetry can be found backlit on street cars and buses in major cities, in commercials run by international companies and crackling out to audiences at open-mike sessions around the world. The variety of opportunities for poets is overwhelming.

Before you decide to submit your work for consideration ask yourself if you've done your job. Have you spent some time learning the craft? Exposed yourself to as many poetry influences as you can? Worked your poems through several drafts? Do you KNOW YOUR MARKET? If so, then you're ready to take the next step and do the work necessary to present your work professionally.

One note before you prepare your work for submission: you must accept that all writers, regardless of their level of experience, receive rejections. Editors receive thousands of submissions from which to choose. However, a submission from someone who has put the time into getting to KNOW THE MARKET and has presented their work in a professional manner will be a welcome reprieve from the crush of inappropriate and poor submissions editors wade through each year. It is in your best interest to follow the guidelines below.

1.1 HOW TO SUBMIT POETRY TO MAGAZINES

1. Start with letter-size white paper and a common font like Times Roman. Avoid unusual fonts. Choose three to six poems which are appropriate to the target market. Print each onto a separate sheet of paper. Include your name and address at the top right hand corner of each. In the case of multi-page poems, number the pages consecutively and include an identifying word from the title beside the page number (i.e. for a poem entitled "Scarlett Feathers" the second page would have Scarlett/p.2 two lines under your name and address).

2. Editors receive many long, anecdotal letters from new writers eager to describe their inspiration. These are unnecessary. Avoid them. Instead, include a short covering letter offering a brief biography of yourself along with two or three selected publishing credits if you have any to offer. Remember to thank the editor for her time.

3. You can assume your submission implies that you accept the licensing of rights as outlined in a publication's writer's guidelines (i.e. first Canadian serial rights). If this is not your intent, indicate this in your cover letter.

4. With respect to e-mail submissions: NEVER e-mail a submission unless a publication's guidelines state that e-mail submissions are welcomed. An editor's e-mail address listed in a market book does NOT imply that e-mail submissions are welcome. However, the editor may be willing to e-mail writer's guidelines to you upon request. Where the website is also listed, take the time to check what information is posted there BEFORE sending questions to a busy editor. A further note about e-mail etiquette: do not use an editor's first name, exclamation points or smiley faces. An e-mail submission is business correspondence.

5. Submissions sent by e-mail should be pasted into the body of the message. Attachments can cause headaches for everyone. If you save your work as a text file before pasting it in, translation glitches will be prevented. For more information on e-mail submissions and e-zines see Chapter Three: Publishing Online.

6. The most important thing to include with your work is a self-addressed stamped envelope (SASE). If you don't include one, you may not get your work back or receive an answer. Foreign editors CANNOT use Canadian stamps so when you submit out-of-country you MUST send International Reply Coupons (IRCs).

When deciding how many IRCs to send you should recognize that although a single IRC will cost you upwards of $3.50 (Can.), an editor can exchange it for only ONE regular stamp. It's up to you to figure out how many IRCs to include to allow sufficient postage for the return of your work. If in doubt, ask the staff at your local Canada Post outlet for help or call the national Canada Post customer service number 1-800-267-1177.

Acquiring US stamps is a chronic problem for Canadian writers. Few people realize you can order US stamps through the Canadian Philatelic Centre in Nova Scotia. Stamps available there are often in odd denominations; for instance only sheets of 32¢ stamps might be available. Still, using two 32¢ stamps on an SASE is much cheaper than purchasing two IRCs. The telephone number for the Canadian Philatelic Centre is 1-800-565-4362.

7. Before you seal the envelope you should proofread your work and reprint it, if there are errors. There is no excuse for sending in work smeared with white-out.

8. NEVER send originals and NEVER illustrate your poems unless visual poetry is your aim.

9. Advise the editor if the poems you submit have also been sent to other editors for consideration. This is called a "multiple" or "simultaneous" submission. If your work gets accepted at another publication, IMMEDIATELY notify all editors who have the same poem under consideration.

10. Keep track of what you've sent out. As I keep most of my work on disk, I find it easier to keep a running commentary across the top of each poem. I type in the date the poem was sent out, which other poems I sent with it, who I sent them to, what return date I expected (generally 3-6 months later) and finally the result. To print the poem, I copy it to another page temporarily.

Other writers have their own methods. Some use a series of notebooks or cards to keep track of what's out, some don't bother to keep track at all. While I won't recommend the latter, you'll have to decide for yourself what works best for you.

Now that you've sent out your work, what can you expect? A long wait. Few publications have the manpower to respond quickly to the volume of mail they receive. Often, submissions are collected then culled through in batches. The average reply time falls somewhere between three and six months but it can take longer. Some editors have listed an approximate time frame; others could only reply "varies." It's not unreasonable to want to follow up your query; however, you should wait at least three months before doing so.

Though most editors do not comment on rejections, if you do receive commentary take the time to evaluate it. After all, you chose that particular market and you may want to submit more work in the future. An editor's comments can help both improve your work and help you decide whether or not that market is appropriate to your work.

If you're looking for instant glory and healthy remuneration you won't find it publishing poetry. Payment is often "on publication" which may come months after acceptance. Payment can range from a minimum of one copy of the issue in which your work appears, to a small honorarium or even a rarely seen $100 or more. Before you send your work, KNOW YOUR MARKET.

1.2 CHOOSING WHERE TO START

A writing coach once said "Start at the top. What do you have to lose?" And to a point, I agree. But it doesn't hurt to work on smaller goals simultaneously. Become involved in your writing community, go to readings, volunteer to help with literary events, attend classes, participate in workshops, poke around on the internet until you find a newsgroup that suits your interests, and take the opportunities that may come your way to contribute to group efforts like anthologies. (Information on writing groups, creative writing programs, and resources for writers appears in Chapter Five.) Every effort you make will inform your understanding of poetry or the publishing business. If, in the meanwhile, you're also submitting work to top notch publications like *ARC*, more power to you.

1.3 COPYRIGHT

The advent of web publications has made rights vs. copyright a murky topic. We'll begin with the basics before tackling the more contentious e-rights issues.

COPYRIGHT

Copyright is, in the simplest terms, ownership of your work. You cannot copyright ideas but you can copyright how those ideas are expressed. Copyright allows you the sole right to control the reproduction and distribution of your work in any and all forms. When you grant a publisher the "right" to publish your work you do not "sell" the work itself, you license its use. Copyright remains yours until your death and remains with your heirs or estate for fifty years afterward. At that point your work enters the public domain.

In Canada, all written work is deemed copyright as soon as it is written. However, a simple way to protect your copyright is to mail yourself a copy of your work by registered mail. Do not open the envelope. File it away with the dated receipt to have it available as evidence should you ever need to prove copyright.

Understand that if you sell the copyright you lose control over your own work. KNOW YOUR MARKETS. Be sure you understand any agreement made with a publisher.

1.4 THE LICENSING OF RIGHTS

ONE-TIME RIGHTS

In this case the publisher wants permission to publish your work one time only. This is a very specific request, (i.e. The ABC Association requests the right to print all or a portion of one of your poems in their company newsletter). Granting one-time rights does not prevent you from licensing other rights, other than if applicable, first-time rights, with regard to the same work.

FIRST SERIAL RIGHTS

The publisher buys the right to be the first to publish your work in a periodical within a specific geographical area. Many publications are distributed in both Canada and the US so the most common request by editors is for first North American serial rights.

SECOND SERIAL RIGHTS

Some publications publish work that has been previously published. In this case, second serial rights, or reprint rights as they are also known, apply. (When you submit work for consideration ALWAYS disclose the publication history of the work.)

FIRST ANTHOLOGY RIGHTS

A number of publications choose to publish anthologies of selected poems previously published in their respective magazines. The editor may ask for these rights at the same time she offers to publish your poem in the magazine or may contact you at some later date to negotiate for this right separately. Being published in an anthology can be an attractive credit and potentially allow more readers to get to know your work.

ALL RIGHTS

If a benefit is to be accrued from your work, it should belong to you. Be very careful when you consider signing away all rights to your work. All rights would now include e-rights, as well as other media like CD ROM or performance rights. Ask questions— KNOW YOUR MARKETS— and avoid signing away all rights.

PERMISSIONS

This generally refers to a request by a publisher to reprint one or more of your poems in a book or anthology. It applies only to the book for which it is granted. Ask if your work will be offered in any other fashion, and negotiate separate terms for this. The least you should expect to receive for the reprinting of your work is a copy of the anthology. Permission fees tend to be negotiable; however, anthologies tend to be expensive undertakings for the publisher so the payment may be small. You must weigh the benefit of having your work included against the potential income of the piece. The anthology fees may be negotiated with either the author or the publisher, depending on where the poem was first published and what rights you granted the original publisher. Your contract should state the title of the work for which your poem has been selected, the estimated press run of the anthology or textbook, and a projected publication date. You may want to include in your contract that a further payment of X amount would be payable should the anthology or textbook publish a second edition.

ELECTRONIC RIGHTS (E-RIGHTS)

You may want to offer first rights within a certain geographic area but the global nature of the internet somewhat negates the attractiveness of this to the publisher.

You may be asked for first worldwide rights.

E-rights should be limited in both scope and time (i.e. "Ode to An Orange" will be posted on the "Plush Poetry" website from April 1, 1999 until March 31, 2000). At that point the electronic rights revert to you and you can sell the work again elsewhere.

Secondary e-rights are the rights we should all be concerned about. Some print magazines are claiming that when they purchase first rights to a work, and then include that work in an online version of their magazine they are not "reprinting the work" but using it for the SAME original purpose for which the writer sold the rights. Writers tend to disagree and there has been an explosion of interest in intellectual property rights. To understand the complexity of e-rights, Canadians writers should contact The Electronic Rights Licensing Agency (TERLA).

When selling your work to a foreign publisher, be wary of whose copyright law will govern your work.

To learn more about copyright issues in Canada and abroad I recommend you join a writers' organization (information on many can be found in Chapter Five) and consult the list of resources below.

Lesley Ellen Harris, a Canadian lawyer specializing in intellectual property, has written two excellent books, *Canadian Copyright Law* (3rd edition, 1997) and *Digital Property: Currency of the 21st Century* (1998). Both are published by McGraw-Hill Ryerson.

1.5 COPYRIGHT INFORMATION RESOURCES

Copyright Policy & Economic Planning
Department of Canadian Heritage
15 Eddy Street, 4th Floor, Hull, Québec K1A 0M5
Telephone: (819) 997-5539 Fax: (819) 997-5685
E-mail: cp_pda@pch.gc.ca
Website: www.pch.gc.ca/culture/cult_ind/copyco_e.htm

Canadian Intellectual Property Office
Industry Canada
50 Victoria Street, Place du Portage, Phase I, Hull, Québec K1A 0C9
E-mail: cipo.contact@ic.gc.ca
Website: cipo.gc.ca

CanCopy: Canadian Reprography Rights
1 Yonge Street, Suite 1900, Toronto, Ontario M5E 1E5
Telephone: (416) 868-1620 or 1-800-893-5777 Fax: (416) 868-1621
E-mail: admin@cancopy.com
Website: cancopy.com

The Electronic Rights Licensing Agency (TERLA)

1 Yonge Street, Suite 1900, Toronto, Ontario M5E 1E5
Telephone: (416) 868-0200 or 1-877-557-4616 Fax: (416) 868-0296
E-mail: rlabossiere@interlog.com
Website: cancopy.com

Copyright Office, Library of Congress

101 Independence Avenue South East, Washington, D.C., USA 20559-6000
Website: lcweb.loc.gov/copyright

The Patent Office in the UK

Website: www.patent.gov.uk/dpolicy/index.html

1.6 CANADIAN PERIODICAL LISTINGS

The listings which follow are an exciting collection of literary ventures which openly welcome you to submit your best work. For specific details on how to submit your work professionally, see the previous section.

Remember, you MUST include a self-addressed stamped envelope (SASE) with every submission if you expect to receive a reply. If you need to follow up your query or submission, it is best to do so by mail detailing the date you submitted your work and listing the titles of each poem submitted. Most publications will respond within the time frame stated.

Congratulations: if you've done your part, sooner or later one of those responses will be an acceptance letter.

Afterthoughts

1100 Commissioners Road East, PO Box 41040, London, Ontario N5Z 4Z7
Editor: Andreas Gripp
Telephone: (519) 474-2409

Since: 1994	Format: Paper	Circ: 500	Sample: $5 with SASE
Time: 1 month	Money: No	Copies: 1	Sub: $16

Authors published: Beryl Baigent, Katherine L. Gordon, Stan Rogal & Lea Littlewolfe.
Associated with Harmonia Press. Send 5–7 poems, up to 3 pages each. Requests first global and reprint rights. Accepts simultaneous submissions. Do not send rhyme, poems about nothing, or boring subject matter. Writers should purchase a sample copy to see what themes are preferred. Occasionally comments on rejections. May use up to 150 of the 1,000 submissions received each year. Interested in 4" x 6" artwork. Query regarding book reviews or translations.

Alias

145 Queen Street East, Toronto, Ontario M5A 1S1
Editor: Cliff Kennedy
Telephone: (416) 364-3171 Ext. 332
E-mail: towndown@hotmail.com

Since: 1993	Format: Paper	Circ: 500	Sample: SASE
Time: 3 Weeks	Money: No	Copies: 1	Sub: Donation

Send 5–6 poems for consideration. Accepts simultaneous submissions. Publishes fiction

and articles up to 1,500 words. Include SASE for response. "*Alias* is published every second month by a collective of low-income community members at Fred Victor Centre, a social agency in downtown Toronto for over 100 years. We reserve the right to refuse any submissions that may be hurtful or offensive to others."

The Amethyst Review

23 Riverside Avenue, Truro, Nova Scotia B2N 4G2

Editors: Penny L. Ferguson & Lenora Steele

Telephone: (902) 895-1345

E-mail: amethyst@col.auracom.com

Website: www.col.auracom.com/~amethyst

Since: 1993	Format: Paper	Circ: Up to 200	Sample: $6
Time: 1-6 months	Money: No	Copies: 1	Sub: $12

Authors published: Liliane Welch, John B. Lee & M. Travis Lane.

Send up to 5 poems with a maximum of 200 lines each. Requests first North American print rights though sometimes requests permission to display selected poems on website. Author receives 1 extra copy as payment. Does NOT accept book reviews, simultaneous submissions or e-mail submissions. Uses 50-80 of the more than 300 poems received each year. Short stories up to 5,000 words considered. "Send only quality contemporary poetry and prose." Black ink artwork considered. No longer responding to submissions without correct postage. Details of annual contest available on website.

The Annals of St. Anne de Beaupré

PO Box 1000, St. Anne de Beaupré, Québec G0A 3C0

Editor: Roch Achard, C.Ss.R.

Telephone: (418) 827-4538 Fax: (418) 827-4530

Since: 1862	Format: Paper	Circ: 50,000	Sample: n/a
Time: n/a	Money: n/a	Copies: n/a	Sub: n/a

"We are not currently accepting or buying poetry and do not anticipate doing so for another 1-2 years due to an overstock."

The Antigonish Review

PO Box 5000, St. Francis Xavier University, Antigonish, Nova Scotia B2G 2W5

Editor: George Sanderson   Poetry Editor: Peter Sanger

Telephone: (902) 867-3962 Fax: (902) 867-5563

E-mail: TAR@stfx.ca

Website: www.stfx.ca/publications/TAR

Since: 1970	Format: Paper	Circ: 800	Sample: $4
Time: 2-3 months	Money: No	Copies: 2	Sub: $22

Authors published: J.S. Porter, Jenni Blackmore, Douglas Lochhead & Barbara Colebrook Peace.

Send up to 5 poems. Requests one-time rights. Does NOT accept simultaneous submissions. Accepts e-mail submissions. Uses up to 200 of the up to 1,500 submissions received each year. Query regarding book reviews or translations. Interested in fiction and non-fiction of 2,500-5,000 words. Also interested in artwork or photos. Please do not send erotica or political material.

ARC: Canada's National Poetry Magazine

PO Box 7368, Ottawa, Ontario K1L 8E4

Co-Editors: John Barton & Rita Donovan

Since: 1978	Format: Paper	Circ: 700	Sample: $8
Time: 3-4 months	Money: $25/page	Copies: 2	Sub: $30/2 yrs

Authors published: Anne Szumigalski, David Donnell, Susan Musgrave, Monty Reid & Elizabeth Brewster.

Send 4–8 poems. Requests first Canadian rights. Does NOT accept simultaneous submissions. Uses about 60 of the 600 submissions received each year. Interested in photography. Has theme issues and runs annual Poem of the Year Contest. Send SASE for details.

Backwater Review

PO Box 222, Station B, Ottawa, Ontario K1P 6C4

Editor: L. Brent Robillard

E-mail: backwaters@cybertap.com

Website: www.cybertap.com/backwaters

Since: 1996	Format: Paper	Circ: 400	Sample: $5
Time: 1-6 months	Money: No	Copies: 2	Sub: $10

Authors published: Stephanie Bolster, Tim Bowling, John B. Lee & Russell Thornton.

Send 3–5 poems. Requests first North American rights. Accepts simultaneous submissions if so noted. Accepts e-mail submissions "begrudgingly." Uses up to 80 poems each year and six or seven short stories of up to 5,000 words each. Please do not send "formula fiction." Interested in translations, book reviews of small press Canadian books, as well as artwork and photography. Runs Hinterland Award for Poetry/Hinterland Award for Prose. Details online or send SASE.

Beneath the Surface

c/o The Department of English, Chester New Hall 321, McMaster University, Hamilton, Ontario L8S 4S8

Editors: Tony Guindon & Erin Poole

Since: 1988	Format: Paper	Circ: 100 copies	Sample: $4
Time: 3 months	Money: No	Copies: Nil	Sub: $8

Send 2–5 poems, totaling no more than 750 words. Requests first-time publishing rights. Does NOT accept simultaneous submissions. Uses up to 30 of 150 submissions received each year. Interested in short stories up to 2,000 words, artwork and photography.

Bywords

c/o University of Ottawa English Department, 70 Laurier Avenue East, Ottawa, Ontario K1N 6N5

Consulting Editor: S. Mayne

Fax: (613) 562-5990

Website: www.writewrights.com/bywords

Since: 1990	Format: Paper/Web	Circ: 500	Sample: $1
Time: 6 weeks	Money: No	Copies: 2	Sub: $12

Authors published: Cyril Dabydeen, Marty Flomen & Enid Rutland.

Send up to 10 poems, maximum 250 words each. Requests e-rights. Accepts simultaneous submissions. Does NOT accept e-mail submissions. Uses up to 80 of the up to 200 submissions received each year. Also publishes postcard fiction (less than 250 words). Has theme issues. Send SASE for details or read announcements on back of magazine.

Cabaret Vert Magazine

PO Box 157, Station P, Toronto, Ontario M5S 2S7

Editors: Beth Learn & Joy Learn

E-mail: cabaretvert@hotmail. com

Website: www.geocities.com/~cabaretvert

Since: 1991	Format: Varies!	Circ: as per venue	Sample: n/a
Time: n/a	Money: provides venue	Copies: n/a	Sub: n/a

Authors published: bill bissett, Steve McCaffery, bpNichol & Yves Troendle.

"Cabaret Vert varies from print to live language festival participation." Associated with learn/yeats & co. production company. Copyright remains with the artist. "We are small and do things differently than a traditional press. We are multi-media language arts == experimental." Query regarding e-mail submissions.

Canada-WYDE: The Lifestyle Magazine
for Large Canadians and Their Admirers

Box 511, 99 Dalhousie Street, Toronto, Ontario M5B 2N2

Editor: Helena Spring

Telephone: (416) 861-0217 Fax: (416) 861-1668

E-mail: cdawyde@interlog.com

Website: www.interlog.com/~cdawyde

Since: 1996	Format: Paper	Circ: 8-20,000	Sample: $5 + tax & ship.
Time: Varies	Money: No	Copies: 1, upon request	Sub: $21.40/yr

Send 1-3 poems, each should be under 200 words. Accepts e-mail submissions. Does NOT accept simultaneous submissions. Often comments on rejections. Interested in fiction and artwork. "We are non-profit, dedicated to size acceptance and self-esteem/body issues for men, women and children."

Canadian Dimension

2B, 91 Albert Street, Winnipeg, Manitoba R3B 1G5

Editor: Collective Poetry Editor: Brenda Austin-Smith

Telephone: (204) 957-1519 Fax: (204) 943-4617

E-mail: info@canadiandimension.mb.ca

Website: www.canadiandimension.mb.ca/cd/index.htm

Since: 1963	Format: Paper	Circ: 2,300	Sample: $4.25
Time: 2 months	Money: No	Copies: 2	Sub: $24.50

Send up to 10 poems, up to 20 lines each. Requests one-time rights. Accepts e-mail submissions and simultaneous submissions. Uses up to 40 of the 200 submissions received each year. Prefers lyric poetry. Comments on rejections. Editor states, "Rejections are often not related to the quality of the work, but rather to the choice and the analysis presented." Selected work is archived, with the author's permission, and linked to the website. Interested in artwork and photography. Runs theme issues. Send SASE for details.

The Canadian Ethnic Studies Journal

University of Calgary, 2500 University Drive NW, Calgary, Alberta T2N 1N4

Editors: James Frideres & Tony Rasporich
Telephone: (403) 220-7257 Fax: (403) 284-5467
E-mail: jcleaver@ucalgary.ca

| Since: 1970 | Format: Paper | Circ: 600 | Sample: $15 |
| Time: 2 months | Money: No | Copies: 1 | Sub: $50 |

Send up to 5 poems. Requests all rights. Does NOT accept e-mail submissions or simultaneous submissions. Uses 4 of the 10 submissions received each year. All submissions must be related to ethnicity, gender or race in Canada. Comments on rejections. "Ethnic Voice" segment publishes short stories and/or poems giving an artistic picture of ethnic life in Canada. Runs theme issues.

The Canadian Forum

35 Britain Street, Toronto, Ontario M5A 1R7
Editor: Robert Chodos   Poetry Editor: Maggie Helwig
Telephone: (416) 362-0726 Fax: (416) 362-3939
E-mail: canadian.forum@sympatico.ca

| Since: 1920 | Format: Paper | Circ: 5,000 | Sample: $4 |
| Time: 3 months | Money: $75/poem | Copies: 2 | Sub: $29. 96 |

Authors published: Margaret Avison, Henry Beissel, Shauna Singh & John Barton.
Send 5–10 poems. Requests first serial rights. Accepts simultaneous submissions if so noted. Does NOT accept e-mail submissions. Uses 30 of the 500 submissions received each year. Interested in book reviews, fiction, artwork and photography.

The Canadian Journal of Contemporary Literary Stuff

PO Box 53106, Ottawa, Ontario K1N 1C5   http://www.litstuff.com
Editors: Tamara Fairchild & Grant Wilkins
Telephone: (416) 463-0703
E-mail: grunge@achilles.net or fairchild@sympatico.ca
Website: www.calnan.com/journal

| Since: 1997 | Format: Paper | Circ: 1,000 | Sample: $4.75 |
| Time: 4-8 months | Money: No | Copies: 3 | Sub: $16/4 issues |

Authors published: Stan Rogal, Catherine Jenkins, Bob Wakulich & Jill Battson.
Send at least 4–6 poems. Likes to run sets of 2–4 poems by a single writer. Requests first North American rights and first e-rights. Does NOT accept simultaneous submissions. Website is now being developed but "we do not intend to ever have a complete version of our mag up." Uses up to 10 of the up to 200 poems received each year. Accepts e-mail submissions in plain text or attached MS Word files. Interested in book reviews 400–800 words, fiction up to 2,000 words, high contrast b/w artwork and photos. "Our mag is dedicated to promoting work from the best new and emerging writers, as well as those already established in the field. As a forum for new ideas, diverse opinions, dialogue, debate and humour, it is our goal to make Canadian literature interesting to read, interesting to read about, and accessible to all."

Canadian Woman Studies/Les Cahiers de la Femme Journal

212 Founders College, York University, 4700 Keele Street, North York, Ontario M3J 1P3
Editor: Luciana Ricciutelli Poetry Editor: Marlene Kadar
Telephone: (416) 736-5356 Fax: (416) 736-5765
E-mail: cwscf@yorku.ca

Website: www.yorku.ca/org/cwscf/home.html

| Since: 1978 | Format: Paper | Circ: 3,500 | Sample: $8 |
| Time: 3 months | Money: No | Copies: 1 | Sub: $30 + GST |

Authors published: Sandra Woolfrey, Renee Norman, Joan Bond & Elisavietta Ritchie.
Associated with Inanna Publications and Education Inc. Send up to 5 poems, up to 90 lines each. Requests one-time rights. Does NOT accept simultaneous submissions. Accepts e-mail submissions within body of e-mail message, NOT as attachments. Uses up to 90 of 225 poems received each year. Interested in book reviews, photography and artwork. Often runs theme issues, calls for papers. Information is online or query with SASE. NOT interested in fiction. "We particularly welcome French-language contributions, as well as work that deals with issues pertaining to the lives of women of colour, Aboriginal women, immigrant women, lesbians, working-class women, women with disabilities, and other marginalized women."

Canadian Writer's Journal

PO Box 5180, New Liskeard, Ontario P0J 1P0

Editor: Deborah Ranchuk

Telephone: (705) 647-5425 or Toll Free 1-800-258-5451 Fax: (705) 647-8366

E-mail: cwj@ntl.sympatico.ca

Website: www.nt.net/~cwj/index.htm

| Since: 1981 | Format: Paper | Circ: 400 | Sample: $5 |
| Time: 2-3 months | Money: Yes | Copies: 1 | Sub: $15 |

Associated with White Mountain Publications. Quarterly digest-sized journal. Send up to 5 poems. Requests one-time rights and does NOT republish on the web. Accepts simultaneous submissions and e-mail submissions. Uses up to 75 of the 500 submissions received each year. Preference given to Canadian writers. Pays $2/short poem, $5/page. "The emphasis in CWJ is on short 'how-to' articles which convey easily understood information useful both to apprentice and professional writers. With the demise of Canadian Author Magazine (June 1998) I believe CWJ is the only national Canadian magazine for writers." Query regarding book reviews. Not interested in fiction outside of contest. See website for details.

Capers Aweigh— Annual Anthology

39 Water Street, Glace Bay, Nova Scotia B1A 1R6

Editor: John MacNeil

Telephone: (902) 849-0822

E-mail: capersaweigh@hotmail.com

| Since: 1992 | Format: Paper | Circ: 500 | Sample: $4.95 |
| Time: 6 months | Money: No | Copies: 1 | Sub: $4.95/yr |

Send 1-3 poems, up to 60 lines each. Requests first rights. Accepts simultaneous submissions. Also interested in fiction by Cape Breton writers. "We publish Cape Breton writers only."

The Capilano Review

2055 Purcell Way, North Vancouver, British Columbia V7J 3H5

Editor: Robert Sherrin

Telephone: (604) 984-1712 Fax: (604) 990-7837

E-mail: tcr@capcollege.bc.ca

Website: www.capcollege.bc.ca/dept/TCR

Since: 1972	Format: Paper/Web	Circ: 600	Sample: $9
Time: 3-4 months	Money: Yes	Copies: 2	Sub: $25

Authors published: Michael Ondaatje, George Bowering, Daphne Marlatt, Erin Mouré & John Newlove.

Associated with The Capilano Press Society. Send a minimum of 5 previously unpublished poems. Requests first North American serial rights. Accepts submissions from August to May. Does NOT accept simultaneous submissions or e-mail submissions. Uses up to 25 of the 800 submissions received each year. Pays $50-200 plus offers author additional copies at half retail price. Interested in translations, artwork and photography, as well as fiction up to 6,000 words. Information on theme issues available online or by SASE. "Submissions without proper, sufficient postage will not be returned."

The Church-Wellesley Review

c/o XTRA Magazine, 491 Church Street, Suite 200, Toronto, Ontario M4Y 2C6

Editors: Jeffrey Round, Rod Heimpel & Hilary Clark

Telephone: (416) 925-6665 Fax: (416) 925-6503

E-mail: cwr@xtra.ca

Website: www.xtra.ca/cwr

Since: 1990	Format: Paper/Web	Circ: See Below.	Sample: Free
Time: 3-6 months	Money: $20-35/poem	Copies: 1	Sub: N/A

Authors published: Timothy Findley, Shyam Selvadurai, Marnie Woodrow & Dale Peck.

Send 5-8 poems. Editor notes, "Shorter poetry seems to be better written." Requests first North American serial rights and, for website, first electronic publication rights. Accepts simultaneous submissions, and prefers e-mail submissions. Uses up to 50 poems of the up to 600 received each year. Interested in translations. Up to 70 per cent of publication is dedicated to fiction but please query first any pieces over 5,000 words. Publishes once a year in Toronto (45,000), Ottawa (20,000), and Vancouver (30,000). NOT interested in greeting card poetry, or first attempts at writing. "All material is now considered for the quarterly website publication first, and selected from that for our annual paper publication. We prefer submissions to arrive in electronic form, either on disk (Wordperfect preferred) or via e-mail. We publish work reflecting the lives and interests of gays and lesbians. Our interests are not limited to sexuality, and we won't ask yours even if we do use your work."

Contemporary Verse 2

Box 3062, Winnipeg, Manitoba R3C 4E5

Editor: Janine Tschuncky Poetry Editor: Clarise Foster

Telephone: (204) 949-1365 Fax: (204) 942-1555

Since: 1975	Format: Paper	Circ: 650	Sample: $7
Time: 4-8 weeks	Money: $20/poem	Copies: 1	Sub: $23.98/yr

Authors published: Catherine Hunter, Laurie Block, Kelly Jo Burke & John Barton.

Send 6-8 poems. Sometimes comments on rejections. Does NOT accept simultaneous submissions. Receives over 800 poems per year and may use up to 250. Interested in translations. Also interested in fiction 800-1,000 words, and artwork. May run theme issues. "Not interested in material that is racist, sexist or homophobic."

The Dalhousie Review

Dalhousie University, Halifax, Nova Scotia B3H 3J5
Editor: Ronald Huebert ~~Ronald Huebert~~ Robert Martin
Telephone: (902) 494-2541 Fax: (902) 494-3561
E-mail: Dalhousie.Review@dal.ca

| Since: 1921 | Format: Paper | Circ: 450 | Sample: $10 |
| Time: 2 months | Money: No | Copies: 2 | Sub: $22.50 |

Authors published: Margaret Atwood & Elizabeth Brewster.
A quarterly digest-sized publication. Send up to 6 poems. Accepts e-mail and simultaneous submissions. Occasionally comments on rejections. Uses about 40 of the 400 submissions received each year. Interested in book reviews, short fiction, and artwork if it accompanies written work. Annual theme issues. Send SASE for details.

Defiance!

1100 Commissioners Road East, PO Box 41040, London, Ontario N5Z 4Z7
Editor: Andreas Gripp
Telephone: (519) 474-2409

| Since: 1998 | Format: Paper | Circ: 250 | Sample: $3 plus SASE |
| Time: 1 month | Money: No | Copies: 1 | Sub: $10 |

Authors published: Anthony Chalk, Gregory Wm. Gunn, Lori A. May & K.A. Corlett.
Associated with Harmonia Press. Send 5-7 poems, up to 3 pages each. Requests first global and reprint rights. Accepts simultaneous submissions, and occasionally comments on rejections. May use up to 50 poems per year. "We are looking for essays, articles, poetry and artwork/photography that are critical of the consumerist lifestyle and capitalist economic system that causes and/or worsens animal exploitation and suffering; world hunger and poverty; environmental destruction; violence and war. We wish to present an alternative to human greed and are a forum for exploring and bringing about equal rights for all peoples and species. We have a vegan, ecologically friendly and non-violent editorial stance."

Ellipse

CP 10, F.L.S.H.— Université de Sherbrooke, Sherbrooke, Québec J1K 2R1
Editor: Charly Bouchara
Telephone: (819) 821-7000 ext.3268 Fax: (819) 821-7285
E-mail: hurlevent@videotron.ca
Website: www.callisto.si.usherb.ca/~ellipse

| Since: 1969 | Format: Paper | Circ: 650 | Sample: $8 |
| Time: Varies | Money: $100 | Copies: 5-10 | Sub: $14 |

Authors published: Many English- and/or French-speaking Canadian poets.
A market for well-established authors. Does NOT accept unsolicited submissions. All of the 45-55 poems used each year, are specifically solicited from the authors by the editorial board. Translations are used but the same limits apply. "Each year, one issue is devoted to the winner of the Governor General's Award for poetry."

Event

PO Box 2503, New Westminster, British Columbia V3L 5B2
Editor: Calvin Wharton Poetry Editor: Gillian Harding-Russell
Telephone: (604) 527-5293 Fax: (604) 527-5095

E-mail: Event@douglas.bc.ca
Website: /www.douglas.bc.ca/Event/event.html

| Since: 1971 | Format: Paper | Circ: 1,000 | Sample: $7 + GST |
| Time: 1-4 months | Money: $22/page | Copies: 2 | Sub: $18 |

Authors published: Lorna Crozier, Stephanie Bolster & Tim Bowling.

Send no more than 7 poems. Requests first North American rights. Does NOT accept previously published submissions or e-mail submissions. Reads submissions all year except July. Interested in translations, and fiction up to 5,000 words. Query first for artwork or photography. Guidelines for SASE. Runs Creative Non-fiction contest annually.

Eyetalian

901 Lawrence Avenue West, A201, Toronto, Ontario M6A 1C3
Editor: John Montesano
Telephone: (416) 787-9598 Fax: (416) 787-9911
E-mail Address: eyetalia@total.net
Website: www.total.net/~eyetalia

| Since: 1993 | Format: Paper/Web | Circ: 12,000 | Sample: $4 |
| Time: 6-8 weeks | Money: $25/poem | Copies: 1-5 | Sub: $18.97 |

Authors published: Gianna Patriarca, Joseph Maviglia, Len Gasparini & Giovanna Riccio.

Send 3-5 poems, up to 200 words each. Requests various rights— please check with editor upon acceptance. Accepts e-mail submissions. Does NOT accept simultaneous submissions. May be interested in small amounts of fiction, book reviews and translations. Query first. Please do not send long prose or overly long poems. "Material must be by a person of Italian descent or deal with an Italian-themed issue. Writers should note ours is a very small market for poetry. We may run poetry in only three of our six issues each year."

Feux Chalins

Université Sainte-Anne, Pointe-de-l'Église, Nova Scotia B0W 1M0
Editor: Ollivier Dyens
Telephone: (902) 769-2114 Fax: (902) 769-2930
E-mail: odyens@hotmail.com
Website: www.geocities.com/~feuxchalinsweb

| Since: 1994 | Format: Paper/Web | Circ: 500 | Sample: $10 |
| Time: 3 months | Money: No | Copies: 2 | Sub: $20 |

Authors published: "We have published 40 authors to date."

Send 1-5 poems. Requests one-time rights as well as non-exclusive e-rights for 2 years. Accepts simultaneous submissions and e-mail submissions. Reads submissions September–December only. Publishes two-thirds in French, one-third in English. Sometimes comments on rejections. Considers fiction up to 2,500 words. Artwork and photography also considered. "*Feux Chalins* is open to any style but because of our sociopolitical and geographical situation (small French sector of Nova Scotia) we have tended to publish texts that explore the many different facets of language (i.e. slang, franglais, Acadian French, chiac, joual, Black English, etc.). Please do not send anything that is not creative. We are not interested in book reviews or essays."

filling Station

Box 22135 Bankers' Hall, Calgary, Alberta T2P 4J5

Editor: Collective

Telephone: (403) 252-8185 Fax: (403) 253-2980

E-mail: cfthomps@cadvision.com

Since: 1994	Format: Paper	Circ: 500	Sample: $6
Time: 6 months	Money: No	Copies: 1	Sub: $15

Authors published: George Bowering, Catriona Strang, Michelle Glennie & Jill Armstrong.

Send no more than 15 poems for consideration. Requests first North American serial rights and non-exclusive e-rights. Uses up to 20 poems each year. Although no cash payment is offered, authors whose work is published receive a one year subscription to *filling Station* starting with the issue in which their work appears. Accepts e-mail submissions. Please note that although *filling Station* accepts simultaneous submissions, editors ask that any accepted piece be withdrawn from other markets. There are three submission deadlines: March 15; July 15; and November 15. Interested in fiction up to 2,500 words, book reviews and translations. Also interested in artwork and photography. Do NOT send racist, misogynist and/or homophobic work.

Firm Noncommittal: An International Journal of Whimsy

5 Vonda Avenue, North York, Ontario M2N 5E6

Editors: Brian Pastoor & Vince Cicchine Poetry Editor: Brian Pastoor

E-mail: firmnon@idirect.com

Website: webhome.idirect.com/~firmnon

Since: 1995	Format: Paper/Web	Circ: 200	Sample: $5
Time: 1-2 months	Money: See below	Copies: 2	Sub: $7

Authors published: bill bissett, John and Mike Erskine-Kellie, Francine Porad & K.V. Skene.

Send up to 6 poems, up to 30 lines each. Requests one-time rights. Will accept simultaneous submissions if so noted. Will NOT accept e-mail submissions. Uses up to 30 of the up to 200 submissions received each year. Pays only for solicited work. Reads submissions in May and June ONLY. Do not send he/she jilted me poems or American stamps. Interested in very short fables, 500 words or less. Will accept artwork queries. "As Canada's only market solely devoted to humour and light verse we seek writers who 'take the utmost trouble to find the right thing to say, and then... say it with the utmost levity' (G. B. Shaw). Interested in seeing more haiku, senryu and clerihew, thank you."

FreeFall

Alexandra Writer's Centre, 922 9th Avenue S.E., Calgary, Alberta T2G 0S4

Editor: Catherine Fuller

Fax: (403) 264-4730

Since: 1990	Format: Paper	Circ: 150	Sample: $7
Time: Up to 6 months	Money: $5/printed page	Copies: 1	Sub: $10

Send up to 5 poems. Requests first North American serial rights. Does NOT accept simultaneous submissions. "We welcome poems in a variety of forms with a strong voice, effective language and fresh images; fiction up to 3,000 words; and interviews or profiles of writers, publishers or those in the business of writing. The magazine is published twice a year, in the spring and fall. Deadlines are March 1 and October 1.

Submissions should be polished, professional and typed on white bond. Double space prose, single space poetry." Black and white photos labeled and titled preferred.

Gaspereau Review *NO LONGER PUBLISHING.*
c/o Gaspereau Press, PO Box 143, Wolfville, Nova Scotia B0P 1X0
Editor: Andrew Steeves *(902) 678-6062*
E-mail: asteeves@gaspereau.com *1-877-230-8232 (GAS. PRESS)*
Website: www.gaspereau.com/review.htm

| Since: 1997 | Format: Paper | Circ: 200 | Sample: $6 |
| Time: 2-3 months | Money: No | Copies: 2 | Sub: $20 |

Send up to 8 poems. Requests first North American serial rights. Accepts e-mail submissions. Does NOT accept simultaneous submissions. Uses up to 60 of the up to 250 submissions received each year. Interested in fiction up to 4,500 words, artwork and photography.

Generation Magazine
Department of English, University of Windsor, 401 Sunset, Windsor, Ontario N9B 3P4
Editor: Tanya Kuzmanovic (Changes yearly)
Telephone: (519) 253-4232 ext.2289 Fax: (519) 971-3676
E-mail: kateq@uwindsor.ca (Changes yearly)

| Since: 1963 | Format: Paper | Circ: 150 | Sample: $1 |
| Time: 3 weeks | Money: No | Copies: 1 | Sub: N/A |

Authors published: Eva Tihanyi, Bronwen Wallace, Phil Hall & Mary DiMichele.

Send any number of poems. Accepts simultaneous submissions and e-mail submissions. Reads submissions between September and early January. Interested in fiction up to 2,000 words as well as artwork and photography.

GirlCult Girlkulturzine
48 Craig Street, London, Ontario N6C 1E8
Editor: Joan Brennan
Telephone: (519) 434-0961
E-mail: girlcult@execulink.com

| Since: 1995 | Format: Paper | Circ: 550 | Sample: $2 |
| Time: Varies | Money: No | Copies: 2 | Sub: N/A |

Send 1-2 poems, up to 200 words each. Requests first rights or reprint rights. Accepts simultaneous submissions and e-mail submissions. Uses up to 12 of the 20 submissions received each year. Interested in translations, short fiction, book reviews, artwork and photography. "Do not send racist, sexist, homophobic drivel. Must be 'female friendly,' prefer edgy work, porn very much okay. *GirlCult* is a literary porn'zine with a good comedic edge. I like to laugh and I encourage others to do so too."

graffito: the poetry poster
Department of English, University of Ottawa, Ontario K1N 6N5
Editor: b stephen harding
E-mail: graffito@uottawa.ca
Website: www.webapps.com/graffito

| Since: 1994 | Format: Paper/Web | Circ: 250 | Sample: $1 |
| Time: 3 months | Money: No | Copies: 3 | Sub: $12 |

Send 4-8 poems, up to 32 lines each. Requests one-time rights, and e-rights. Does

NOT accept simultaneous submissions. Accepts e-mail submissions but "preference given to submissions received by regular mail." Reads submissions 15th of every month. Generally publishes once a month. Uses only 62 of the thousands of submissions received each year. Interested in translations, books reviews of books by Canadian writers, artwork and photography.

GRAIN Magazine

PO Box 1154, Regina, Saskatchewan S4P 3B4

Editor: Elizabeth Philips Poetry Editor: Sean Virgo

Telephone: (306) 244-2828 Fax: (306) 244-0255

E-mail: grain.mag@sk.sympatico.ca

Website: www.skwriter.com/grain

Since: 1973	Format: Paper	Circ: 1,300	Sample: $7.95
Time: 3-4 months	Money: $30-100/page	Copies: 2	Sub: $26.95

Send 4-6 poems, totaling up to six pages. Requests first Canadian serial rights. Does NOT accept simultaneous submissions. Accepts previously unpublished translations in English. Uses only 120 of the 1,500 poems received each year. Author receives 40% discount on additional copies. Considers literary work ONLY. "Writers: Save your stamps and IRCs: Include an e-mail address with your submissions and we won't require an SASE to respond to your submission." Also interested in fiction, artwork and photography. Runs annual poetry contest with total prizes of $1,000.

Green's Magazine

Box 3236, Regina, Saskatchewan S4P 3H1

Editor: David Green

Since: 1972	Format: Paper	Circ: 250	Sample: $5
Time: 8 weeks	Money: No	Copies: 2	Sub: $15

Authors published: Pheryne Thatcher Williams, Brian Burke, Jill Williams & Sheila Hyland. Send 4-6 poems, up to 40 lines each. Requests first North American rights. Does NOT accept simultaneous submissions. Not interested in sexually explicit material. Uses up to 150 poems of the 600 received each year. Interested in fiction. Will consider artwork and photography. Send SASE for guidelines.

Hook & Ladder Magazine

PO Box 78, Station B, Ottawa, Ontario K1P 6C3

Editor: Victoria Martin Poetry Editors: G. T. Fougere & Victoria Martin

Telephone: (613) 823-6585 Fax: (613) 823-7372

E-mail: martinv@electricgarden.com

Website: www.electricgarden.com/h&l/index.html

Since: 1993	Format: Paper	Circ: 500	Sample: $3.50
Time: 2-3 months	Money: No	Copies: 2	Sub: $6

Authors published: R.D. Patrick, Lea Littlewolfe, Susan McCaslin, Lorrette C. Thiessen & Aidan Baker. Associated with Electric Garden Press. Send 6-8 poems, not more than four pages each. Requests first North American serial rights. Accepts e-mail submissions. Uses about 50 of the up to 300 poems received each year. Also interested in fiction, and small-press comics. "Please do not send previously published poems, poems that recycle cliches, anything trite, banal, or something we've heard before." Does NOT accept simultaneous submissions. Comments on rejections whenever possible. The editor writes, "It might be helpful to know what we read in our spare time: 'early '60's' Leonard Cohen; Irving Layton; Margaret Atwood; Gwendolyn MacEwen; Susan Musgrave; Stephanie Bolster; Lorna Crozier and Karen Connelly. Powerful writing. Imagery that leaps off the page." Runs a writing contest. Details available online or by SASE.

IN 2 PRINT Magazine

PO Box 102, Port Colborne, Ontario L3K 5V7
Editor: Jean Baird
Telephone: (905) 834-1539 Fax: (905) 834-1540

| Since: 1995 | Format: Paper | Circ: 25,000 | Sample: $4 |
| Time: 3 months | Money: $50+ | Copies: 1 | Sub: $14.95 + GST |

Send up to 4 poems. Requests one-time rights. Receives more than 6,000 submissions per year, can use only about 100. Comments on rejections. "*IN 2 PRINT* is a national forum for emerging artists ages 12 to 21. It is a high quality, four-colour glossy magazine which promotes and showcases the creativity of young Canadians: the magazine publishes original works of poetry, short stories, plays, painting, photography, computer art and cartoons. *IN 2 PRINT* also publishes an eclectic array of interviews and reviews of books, music and theatre." Runs writing contest.

Jones Av

88 Dagmar Avenue, Toronto, Ontario M4M 1W1
Editors: Paul Schwartz, Allan Brown & Sophia Kaszuba
Telephone: (416) 461-8739
E-mail: oel@interlog.com

| Since: 1994 | Format: Paper | Circ: 50 | Sample: $2 |
| Time: 3 months | Money: No | Copies: 1 | Sub: $8 |

Authors published: Greg Evason, Eric Folsom, Jennifer Footman & Stan Rogal.
Associated with Oel Press. Send 5-6 poems. May request e-rights for use on their website. Accepts e-mail submissions. Does NOT accept simultaneous submissions or prose. Often comments on rejections. Uses up to 70% of the up to 200 submissions received each year. Very interested in artwork and photos. Editor states, "I find most rhymed poetry that comes our way to be unsatisfactory and amateurish. It better be good or don't send it."

Kinesis

#309-877 East Hastings Street, Vancouver, British Columbia V6A 3Y1
Editor: Agnes Huang
Telephone: (604) 255-5499 Fax: (604) 255-7508
E-mail: kinesis@web.net

| Since: 1974 | Format: Paper | Circ: 2,000 | Sample: $2.25 |
| Time: 2 weeks | Money: No | Copies: 1 | Sub: $21.40 |

Kinesis is a review market only. "We do not publish poetry or any genres of fiction." Query. Requests one-time rights.

The Lazy Writer

Box 977, Station F, 50 Charles Street East, Toronto, Ontario M4Y 2N9
Editor: Cheryl Carter Portfolio Editor: Alexandra Leggat

Telephone: (416) 538-0559
E-mail: lzwriter@interlog.com

| Since: 1997 | Format: Paper | Circ: 2,500 | Sample: $6 |
| Time: 3 months | Money: $25/printed page | Copies: 2 | Sub: $32.05 |

Authors published: Sandra Alland, Heather Cadsby, Linda Gabris & P.K. Page.

Send 3–12 poems. Requests first North American serial rights. Accepts e-mail queries but NOT e-mail submissions. Accepts simultaneous submissions if so noted. Uses up to 25 of the up to 500 submissions received each year. Query regarding translations. Interested in fiction up to 4,000 words, and book reviews of books for writers. May be interested in artwork or photography. Query.

The Malahat Review

Box 1700, University of Victoria, Victoria, British Columbia V8W 2Y2
Editor: Marlene Cookshaw
Telephone: (250) 721-8524
E-mail: malahat@uvic.ca
Website: www.uvic.ca/malahat

| Since: 1967 | Format: Paper | Circ: 1,000 | Sample: $8 |
| Time: 2–3 months | Money: $30/page +sub. | Copies: 2 | Sub: $25 |

Authors published: Don McKay, Rhea Tregebov & Pain not Bread.

Send 6–12 pages of poetry. Requests first world rights in English. Does NOT accept e-mail submissions. Accepts simultaneous submissions. Uses up 50 of the up to 1,200 poetry submissions received each year. Occasionally comments on rejections. Interested in translations, fiction, book reviews of recent Canadian fiction and poetry, as well as colour artwork or photos for cover. Runs Long Poem Contest or Novella Contest in alternating years. Details online or send SASE.

New Muse of Contempt

Box 596, Station A, Fredericton, New Brunswick E3B 5A6
Editor: Joe Blades
Telephone: (506) 454-5127 Fax: (506) 454-5127
E-mail: jblades@nbnet.nb.ca

| Since: 1987 | Format: Paper | Circ: 200 | Sample: $5 |
| Time: 3 months | Money: No | Copies: 1–2 | Sub: $12/yr |

Authors published: Tim Landers, Kath MacLean, rob mclennan & Marijan Megla.

Associated with Maritimes Arts Projects Productions. Send 4–8 poems. Requests one-time rights. May ask for one-time anthology rights. Uses between 6 and 40 poems each year. Does NOT accept e-mail submissions or simultaneous submissions. Please do not send devotional, greeting card platitudes. Interested in book reviews, translations, fiction, artwork and photography.

The New Quarterly

ELPP, PAS 2082, University of Waterloo, Waterloo, Ontario N2L 3G1
Editor: Mary Merikle Poetry Editors: Charlene Diehl-Jones, Randi Patterson, Gary Draper & John Vardon.
Telephone: (519) 888-4567 ext.2837
E-mail: mmerikle@watarts.uwaterloo.ca
Website: watarts.uwaterloo.ca/~mmerikle/newquart.html

Since: 1981	Format: Paper	Circ: 300	Sample: $6.42
Time: 4-6 months	Money: $25/poem	Copies: 1	Sub: $21.40

Send 5 poems. Requests first Canadian rights. Accepts e-mail submissions. Does NOT accept simultaneous submissions. Uses up to 100 of the up to 500 poems received each year. Interested in translations and fiction. Occasionally runs theme issues. Details online or send SASE.

NeWest Review
Box 394, RPO University, Saskatoon, Saskatchewan S7N 4J8
Editor: Verne Clemence Poetry Editor: Sylvia Legris
Telephone: (306) 934-1444 Fax: (306) 343-8579
E-mail: sylleg@artslab.usask.ca

Since: 1975	Format: Paper	Circ: 800	Sample: Free
Time: 2 months	Money: $15/poem	Copies: 1	Sub: $19.26

Authors published: John Livingstone Clarke, Thomas Trofimuk, Rahel Zolf & Trevor Roberts.

Send 4-6 poems. Requests first publication rights. Accepts simultaneous submissions if so noted. Accepts e-mail submissions. "Please do not send work that is too amateurish." Interested in book reviews and fiction. May be interested in artwork and photography. Query. Runs theme issues and a short story contest for writers 40 and over. Details online or send SASE.

On Spec— More Than Just Science Fiction
Box 4727, Edmonton, Alberta T6E 5G6
Editorial Collective: Barry Hammond (Poetry Editor), Susan MacGregor, Hazel Sangster, Jena Snyder & Diane L. Watson
E-mail: onspec@earthling.net
Website: www.icomm.ca/onspec

Since: 1989	Format: Paper	Circ: 1,500	Sample: $6
Time: 2 months	Money: $20/poem	Copies: 1	Sub: $19.95

Authors published: Sandra Kasturi & Eileen Kernaghan.

On Spec is a digest-sized quarterly publication. Send up to 5 poems, up to 100 lines each. Requests first North American serial rights. Accepts simultaneous submissions if so noted. Does NOT accept e-mail submissions. Uses 5-7 of the up to 50 poems received each year. Always comments on rejections. Also interested in fiction. All artwork is commissioned— guidelines available online or send SASE. Spring issue is always a theme issue. "We are open to submission of any speculative poems: science fiction; fantasy; horror; magic realism or any other kind of speculative material. Please, no religious or rhyming poetry."

Other Voices
Garneau PO Box 52059, 8210-109th Street, Edmonton, Alberta T6G 2T5
Editing done by collective
E-mail: kpress@gpu.srv.ualberta.ca
Website: www.ualberta.ca/~kpress/OtherVoices.html

Since: 1988	Format: Paper	Circ: 550	Sample: $8
Time: See below	Money: $25 honorarium	Copies: 1*	Sub: $15

Authors published: Kath MacLean, Robin S. Chapman, Zoe Landale, Heidi Greco & Anne LeDressay.

Send 2-10 poems, up to 2 pages each. Requests first North American serial rights. Uses the work of about 15 poets out of the 300 submissions received each year. May ask for short-term e-rights for use on website. Do NOT send popular verse or simultaneous submissions. Responds to submissions April/May and October/November. Sometimes comments on rejections. Interested in book reviews. May be interested in translations. Often runs theme issues. Details online or send SASE. Interested in fiction, artwork and photography. Artwork intended for the cover may be in b/w or colour and should be available on a slide. Photos or artwork for inside the magazine must be in b/w. *Other Voices* is "open to work by both experienced and beginning writers. We encourage submissions by women and members of minorities." ★Contributors receive one copy of the issue in which their work appears plus one copy of the next consecutive issue. Runs annual contest. Details online or send SASE.

Our Family

Box 249, Battleford, Saskatchewan S0M 0E0
Editor: Marie-Louise Ternier-Gommers
Telephone: (306) 937-7771 Fax: (306) 937-7644
E-mail: ourfamily@marianpress.sk.ca
Website: www.marianpress.sk.ca/ourfamily/

Since: 1949	Format: Paper/Web	Circ: 8,000	Sample: $2.50
Time: 4-5 weeks	Money: $.75/line	Copies: 2	Sub: $15.98 + GST

Member of the Canadian Church Press Association. Send any number of poems, "even one is okay," up to one page each. Plans content one year in advance. Requests first North American serial rights. Uses up to 25 of the 100 poems received each year. Comments on rejections. Accepts e-mail submissions. Does NOT accept simultaneous submissions. Please do NOT send fiction. Interested in artwork and photography. Has theme issues. Send SASE for details. "*Our Family Magazine* is read primarily by a Roman Catholic readership. Christian faith reflections are particularly welcomed. Topics vary from parenting, marriage breakdown, church issues, spirituality of artists, aging, and social justice."

The Poem Factory/Usine de Poem

Box 3655, Vancouver, British Columbia V6B 3Y8

Since: 1990	Format: Paper	Circ: Varies	Sample: $3
Time: 1 year	Money: No	Copies: 20	Sub: $25

The Poem Factory produces small runs of 8 page publications. No set format. Send up to 5 poems for consideration. Requests first publication rights. Does NOT accept simultaneous submissions. Uses many of the submissions received.

The Plowman

Box 414, Whitby, Ontario L1N 5S4
Editor: Tony Scavetta
Telephone: (905) 668-7803

Since: 1988	Format: Paper	Circ: 1,000	Sample: Free
Time: 3-4 weeks	Money: No	Copies: 1	Sub: $10

Associated with Plowman Press. Send 2-5 poems. Requests one-time rights. Uses up to 50 of the up to 150 poems received each year. Accepts simultaneous submissions. Usually comments on rejections. Do NOT send satanic poems or poems using bad language. Interested in fiction, book reviews, artwork and photography. Runs monthly poetry contest.

Pottersfield Portfolio

PO Box 40, Station A, Sydney, Nova Scotia B1P 6G9

Editor: Douglas Arthur Brown

Since: 1979	Format: Paper	Circ: 700	Sample: $6
Time: 3 months	Money: $5/page	Copies: 1	Sub: $19.95

Authors published: David Zieroth, Steven Heighton, Don McKay & Don Domanski.

Send a maximum of 6 poems. Requests first Canadian serial rights. Accepts simultaneous submissions if so noted. Uses up to 50 of the up to 300 poems received each year. Interested in fiction. May be interested in translations. Do NOT send religious verse, doggerel, or poetry for children. Occasionally comments on rejections. "*Pottersfield Portfolio* is always open to submissions of new work by unpublished writers or established writers. Poetry should be fresh and deliver the unexpected."

Prairie Fire

423-100 Arthur Street, Winnipeg, Manitoba R3B 1H3

Editor: Andris Taskans Poetry Editors: Catherine Hunter & Robert Budde.

Telephone: (204) 943-9066 Fax: (204) 942-1555

Since: 1978	Format: Paper	Circ: 1,600	Sample: $10
Time: 4-5 months	Money: See below.	Copies: 1	Sub: $25

Authors published: Lorna Crozier, Patrick Lane, Al Purdy & Anne Szumigalski.

Send up to 6 poems. Requests first Canadian serial rights. Does NOT accept simultaneous submissions. Uses up to 40 of the 400 poems received each year. Detailed rates of payment schedule available with guidelines. Send SASE. Please do not send rhyming poetry, religious poetry or haiku. Interested in fiction up to 5,000 words. For details of theme issues send SASE. "Because we do frequent special issues, we're not as receptive to unsolicited submissions as we'd like to be. Some years, two of the four issues might be on a special topic. That also means that we don't usually publish accepted work in the 'next' issue but might hang onto it for months until space permits." Interested in translations and book reviews. Runs annual writing contests in poetry, long short fiction, short fiction, and creative non-fiction.

Prairie Journal

PO Box 61203, Brentwood PO, Calgary, Alberta T2L 2K6

Editor: A. Burke

Since: 1983	Format: Paper	Circ: 500	Sample: $6
Time: Varies	Money: $5-50	Copies: 1	Sub: $7

Send 6-8 poems. Requests first North American serial rights. Does NOT accept simultaneous submissions. Reads submissions only twice a year. Uses up to 30 of the 200 poems received each year. Interested in fiction, artwork and photography. Send copies only. Occasionally runs theme issues. Send SASE for details. "A good home for poetry, sometimes features work of one poet; reviews books of poetry especially if reviewed by fellow poets. Also interested in translations, interviews, bibliography, etc. Query first for reviews, otherwise send submissions with SASE for reply/return by snail mail."

Prism International

Creative Writing Program, UBC, Buch. E462, 1866 Main Mall, Vancouver, British Columbia V6T 1Z1

Editor: Jeremiah Aherne Poetry Editor: Natalie Meisner

Telephone: (604) 822-2514 Fax: (604) 822-3616

E-mail: prism@unixg.ubc.ca

Website: www.arts.ubc.ca/prism

Since: 1959	Format: Paper/Web	Circ: 1,100	Sample: $5
Time: 2-6 months	Money: $40/printed page	Copies: 1 year sub.	Sub: $16

Authors published: Di Brandt, Esta Spalding, Coral Hull, Beth Goobie, Tom Wayman & Ken Babstock.

Send up to 5 poems, with a limit of 25 pages total. Requests first North American serial rights, and limited e-rights ($10 per printed page) for use in the web version of the magazine. Accepts e-mail submissions. Accepts simultaneous submissions if so noted. Uses up to 100 of the 1,200 submissions received each year. Interested in translations, fiction, artwork and photography. "Do not send genre fiction or previously published work." Editors award Earle Birney Prize for Poetry annually to a poet published within a regular volume of the magazine.

Queen's Quarterly

184 Union Street, Kingston, Ontario K7L 3N6

Editor: Boris Castel

Telephone: (613) 545-2667 Fax: (613) 545-6822

E-mail: qquartly@post.queensu.ca

Website: www.queensu.ca/quarterly

Since: 1893	Format: Paper/Web	Circ: 3,100	Sample: $6.50
Time: 4-6 weeks	Money: No	Copies: 2	Sub: $20

Send up to 6 poems. Requests first North American serial rights. Accepts e-mail submissions. Does NOT accept simultaneous submissions. Uses up to 40 of the 500 submissions received each year. Interested in articles up to 2,500 words. Also interested in translations, book reviews, artwork and photography. Runs theme issues. Details online or send SASE.

Queen Street Quarterly

Box 311, Stn. P, 704 Spadina Avenue, Toronto, Ontario M5S 2S8

Editor: Suzanne Zelazo

Telephone: (416) 657-1637

E-mail: zelazo@psych.utoronto.ca

Website: psych.utoronto.ca/~zelazo/~qsq.htm

Since: 1997	Format: Paper	Circ: 500	Sample: $6.75
Time: 3 months	Money: $5	Copies: 2	Sub: $20

Authors published: Victor Coleman, Jeff Derksen, Patrick Friesen & A.F. Moritz.

Send up to 10 poems, each of which should not exceed three double-spaced pages. Encourages e-mail submissions. "However, each page must be clearly marked with author identification info." Does NOT accept simultaneous submissions. Sometimes comments on rejections. Interested in translations, fiction, artwork and photography.

QWERTY

c/o University of New Brunswick English Department, PO Box 4400, Fredericton, New Brunswick E3B 5A3

Editor: Eric Hill
E-mail: qwerty@unb.ca
Website: www.unb.ca/QWERTY

Since: 1996	Format: Paper/Web	Circ: 250	Sample: $5
Time: 3 months	Money: No	Copies: 1	Sub: $12

Authors published: Steven Heighton, John B. Lee & Michael Ondaatje.

Send up to 6 poems. Requests first North American serial rights. Accepts simultaneous submissions. Does NOT accept e-mail submissions. Interested in fiction up to 4,000 words. Also interested in translations, artwork and photography.

Raddle Moon

518-350 East Second Avenue, Vancouver, British Columbia V5T 4R8

Editor: Susan Clark
E-mail: clarkd@sfu.ca

Since: 1984	Format: Paper	Circ: 700	Sample: $8
Time: 3 months	Money: No	Copies: 1	Sub: $15

Authors published: Aaron Shurin, Anne Talvez, Dan Farrell & Diane Ward.

Associated with Sprang Texts, a chapbook series. First time submitters should send up to ten pages of work. Requests one-time rights. Does NOT accept e-mail submissions or simultaneous submissions. Uses up to 50 of the up to 500 submissions received each year. NOT interested in fiction but does publish prose. "We have a strong interest in rigorous experimental work by women, collaborative works, long poems, image/text, translations, and engaged criticism. Though we favour experimental work by women this is by no means exclusive. Before submitting please become familiar with our magazine."

RAMPIKE

81 Thornloe Crescent, Sault-Ste-Marie, Ontario P6A 4J4

Editor: Karl E. Jirgens Poetry Editor: Carole E. Turner
Telephone: (705) 949-6498 Fax: (705) 949-4734
E-mail: jirgens@thunderbird.auc.on.ca

Since: 1979	Format: Paper/Web	Circ: 2,000	Sample: $7
Time: 6 months	Money: $25/poem	Copies: 2	Sub: $16

Authors published: "The who's who of Canadian literature, plus a sterling contingent of some of the finest authors in the English speaking world."

Associated with Coach House Press. Send up to 12 poems. Requests first Canadian publishing rights and one-time web-page rights with permission of author. Does NOT accept simultaneous submissions. Uses up to 100 of 2,000 submissions received each year. Sometimes comments on rejections. Interested in translations "especially of works by high profile authors;" fiction up to 3,500 words. Pays $75 for short stories. May be interested in book reviews. Query first. Also interested in artwork and photography provided they "suit our themes." Every issue is a theme issue. Details online or send SASE. "We are not interested in works from people who have no familiarity with our editorial mandate or stylistic preferences."

Raw Nervz Haiku

67 Court Street, Aylmer, Québec J9H 4M1
Editor: Dorothy Howard
Telephone: (819) 684-1345

Since: 1994	Format: Paper	Circ: 200	Sample: $6
Time: 1-3 months	Money: No	Copies: Nil	Sub: $20

Authors published: LeRoy Gorman, Marco Fraticelli, Janice Bostok & Marlene Mountain.
Send up to 10 poems. Requests either one-time or first-time publication rights. Does NOT accept simultaneous submissions. Accepts only five haiku per quarter from any one subscriber. Uses up to 800 of the 5,000 submissions received each year. Please do not send work that is too linear, cute, banal or preachy. Interested in book reviews of 250–500 words, translations and fiction. All submissions must directly relate to haiku or related form. Interested in proof-ready b/w graphics suitable for 5.5 x 8.5 inch format.

Room of One's Own

PO Box 46160, Station D, Vancouver, British Columbia V6J 5G5
Editor: Collective
Website: www.islandnet.com/Room/enter

Since: 1975	Format: Paper	Circ: 800	Sample: $7
Time: 3-6 months	Money: $25*	Copies: 2	Sub: $22

Authors published: Emerging and developing writers and well as established women writers.
Send 4–6 poems. Requests first North American rights. Does NOT accept simultaneous submissions or e-mail submissions. Uses up to 120 of the 1,000 submissions received each year. *Pays $25 total regardless of the number of poems used. Occasionally comments on rejections. Please do not send work that does not center around women. Interested in translations, fiction up to 5,000 words, artwork and photography. Also interested in book reviews but please query first. Runs theme issues. Send SASE for details.

Scrivener Creative Review

853 Sherbrooke Street West, Montréal, Québec H3A 2T6
Coordinating Editors: Konstantine Stavrakos & Michelle Syba Poetry Editors: Claire Ezzeddin & Jesse Newman
Telephone: (514) 398-6588

Since: 1980	Format: Paper	Circ: 500	Sample: $5
Time: 2-6 months	Money: No	Copies: 1	Sub: $5

Authors published: Leonard Cohen, Heather Hernant, P.K. Page & Gail Scott.
Associated with Scrivener Press. Send up to 15 poems, with a limit of 30 pages total. Reads submissions between September and January 15th. Requests one-time rights. Accepts simultaneous submissions if so noted. Uses up to 60 of the 500 submissions received each year. Up to 16 of these are poems. Interested in book reviews, fiction, artwork and photography. Occasionally plans theme issues.

SEEDS Poetry Magazine

412-701 King Street West, Toronto, Ontario M5V 2W7
Editor: Richard M. Grove
Telephone: (416) 504-3966

E-mail: writers@pathcom.com
Website: www.pathcom.com/~writers/

| Since: 1993 | Format: Paper/Web | Circ: Varies | Sample: $3 |
| Time: Varies | Money: No | Copies: 2 | Sub: $10 |

Authors published: Al Purdy, Stan Rogal, Jennifer Footman & John B. Lee.

Associated with Hidden Brook Press. Send up to 5 poems. Requests one-time rights. Accepts simultaneous submissions if so noted. Accepts e-mail submissions. Uses up to 40 poems in each of their quarterly issues. Uses different work in the e-zine *SEEDS*. Please do not send sex, porno, science-fiction or fantasy work. Interested in b/w artwork only. "We publish well crafted poetry from around the world, so send us any style of poetry you love to write. Be sure it is your absolute top shelf, best stuff. We pride ourselves on presenting a mix of emerging writers with more established published writers." Guidelines online or send SASE. Runs writing contest.

Smoke, A Journal of Literary Prose
Box 73587, 509 St. Clair Avenue West, Toronto, Ontario M6C 2K7
Editor: George Murray
Telephone: (416) 651-6679
E-mail: bsp@yesic.com
Website: www.yesic.com/~gmurray/smokhome.html

| Since: 1997 | Format: Paper/Web | Circ: 500 | Sample: $6 |
| Time: 1-4 months | Money: No | Copies: 2 | Sub: $18 |

Authors published: Susan Swan, George Bowering, Maggie Helwig & rob mclennan.

Associated with Bathurst Street Press. Send up to 3,500 words. Accepts ONLY prose poetry, fiction, micro fiction, creative non-fiction, etc. Requests first North American serial rights. Negotiates e-rights. Accepts simultaneous submissions if so noted. Does NOT accept e-mail submissions. Uses up to 45 of the hundreds of submissions received each year. Very interested in translations. These should be accompanied by original and letter of permission from the author. Query regarding artwork or photography. "We are interested in PROSE, which, for sanity's sake, we are defining as anything that word wraps. We have no requirements for genre, ideology, geography, politics, gender, orientation or language. Send us pieces which use to the fullest extent, the traditional precepts of prose writing (voice, event, narrative, character, dialogue, etc.) or pieces which challenge these precepts in a thought-provoking, intelligent manner. We accept and encourage translations of all languages, as well as writers working in French to submit original French manuscripts or translations in French."

STANZAS
c/o above/ground press, RR#1, Maxville, Ontario K0C 1T0
Editor: rob mclennan
Telephone: (613) 235-2783
E-mail: az421@freenet.carleton.ca
Website: www.nonlinear.ca/aboveground

| Since: 1993 | Format: Paper | Circ: 750 | Sample: $2 |
| Time: 6 months | Money: No | Copies: 40 | Sub: $10/5 issues |

Authors published: Judith Fitzgerald, Ian Whistle, carla milo & Greg Evason.

Associated with above/ground press. *STANZAS* is a long poem/sequences magazine. Send up to 28 pages of work by a single author. NOT interested in anything else.

Requests first Canadian rights. Do NOT send e-mail submissions or simultaneous submissions. Interested in translations. Receives up to 100 submissions each year, uses very few. Rarely comments on rejections.

Teak Roundup

#5-9060 Tronson Road, Vernon, British Columbia V1H 1E7 *SUBS. ONLY*
Editor: Yvonne Anstey
Telephone: (250) 545-4186 Fax: (250) 545-4194

Since: 1994	Format: Paper	Circ: 200	Sample: $5
Time: 1 week	Money: No	Copies: N/A	Sub: $17

Authors published: George Kuhn, Rita Campbell & Robert G. Anstey.

Associated with West Coast Paradise Publishing. "*Teak Roundup* is an international prose and poetry quarterly magazine dedicated to showcasing the work of our subscribers." Send up to 5 poems, of up to 40 lines each. Requests one-time rights. Uses all submissions. Interested in fiction up to 1,000 words as well as book reviews, artwork and photography. Accepts simultaneous submissions. Please do NOT send uncouth work or porn.

Textshop

First Year Services, University of Regina, Regina, Saskatchewan S4S 0A2
Editor: Andrew Stubbs
Telephone: (306) 585-4316
E-mail: Andrew.Stubbs@uregina.ca

Since: 1992	Format: Paper	Circ: 200	Sample: $2.50*
Time: 6-8 weeks	Money: No	Copies: 2	Sub: $10

Authors published: Both new and established.

Send 5-6 poems, up to 2 pages each. Requests first Canadian serial rights. Accepts simultaneous submissions. Reads submissions up to October 1. Uses up to 40 of the up to 200 submissions received each year. Often comments on rejections. Interested in fiction up to 1,000 words. *Special rate for back issue sample copy. "What *Textshop* publishes is eclectic but we encourage personal narratives, life writing. We provide 'reviews' or, more specifically, 'reactions,' to published material inside the issue. These are positive, supportive, analytical, not 'critical' in a negative sense. The purpose is to generate dialogue among writers and editors."

Thalia: Studies in Literary Humor

University of Ottawa, Ottawa, Ontario K1N 6N5
Editor: Dr. Jaqueline Tavernier-Courbin
Telephone: (613) 230-9505 Fax: (613) 565-5786
E-mail: jtaverni@aix1.uottawa.ca

Since: 1978	Format: Paper	Circ: 500	Sample: $23
Time: 2-4 months	Money: No	Copies: 2+sub.	Sub: $23

All submissions must deal with humour or be humourous. Requests first rights. Accepts simultaneous submissions if so noted. Does NOT accept e-mail submissions. May use up to 20 of the 60 submissions received each year. Comments on rejections. Interested in fiction, book reviews, artwork and photography. Runs theme issues. Uses the Chicago Style Sheet. Submit hard copy in triplicate. Disk copy requested if accepted. Be sure your submission includes an SASE or IRC for reply.

NO LONGER
TAKEN UNSOL
ShB.

THIS Magazine

396-401 Richmond Street, Toronto, Ontario M5V 3A8
Editor: Andrea Curtis Poetry Editor: R.M. Vaughan
Telephone: (416) 979-8400 Fax: (416) 979-1143
E-mail: thismag@web.net
Website: www.THISmag.org

| Since: 1966 | Format: Paper/Web | Circ: 6,000 | Sample: $4.50 |
| Time: 6 weeks | Money: $75/poem | Copies: 2 | Sub: $23.99 |

Authors published: Michael Holmes, Lynn Crosbie, Derek McCormack & Heather Browne Prince.

Send up to 3 poems. Requests first North American rights. Does NOT accept e-mail submissions. Accepts simultaneous submissions. Uses up to 10 of the 40 submissions received each year. Interested in translations, fiction, artwork and photography. Runs "The Great Canadian Literary Hunt" every year which awards the largest Canadian prize offered ($1,500) to the author of the winning poem.

TickleAce

PO Box 5353, St. John's, Newfoundland A1C 5W2
Editor: Bruce Porter Poetry Editors: Susan Ingersoll & Bruce Porter
Telephone: (709) 754-6610 Fax: (709) 754-5579
E-mail: tickleace@nfld.com

| Since: 1977 | Format: Paper | Circ: 1,000 | Sample: $8 |
| Time: 4 months | Money: $25 | Copies: 1 | Sub: $26/2 years |

Authors published: We publish big name authors as well as emerging and brand new writers.

Send 6–8 poems. Requests first Canadian rights only. Accepts e-mail submissions. Tends to read submissions in March and September, though this varies. Does NOT accept simultaneous submissions. Uses up to 80 of the 1,500 submissions received each year. Offers additional copies at discount. Do NOT send greeting card verse. Interested in fiction up to 5,000 words. Query regarding artwork or photography. Runs occasional theme issues. Send SASE for details. May run occasional contest.

Tickled By Thunder

7385-129 Street, Surrey, British Columbia V3W 7B8
Editor: Larry Linder
Telephone: (604) 591-6095
E-mail: thunder@istar.ca
Website: www.home.istar.ca/~thunder

| Since: 1990 | Format: Paper/Web | Circ: 1,000 | Sample: $2.50 |
| Time: 3-6 months | Money: No | Copies: 1 | Sub: $12 |

Associated with Tickled By Thunder Publishing Company. Send 3–6 poems. Requests first-time rights, e-rights optional. Accepts simultaneous submissions. Does NOT accept e-mail submissions. Uses up to 20 poems each year. Occasionally comments on rejections. Interested in book reviews, and fiction up to 2,000 words. Interested in artwork or photography ONLY if it accompanies manuscript. Send "writing that tears itself from the page, grabs readers by the throat and demands to be read. 'Religious' fiction and poetry must stand on its own, not using its genre for a crutch. I don't necessarily publish the best stuff. I publish whatever I like best." Runs annual fiction, poetry and article contests. Writer's guidelines and contest details online or send SASE.

Time For Rhyme

c/o Richard W. Unger, PO Box 1055, Battleford, Saskatchewan S0M 0E0

Editor: Richard W. Unger

Telephone: (306) 445-5172

| Since: 1994 | Format: Paper | Circ: Varies | Sample: $3.25 |
| Time: 4-6 weeks | Money: No | Copies: 1 | Sub: $12 |

Authors published: Elizabeth Symon, Sharon R. McMillan & J. Alvin Spears.

Send up to 5 poems, of up to 32 lines each. Include a short bio. Requests first North American rights. Does NOT accept simultaneous submissions. Uses up to 54 of the hundreds of submissions received each year. Almost always comments on rejections. Please do NOT send "porn, obscenities, profanity or racism." Seasonal poems welcome. "All poems must rhyme. Can be in couplet or quatrain forms, or one of the older traditional forms like sonnet. Open to light verse, if in good taste. This is a family-oriented publication with old-fashioned values. Not particularly open to intellectual/philosophical poetry— prefer experiential poetry with vivid images. Help me experience your experience: to see; hear; and feel it. Each issue contains a book review. Authors of books with rhyming poems may submit a copy for review."

Tower Poetry

c/o Dundas Public Library, 18 Ogilvie Street, Dundas, Ontario L9H 2S2

Editor: Joanna Lawson

| Since: 1951 | Format: Paper | Circ: 250 | Sample: $4 |
| Time: 6 months | Money: No | Copies: 1 | Sub: $8 |

Authors published: Poets from around the world.

Send up to 4 poems. Requests one-time rights. Accepts simultaneous submissions. Uses up to 80 of the 140 submissions received each year. Please do not send haiku or prose poetry. "We look for concrete images, attention to space, sound and sense."

TROUT

PO Box 4017, Station E, Ottawa, Ontario K1S 5B1

Editor: John Gillies Poetry Editor: Loredana Rancatore

E-mail: ap368@freenet.carleton.ca

Website: www.ncf.carleton.ca/~ap368/

| Since: 1997 | Format: Paper | Circ: Up to 500 | Sample: $4 |
| Time: 2 months | Money: $20 | Copies: 3 | Sub: $10 |

Authors published: Paul Keen & Khaled Kurodvic.

TROUT publishes 2-3 times each year. Send up to 8 poems. Requests first North American rights. Uses up to 45 of the 250 submissions received each year. Accepts simultaneous submissions and e-mail submissions. Comments on rejections. Please do NOT send "men's movement literature, -ist and -ism poetry, hypermystical and neo-mythical poetry, gothic, sci-fi fiction shorts." Interested in fiction up to 3,000 words, micro-fiction up to one page and book reviews. Interested in artwork and photography. "We are interested in francophone and anglophone writing as well as translations. TROUT publishes writing in both official languages. Humour, parody and satire are all welcome. ('TROUT is not afraid to bite.') Essays and sometimes even rants are published." Contest planned for year 2000.

Urban Graffiti

PO Box 41164, Edmonton, Alberta T6J 6M7

Editor: Mark McCawley

E-mail: cogwheels@worldgate.com

| Since: 1993 | Format: Paper | Circ: 200-500 | Sample: $2 |
| Time: 8 weeks | Money: No | Copies: 2+ | Sub: N/A |

Authors published: Daniel Jones, Clint Burnham, David Pahn & Lorrette Thiessen.

Send up 5-8 poems. Requests first North American rights, and first anthology rights. Accepts e-mail submissions. Does NOT accept simultaneous submissions. Uses up to 10 per cent of the hundreds of poems received each year. Please do NOT send religious, sexist, homophobic or nature poems. Interested in fiction, artwork and photography. "*Urban Graffiti* is a litzine of transgressive, discursive, post-realist writing concerned with the struggles of hard-edge urban living, deviance and alternative lifestyles presented in their most raw and unpretentious form."

VOX FEMINARUM

38-200 Elm Ridge Drive, Kitchener, Ontario N2N 2G4

Editor: Ginny Freeman MacOwan

Telephone: (519) 576-4588

E-mail: voxfeminarum@sympatico.ca

Website: www3.sympatico.ca/voxfeminarum

| Since: 1996 | Format: Paper | Circ: 1,500 | Sample: $7 |
| Time: 3-6 months | Money: No | Copies: 1+ | Sub: $25/2 yrs |

Authors published: Priyamvada Sankar, Rita Shelton Deverell, Susan L. Scott & Beth Powning.

Send up to five poems. Requests first North Amercian rights. Policy for e-rights is currently being developed. Poems used are often part of longer texts. Accepts e-mail submissions but please include regular mailing address and telephone number. Accepts simultaneous submissions if so noted. Often comments on rejections. All issues are thematic. Details online or send SASE. Interested in translations and book reviews. "*VOX FEMINARUM* is a forum for women; therefore we are primarily interested in publishing women writers. Submissions must reflect aspects of feminist spirituality." Authors get discount on additional copies.

West Coast Line

2027 East Academic Annex, Simon Fraser University, Burnaby, British Columbia V5A 1S6

Editor: Roy Miki Managing Editor: Jacqueline Larson

Telephone: (604) 291-4287 Fax: (604) 291-5737

E-mail: jlarson@sfu.ca (subject to change late '99)

| Since: 1990 | Format: Paper | Circ: 700 | Sample: $10 |
| Time: 4 months | Money: $10/page | Copies: 2 | Sub: $25 |

Authors published: Roy Kiyooka, Nicole Brossard, Lola Lemire Tostevin & Hiromi Goto.

Send 4-8 poems. Requests first-time rights. Uses up to 25 of the up to 600 submissions received each year. Does NOT accept simultaneous submissions or e-mail submissions. Please do NOT send "straight" sentimental or lyrical poetry, no haiku or traditional verse. Interested in fiction up to 5,000 words. Interested in book reviews, translations, artwork and photography. May run theme issues. Send SASE for details. "We are interested in formally innovative writing that experiments with or expands the boundaries of conventional forms of poetry, fiction and criticism. Most of the writers we publish are familiar with the journal."

Western People

Box 2500, 2310 Millar Avenue, Saskatoon, Saskatchewan S7K 2C4
Editor: Michael Gillgannon
Telephone: (306) 665-9611 Fax: (306) 934-2401
E-mail: people@producer.com
Website: www.producer.com

| Since: 1978 | Format: Paper | Circ: 95,000 | Sample: Free |
| Time: 3 weeks | Money: $10-50 | Copies: 2 | Sub: $41* |

Western People is a supplement to *Western Producer* newspaper. Send up to 5 poems, up to 100 words each. Requests one-time rights. Accepts simultaneous submissions and e-mail submissions, though prefers hard copy. Do NOT send drivel. Uses up to 60 poems each year. Publishes fiction once a month. Theme issues revolve around occasions like Remembrance Day, Christmas, Mother's Day. Overall, "prairie flavour preferred."

Whetstone

University of Lethbridge, c/o the English Department, 4401 University Drive, Lethbridge, Alberta T1K 3M4
Editor: Steve Marlow
Telephone: (403) 329-2367 Fax: (403) 382-7191
E-mail: whetstone@uleth.ca
Website: www.home.uleth.ca/~whetstone

| Since: 1971 | Format: Paper | Circ: 500 | Sample: $3 |
| Time: 2-6 months | Money: No | Copies: 1 | Sub: $15 |

Authors published: Lyn Lifshin, Dorothy Livesay, W.P. Kinsella & m. oordt.
Associated with the University of Lethbridge Press. Send up to 6 poems. Accepts e-mail submissions. Does NOT accept simultaneous submissions. Reads submissions from September–March only. Interested in fiction up to 2,500 words. Also interested in b/w artwork and photography.

Windsor Review

Department of English, University of Windsor, Windsor, Ontario N9B 3P4
Poetry Editor: John Ditsky
Telephone: (519) 253-4232 ext.2332 Fax: (519) 973-7050
E-mail: uwrevu@uwindsor.ca

| Since: 1965 | Format: Paper | Circ: 250 | Sample: $8 |
| Time: 2 months | Money: $15/poem | Copies: 1 | Sub: $19.95+GST |

Authors published: Walter McDonald, Lyn Lifshin, W.P. Kinsella & Deborah Joy Cory.
Send 5-10 poems. Requests one-time rights. Reads submissions September–April. Does NOT accept simultaneous submissions. Prefers hard copy or submissions on disk. Uses up to 40 poems each year. Please do not send "epics." Interested in fiction, artwork and photography. Runs theme issues. For details send SASE.

Writer's Block Magazine

Box 32, 9944-33 Avenue, Edmonton, Alberta T6N 1E8

Editor: Shaun Donnelly
Telephone: (780) 464-6623 Fax: (780) 464-5524

Since: 1994	Format: Paper	Circ: 5,000	Sample: $5
Time: 4-6 weeks	Money: $25/poem	Copies: 3	Sub: $12

Authors published: J.A.H. Rice, Anna Best & Pierre Berton.

Writer's Block is published biannually in March and September. Send 3-5 poems. Requests first or second North American serial rights. Accepts simultaneous submissions. Uses up to 30 of the up to 800 submissions received each year. Occasionally comments on rejections. Interested in fiction up to 5,000 words, as well as book reviews, artwork and photography. "Our magazine spotlights exceptional poetry and stories in the following genres: horror, mystery, science fiction/fantasy; romance and western." Runs two contests biannually. Send SASE for details.

The Writer's Publisher

Box 55, Tofino, British Columbia V4R 2Z4
Editor: R. Tuck
Telephone: (250) 725-2588 Fax: (250) 725-2588
E-mail: thewp@island.net

Since: 1997	Format: Paper	Circ: 200	Sample: SASE
Time: 2 weeks	Money: $25/poem	Copies: 1	Sub: $16

Send any number of poems. Requests one-time rights. Accepts e-mail submissions as well as simultaneous submissions. Uses up to 30 of the 200 submissions received each year. Interested in fiction up to 1,000 words.

Zygote Magazine

1474 Wall Street, Winnipeg, Manitoba R3E 2S4
Editors: Tom Schmidt, Cindy Little & Brent Pahl.
E-mail: tschmidt@mail.escape.ca

Since: 1993	Format: Paper	Circ: 1,000	Sample: $3.95
Time: 3-4 months	Money: $5-10/poem	Copies: 2	Sub: $16

Authors published: Beth Goobie, Patrick Friesen, Carol Rose, Anne Szumigalski & Wally Jansen

Send 5-8 poems, up to 55 lines each. Requests first print and first e-rights. Prefers e-mail submissions and accepts simultaneous submissions. Uses up to 100 of the more than 600 submissions received each year. Interested in translations, book reviews, fiction up to 2,500 words, as well as b/w artwork and photography or colour work with good contrast. "Our magazine is distributed nationally. We publish all genres and both new and established writers. (We focus on new writers!) Our criteria is good writing." Runs a writing contest in every issue.

The following periodicals have ceased publication since the sixth edition of this book:

Amber, Black Cat 115, Canadian Author Magazine, Dandelion, Exhumed, Impulse, Madame Bull's Tavern, The Muse Journal, Musk Gland Sally, paperplates, PARA*phrase, Poem, Women's Education des Femmes

The following periodicals no longer publish poetry or they have asked to be delisted:

Abilities Magazine, absinthe, Blood & Aphorisms, Canabis Culture, letters, Missing Jacket, Musicworks Magazine, The Mystery Review, Open Letter, Paragraph, Unmuzzled Ox, Windspeaker

The following periodicals believed to still be active, failed to respond to requests for information:

Arachne: A Literature Journal, Atlantis: A Womens' Studies Journal, Bardic Runes, blue buffalo, Carleton Arts Review, Carousel, Chickadee, The Claremont Review, The Country Connection, descant, Exile, The Fiddlehead, Fireweed: a feminist quarterly, Geist, The Harpweaver, Hecate's Loom, Herizons, Ink Magazine, Matriart, Matrix, Minus Tides Magazine, McClung's Magazine, Pearls, People's Poetry Letter, Poetry Canada, Possibilitiis Literary Arts Magazine, Quarry, RIM, Rungh Magazine, Scarborough Fair, Toronto Life, The Toronto Review of Contemporary Writing Abroad, White Wall Review

1.7 US PERIODICAL LISTINGS *U.S. STAMPS #*

American publications have been steady consumers of Canadian literary work. Many at some point in their publishing history have devoted an entire issue to the work of Canadians. Listed here is an eclectic collection of American literary magazines whose editors expressed a clear desire to see more Canadian work.

An organized submission allows an editor more time to consider your work. As with all submissions, you MUST include a self-addressed stamped envelope (SASE) to receive a reply or return of your work. It is a standard of the publishing industry and therefore would have been redundant to include in each listing.

Remember to include either US stamps or sufficient IRCs when dealing with US publications. Do NOT send Canadian postage. (For more information on US postage and IRCs see Chapter One.)

Aethlon: Journal of Sport Literature

Box 70720 ETSU, Johnson City, Tennessee, USA 37614
Editor: Don Johnson Poetry Editor: Robert Hamblin
Telephone: (423) 439-5995 Fax: (423) 439-7193
E-mail: sla@etsu.edu
Website: www.etsu.edu/English/English/aethlon.htm

| Since: 1984 | Format: Paper | Circ: 300 | Sample: $15 US |
| Time: 1-2 months | Money: No | Copies: 1 | Sub: Varies |

Associated with ETSU University Press. Concentrates on sports literature. Accepts simultaneous submissions. Does NOT accept e-mail submissions. Uses some of the

50 submissions received each year. May comment on rejections. Interested in translations, book reviews and fiction. Not interested in memoirs.

a gathering of the tribes

PO Box 20693, Tompkins Square Station, New York, New York, USA 10009
Editor: Steve Cannon Poetry Editor: Amy Ouzoonian
Telephone: (212) 674-3778 Fax: (212) 674-5576
E-mail: tribes@info.org
Website: www.tribes.org

Since: 1991	Format: Paper	Circ: 2,000	Sample: $12.50 US
Time: 90 days	Money: No	Copies: 1	Sub: $25 US

Authors published: Victor Cruz, Edwin Torres, Ishmael Reed & Paul Beatty.
Send up to 5 poems. Requests first-time rights. Accepts simultaneous submissions if so noted. Does NOT accept e-mail submissions. Uses 100 of the 4,000 submissions received each year. Comments on rejections. Interested in book reviews, translations, artwork and photography. Will consider fiction up to 2,500 words. Please send only one story per submission. "Our magazine is a place for other arts disciplines, such as the whole range of visual and performing arts."

AGNI

236 Bay State Road, Boston University, Boston, Massachusetts, USA 02215
Editor: Askold Melnyczuk Managing Editor: Valerie Duff
Telephone: (617) 353-5389 Fax: (617) 353-7136
E-mail: AGNI@bu.edu
Website: www.webdelsol.com/AGNI

Since: 1972	Format: Paper	Circ: 2,000	Sample: $9 US
Time: 3-4 months	Money: $20US min.	Copies: 2	Sub: $18 US

Authors published: Olena Kalytiak, Charles Simic, Jill McCorkle & Chinua Achebe.
Send 3-5 poems. Requests first publication rights and e-rights. Accepts simultaneous submissions if so noted. Does NOT accept e-mail submissions. Reads submissions October-January. Please do not send unsolicited non-fiction work. Interested in translations, and fiction. Occasionally runs theme issues. Details online or send SASE.

Alpha Beat Press

31 Waterloo Street, New Hope, Pennsylvania, USA 18938-1210
Editor: Dave Christy
Telephone: (215) 862-0299

Since: 1986	Format: Paper	Circ: 500	Sample: $10 US
Time: 1 week	Money: No	Copies: 1	Sub: $17 US

Authors published: A.D. Winans, Steve Richmond & Ana Christy.
Send 3-4 poems. Requests one-time rights. Accepts simultaneous submissions. Interested in translations, book reviews, fiction, artwork and photography. Uses up to 300 of the up to 800 submissions received each year. Comments on rejections. Please do not send traditional poetry or Christian poetry. "We publish 'Beat Generation', Post-Beat Independent and other modern writings, poetry, reviews and essays."

Amaranth

PO Box 184, Trumbull, Connecticut, USA 06611
Editors: Becky Rodia & Christopher Sanzeni

Telephone: (203) 452-9652 Fax: (203) 268-1619
E-mail: brodyjean@aol.com

| Since: 1995 | Format: Paper | Circ: 1,000 | Sample: $6 US |
| Time: 4-6 months | Money: No | Copies: 2* | Sub: $10 US |

Authors published: Gary Young, Charles H. Webb & Gray Jacobik.

Send 3-5 poems. Requests first-time rights. Accepts simultaneous submissions if so noted. Does NOT accept e-mail submissions. Uses 50 of the 2,000 submissions received each year. *Additional copies may be purchased at a discount. May be interested in artwork and photography. Query. Runs occasional writing contests. Details published in trade publications. "*Amaranth* seeks poetry with a human element— we prefer portraits of people rather than abstracts and landscapes. Send work with LINE-BY-LINE energy! Most of the work we reject is technically fine, it's just not very interesting. Snappy language in every line will get our attention."

AMELIA Magazine

329 "E" Street, Bakersfield, California, USA 93304-2031

Editors: Frederick A. Raborg, Jr.

Telephone: (805) 323-4064 Fax: (805) 323-5326

E-mail: amelia@lightspeed.net

| Since: 1983 | Format: Paper | Circ: 1,750 | Sample: $10.50 US |
| Time: 1-3 months | Money: $2-$25 US | Copies: 2 | Sub: $32 US |

Authors published: Pattiann Rogers, David Ray, Maxine Kumin & Matt Mulhern.

Associated with Amelia Press. Send 3-6 poems. Requests first North American serial rights. Accepts simultaneous submissions if so noted. Does NOT accept e-mail submissions. Uses 800 of the 30,000+ poems received each year. Usually comments on rejections. Please do not send overtly religious or political material. "We look for a strong sense of kinship with the reader, a feeling of importance and worth, stance and control in our poetry, any form to 100 lines." Interested in translations, book reviews, fiction, artwork and photography. Runs annual contest. Note: Excellent guidelines available. Send SASE.

American Poetry Review

1721 Walnut Street, Philadelphia, Pennsylvania, USA 19103

Editor: David Bonanno Poetry Editor: Arthur Vogelsang

Telephone: (215) 496-0435 Fax: (215) 569-0808

| Since: 1977 | Format: Paper | Circ: 18,000 | Sample: $3.95 US |
| Time: 2-3 months | Money: $2 US/line | Copies: Nil | Sub: $18 US |

Authors published: Louise Gluck, Kenneth Koch & Gerald Stern.

Send 1-6 poems. Requests first rights, anthology rights and electronic promotion rights. Does NOT accept simultaneous submissions. Uses 120 of the 14,000 submissions received each year. Interested in fiction, book reviews and translations.

American Tanka

PO Box 120-024, Staten Island, New York, USA 10312

Editor: Laura Maffei

E-mail: editor@americantanka.org

Website: www.americantanka.org

| Since: 1996 | Format: Paper | Circ: 200+ | Sample: $8 US |

| Time: 4-6 weeks | Money: No | Copies: I | Sub: $16 US |

Authors published: Sanford Goldstein, ai li & Marianne Bluger.

Send up to 5 poems. Requests first North American serial rights. Accepts e-mail submissions. Does NOT accept simultaneous submissions. Uses 50 of the 250 submissions received each year. "We are interested in five-line, 31 syllables or less, untitled single tanka ONLY."

The Atlantic Monthly

77 North Washington Street, Boston, Massachusetts, USA 02114
Editor: William Whitworth Poetry Editor: Peter Davison
Telephone: (617) 854-7700 Fax: (617) 854-7877
Website: www.theatlantic.com

| Since: 1857 | Format: Paper/Web | Circ: 550,000 | Sample: $3.50 (Can.) |
| Time: 3 weeks | Money: $4 US/line | Copies: 2 | Sub: $25.95 (Can.) |

Authors published: W.S. Merwin, Philip Levine, Yusef Komunyakaa & Wislawa Szymborska.

Send up to 6 poems. Requests first North American serial rights. Does NOT accept simultaneous submissions. Uses up to 50 of the 50,000 submissions received each year. NOT interested in long poems. May be interested in translations. Interested in fiction. May run theme issues.

Atom Mind

PO Box 22068, Albuquerque, New Mexico, USA 87154
Editor: Gregory Smith

| Restarted: 1991 | Format: Paper | Circ: 1,200+ | Sample: $6 US |
| Time: 1-2 months | Money: No | Copies: 2+ | Sub: $20 US |

Authors published: Wilma Elizabeth McDaniel, Lawrence Ferlinghetti & Edward Field.

Associated with Mother Road Publications. Send 6–8 poems, 20–80 lines each. Requests first North American rights. Uses up to 150 of the 3,000+ submissions received each year. Occasionally comments on rejections. Does NOT accept simultaneous submissions. Interested in fiction 2,000–4,000 words, translations, artwork and photography.

Bathtub Gin

PO Box 2392, Bloomington, Indiana, USA 47402
Editors: Christopher Harter & Tom Maxedon
Telephone: (812) 323-2985
E-mail: charter@bluemarble.net
Website: www.bluemarble.net/~charter/btgin.htm

| Since: 1997 | Format: Paper | Circ: 200+ | Sample: $6 US |
| Time: 1-2 months | Money: No | Copies: I | Sub: $10 US |

Authors published: T.K. Splake, B.Z. Niditch, Arthur Knight & Mark Sonnenfeld.

Associated with Pathways Press. Send 3–5 poems. Requests one-time rights. Accepts e-mail submissions, and simultaneous submissions if so noted. Two reading periods: July 1–September 15 and December 1–March 15. Uses 50 of the 500 submissions received each year. Usually comments on rejections. Please do not send horror, sci-fi, historical, academia, or Bukowski wanna-be work. Interested in book reviews, translations, fiction, artwork and photography.

The Beloit Poetry Journal

24 Berry Cove Road, Lamoine, Maine, USA 04605

Editor: Marion K. Stocking

Telephone: (207) 667-5598

Website: violet.umf.maine.edu/~sharkey/bpj

| Since: 1950 | Format: Paper | Circ: 1,200 | Sample: $4 US |
| Time: 1-4 months | Money: No | Copies: 3 | Sub: $15.52 US |

Authors published: Sherman Alexic, Mary Leader & A.E. Stallings.

Send up to 8 poems. Requests first serial rights. Does NOT accept simultaneous submissions. Uses 80 of the 12,000 submissions received each year. Interested in translations. "We publish the best poems we receive without bias as to form, subject, length or tradition. They need to be strong, fresh, imaginative poems, with accurate, unsentimental language."

Bellingham Review

MS9053, WWU, Bellingham, Washington, USA 98225

Editor: Robin Henley Poetry Editors: Bruce Beasley & Suzanne Paolo

Website: www.wwu.edu/~bhreview

| Since: 1977 | Format: Paper/Web | Circ: 1,500 | Sample: $5 US |
| Time: 6-8 weeks | Money: No | Copies: 2 | Sub: $10 US |

Authors published: Charles Wright, Timothy Liu, Claudia Keelan & Lyn Hejinian.

Associated with Signpost Press. Send 3-5 poems. Requests first North American serial rights and/or e-rights. Uses 20 of the 2,000 poetry submissions received each year. Accepts simultaneous submissions if so noted. Reads submissions October 1–May 1. Interested in book reviews, translations, fiction up to 10,000 words, as well as artwork and photography. Runs poetry contest. Send SASE for details.

Black Warrior Review

PO Box 862936, Tuscaloosa, Alabama, USA 35486-0027

Editor: Christopher Chambers Poetry Editor: Matt Doherty

Telephone: (205) 348-4518

Website: www.sa.ua.edu/osm/bwr

| Since: 1974 | Format: Paper | Circ: 2,000 | Sample: $8 US |
| Time: 1-4 months | Money: $45 US | Copies: 2 | Sub: $14 US |

Authors published: Bob Hicok, C.D. Wright, Nicole Cooley & Billy Collins.

Send 5-7 poems, up to 10 pages total. Requests copyright, returned to writer upon request following publication. Uses up to 50 of the 3,500 submissions received each year. Accepts simultaneous submissions if so noted. Sometimes comments on promising work. Interested in book reviews, translations, fiction up to 10 pages, artwork and photography.

BOGG

PO Box 23148, 380 Wellington Street, London, Ontario, Canada N6A 5N9

Canadian Editor: Sheila Martindale

Telephone: (519) 764-2647 Fax: (519) 764-2935

E-mail: sheila.martindale4@sympatico.ca

| Since: 1968 | Format: Paper | Circ: 800 | Sample: $4.50 (Can.) |
| Time: Varies | Money: No | Copies: 2 | Sub: $12 (Can.) |

Authors published: George Amabile, Chad Norman, K.V. Skene & Norma West Linder.

Send 6–8 poems, up to one page each. Requests first North American rights. Uses up to 12 poems each year. Accepts e-mail submissions. Does NOT accept simultaneous submissions. Please do NOT send long poems. Interested in book reviews and translations. "We look for poems which are composed with technical skill, work on more than one level, capture the personal experience but also rise above it, and are witty, but this does not mean we publish only humor."

BOMB Magazine
594 Broadway, Suite 905, New York, New York, USA 10012
Editor: Betsy Sussler Poetry Editor: Suzan Sherman
Telephone: (212) 431-3943 Fax: (212) 431-5880
E-mail: bombmag@bombsite.com
Website: www.bombsite.com

| Since: 1988 | Format: Paper | Circ: 25,000 | Sample: $4 US |
| Time: 8-10 weeks | Money: $100 US | Copies: 2 | Sub: $18 US |

Authors published: Rick Bass, Carole Maso, Peter Carey & Padgett Powell.

Send up to 8 poems. Requests first serial rights. Accepts simultaneous submissions if so noted. Does NOT accept e-mail submissions. Uses 20 of the 3,500 submissions received each year. Occasionally comments on rejections. Please do not send genre work. Interested in translations, and fiction up to 25 pages. "We look for work with a literary quality which is unconventional, and contains an edge, whether it be style or subject matter."

Boston Review
E53-407 MIT, Cambridge, Massachusetts, USA 02139
Editor: Joshua Cohen Poetry Editors: Timothy Donnelly & Mary Jo Bang
Telephone: (617) 253-3642 Fax: (617) 252-1549
E-mail: bostonreview@mit.edu
Website: www.bostonreview.mit.edu

| Since: 1975 | Format: Paper/Web | Circ: 30,000 | Sample: $4.50 US |
| Time: 4 months | Money: Varies | Copies: 5 | Sub: $17 US |

Authors published: Harold Brown, Mark Doty, Thylias Moss & Rita Dove.

Send up to 10 pages total. Rights revert to author after publication. Accepts simultaneous submissions if so noted. Does NOT accept e-mail submissions. Interested in fiction. April/May is poetry issue. Runs contest. Details online or send SASE.

Boulevard
4579 Laclede Avenue, #332, St. Louis, Missouri, USA 63130
Editor: Richard Burgin
Telephone: (314) 361-2986

| Since: 1986 | Format: Paper | Circ: 3,000 | Sample: $8 US |
| Time: 3 months | Money: $25-$150 US | Copies: 1 | Sub: $15 US |

Send up to 5 poems, up to 200 lines each. Rights revert to author after publication. Accepts simultaneous submissions if so noted. Reads submissions October–March. Uses 100 of 8,000 submissions received each year. Do not send "light verse." Interested in translations, fiction up to 8,000 words, artwork and photography. "We are very interested in publishing less experienced or unpublished writers with exceptional promise." Runs writing contest.

The Cape Rock

Southeast Missouri State University, Cape Girardeau, Missouri, USA 63701

Editor: Harvey Hecht

Telephone: (573) 651-2500

E-mail: hhecht@semovm.semo.edu

| Since: 1964 | Format: Paper | Circ: 400 | Sample: $3 US |
| Time: 2-4 months | Money: See below | Copies: 2 | Sub: $7 US |

Send 3-6 poems. Requests ALL rights "but will release rights to individual authors upon request, provided they give proper credit to *The Cape Rock* as the original publisher whenever and wherever the work is placed." Uses about 90 poems per year. Pays $100 US for best poem in each issue. Pays $200 US for photography in each issue, (uses 12 photos from a single photographer). Reads submissions September–April. Runs writing contest. For details send SASE.

The Carolina Quarterly

CB#3520, Greenlaw Hall, Chapel Hill, North Carolina, USA 27599-3520

Editor: Robert West Poetry Editor: Al Benthall

Telephone: (919) 962-0244 Fax: (919) 962-3520

E-mail: cquarter@unc.edu

Website: www.unc.edu/student/orgs/cquarter

| Since: 1948 | Format: Paper | Circ: 1,100 | Sample: $5 US |
| Time: 4 months | Money: No | Copies: 2 | Sub: $12 US |

Authors published: Albert Goldbarth, Robert Morgan & Eleanor Ross Taylor.

Send up to 6 poems. Requests first publications rights, print or electronic. Does NOT accept simultaneous or e-mail submissions. Uses about 45 of the 5,000 submissions received each year. Interested in translations and fiction. For artwork and photography please "send a sample we can keep." Annually awards the Charles B. Wood Award, a $500 prize, for the best short story or poem by an unestablished writer.

The Chattahoochee Review

Georgia Perimeter College, 2101 Womack Road, Dunwoody, Georgia, USA 30338-4497

Editor: Lawrence Hetrick Poetry Editors: Collie Owens & J. Steven Beauchamp

Telephone: (770) 551-3019

E-mail: lhetrick@gpc.Peachnet.edu

Website: www.dc.peachnet.edu/~twadley/cr/index.htm

| Since: 1981 | Format: Paper | Circ: 1,250 | Sample: $6 US |
| Time: 3 months | Money: $50 US/poem | Copies: 3 | Sub: $16 US |

Authors published: Nola Perez-Wyatt Prunty, John Stone, Judson Mitcham & Caroline Wright.

Send 1-5 poems. Requests first rights. Does NOT accept e-mail submissions or simultaneous submissions. Uses up to 36 of the hundreds of submissions received each year. Occasionally comments on rejections. Interested in book reviews, translations, fiction, artwork and photography. Runs theme issues. Send SASE for details.

Chicago Review

5801 South Kenwood Avenue, Chicago, Illinois, USA 60637

Editor: Andrew Rathman Poetry Editor: Deven Johnson

Telephone: (773) 702-0887 Fax: (773) 702-0887

E-mail: chicago-review@uchicago.edu
Website: humanities.uchicago.edu/humanities/review

| Since: 1946 | Format: Paper | Circ: 2,500 | Sample: $6 US |
| Time: 3 months | Money: No | Copies: 3 | Sub: $18 US |

Authors published: Peter Dale Scott, Tomaz Salamun, Tom Pickard & Eleanor Wilner.

Send 3-6 poems. Requests first North Amercian and electronic rights. Accepts simultaneous submissions if so noted. Does NOT accept e-mail submissions. Uses up to 60 of the 2,000 submissions received each year. Occasionally comments on rejections. Interested in book reviews, translations and fiction. Special interest in experimental traditions. Runs theme issues. Send SASE for details.

Chiron Review

702 North Prairie, St. John, Kansas, USA 67576-1516
Editor: Michael Hathaway Poetry Editors: Michael Hathaway & Gerald Locklin
Telephone: (316) 549-6156 or (316) 786-4955
E-mail: chironreview@hotmail.com

| Since: 1982 | Format: Paper | Circ: 1,000 | Sample: $4 US |
| Time: 1-2 months | Money: No | Copies: 1 | Sub: $12 US |

Authors published: Janine Pommy Vega, Geezus Lee, Charles Plymell & Lyn Lifshin.

Send 3-5 poems. Requests one-time rights. Does NOT accept simultaneous submissions or e-mail submissions. Uses 100 of the "tons" of submissions received each year. Please do not send religious, didactic, overtly political, rhyming poetry or haiku. Interested in translations, fiction, artwork and photography.

Cimarron Review

205 Morrill Hall, Oklahoma State University, Stillwater, Oklahoma, USA 74078
Editor: E.P. Walkiewicz Poetry Editor: Lisa Lewis
Telephone: (405) 744-9476

| Since: 1967 | Format: Paper | Circ: 500 | Sample: $5 US |
| Time: 2-3 months | Money: $15/poem US | Copies: 1 | Sub: $20 US |

Authors published: David Kirby, Diane Glancy, Carter Revard & Maurice Kenny.

Send 3-6 poems. Requests ALL rights. Does NOT accept simultaneous submissions. Uses up to 75 of the 2,500 submissions received each year. Please do not send greeting-card verse that attempts to be profound, or sci-fi work. "Try to be fresh—with language, imagery, perspective, tone, etc.." Interested in fiction up to 3,000 words, book reviews, translations, artwork and photography.

Cottonwood

400 Kansas Union, Box J, University of Kansas, Lawrence, Kansas, USA 66045
Editor: Tom Lorenz Poetry Editor: Philip Wedge
Telephone: (785) 864-3777
E-mail: cottonwd@falcon.cc.ukans.edu
Website: falcon.cc.ukans.edu/~cottonwd

| Since: 1965 | Format: Paper | Circ: 500 | Sample: $4 US |
| Time: 3-6 months | Money: No | Copies: 1 | Sub: $15 US |

Authors published: William Stafford, Rita Dove, Antonya Nelson & Thomas Fox Averill.

Associated with Cottonwood Press. Send 1-6 poems. Requests first North American serial rights. Does NOT accept simultaneous or e-mail submissions. Uses 30 of the 3,000 submissions received each year. Occasionally comments on rejections. Please do not send rhymed poetry or trite diction. Interested in book reviews and fiction. "We are interested in mainstream contemporary fiction and poetry, not genre-oriented material."

CutBank

English Department, University of Montana, Missoula, Montana, USA 59802
Editors: Josh Corey & Nicole Cordrey Poetry Editor: Matt Byrne
Telephone: (406) 243-6156
E-mail: cutbank@selway.umt.edu
Website: www.umt.edu/cutbank

Since: 1973	Format: Paper/Web	Circ: 500	Sample: $4 US
Time: 2 months	Money: No	Copies: 2	Sub: $12 US

Authors published: Eamon Grennan, Pattiann Rogers, Jack Gilbert & Sheryl Noethe.
Send 4-6 poems. Requests first rights. Accepts simultaneous submissions if so noted. Does NOT accept e-mail submissions. Reads submissions August 15–April 1. Uses up to 30 of the 1,000 submissions received each year. "*CutBank* is interested in art, poetry and fiction of high quality and serious intent." Runs writing contest. Details online or send SASE.

Denver Quarterly

University of Denver, Department of English, Denver, Colorado, USA 80208
Editor: Bin Ramke
Telephone: (303) 871-2892 Fax: (303) 871-2853

Since: 1966	Format: Paper	Circ: 1,000	Sample: $6 US
Time: 6 months	Money: $5/page US	Copies: 2	Sub: $24 US

Authors published: James Tate, Gustaf Sobin & Jorie Graham.
Send 3-5 poems. Requests first North American rights. Does NOT accept simultaneous submissions. Uses 120 of the 20,000 submissions received each year. Reads submissions September 15-May 15. Please do not send confessional poetry. Interested in book reviews, translations, fiction up to 1,700 words, and poetry with "interesting language."

descant

TCU Box 297270, Fort Worth, Texas, USA 76129
Editor: Neil Easterbrook
Telephone: (817) 257-7240
E-mail: descant@tcu.edu
Website: www.eng.tcu.edu/eng/descant.htm

Since: 1958	Format: Paper/Web	Circ: 400	Sample: $6 US
Time: 10-12 weeks	Money: No	Copies: 2	Sub: $10 US

Send 4-10 poems. Requests first publication rights. Accepts short poetry submissions by e-mail. Please do not send fiction by e-mail. Does NOT accept simultaneous submissions. Reads submissions September-May. Uses 50 of the 1,000 submissions received each year. Awards the $500 Frank O'Conner Memorial Award for Fiction and the $500 Betty Colquitt Prize for Poetry; annual winners are selected from work previously published in *descant*.

The Eckerd College Review

Box 1514, Eckerd College, 4200 54th Avenue South, St. Petersburg, Florida, USA 33711

Editor: Fritz Ward

| Since: 1993 | Format: Paper | Circ: 1,200 | Sample: $6 US |
| Time: 1-3 months | Money: No | Copies: 1-2 | Sub: $6 US |

Authors published: Peter Meinke, R.T. Smith, Fred Chappell & Kathryn Stripling Byer.

Send 3-5 poems. Requests first rights. Does NOT accept simultaneous submissions. Reads submissions September-January 15. Uses up to 25 of the 1,200 submissions received each year. Interested in book reviews up to 1,000 words, translations, fiction, artwork and photography. Please do not send ranting, raving or preaching verse. "Editors favor authors who have studied other poets as well as their craft."

Ellery Queen's Mystery Magazine

1270 Avenue of the Americas, New York, New York, USA 10020

Editor: Janet Hutchings

Telephone: (212) 698-1313

Website: www.mysterypages.com/EQMM.html

| Since: 1941 | Format: Paper | Circ: 500,000 | Sample: $2.95 US |
| Time: 3 months | Money: Varies | Copies: 3 | Sub: $33.97 US |

Send 1-3 poems. Requests first North American serial rights. Accepts simultaneous submissions if so noted. Uses up to 14 of the many submissions received each year. "Although primarily a fiction magazine, *Ellery Queen's Mystery Magazine* accepts all types of short poems dealing with mystery, crime, suspense, police procedurals, etc. Poetry may also take the form of a pastiche of well-known characters, writers, etc.."

Field

Rice Hall, Oberlin College, Oberlin, Ohio, USA 44074

Editor: David Young

Telephone: (440) 775-8408 Fax: (440) 775-8124

E-mail: oc.press@oberlin.edu

Website: www.oberlin.edu/~ocpress

| Since: 1969 | Format: Paper | Circ: 2,500 | Sample: $7 US |
| Time: 1 month | Money: $10-15/page US | Copies: 2 | Sub: $14 US |

Authors published: Carol Muske, Charles Simic, Carl Phillips & W.S. Merwin.

Send up to 6 poems. Requests first printed rights. Does NOT accept e-mail submissions or simultaneous submissions. Uses 100 of the 5,000 submissions received each year. Sometimes comments on rejections. Interested in translations. Runs FIELD Poetry Prize. Details online or send SASE.

Fine Madness

PO Box 31138, Seattle, Washington, USA 98103-1138

Editors: Bentley/Brewster/Malek/Ditkin/Wald

Website: www.scn.org/arts/finemadness

| Since: 1982 | Format: Paper/Web | Circ: 800 | Sample: $4 US |
| Time: 3 months | Money: No | Copies: 1+sub. | Sub: $9 US |

Authors published: Albert Goldbarth, Caroline Knox & Christopher Howell.

Send 3-8 poems. Requests first North American serial rights. Does NOT accept simultaneous submissions. Uses up to 75 of the 1,500 submissions received each year. Please do not send essays, doggerel or formal verse. Interested in translations.

The Florida Review

Department of English, University of Central Florida, Orlando Florida, USA 32816

Editor: Russ Kesler

Telephone: (407) 823-2038 Fax: (407) 823-6582

Website: www.pegasus.cc.ucf.edu/English/floridareview/home.htm

| Since: 1972 | Format: Paper | Circ: 750 | Sample: $6 US |
| Time: 3 months | Money: No | Copies: 3 | Sub: $10 US |

Authors published: Colin Morton, Alan Peterson, Elton Glaser & William Trowbridge.

Send 1-5 poems. Requests first-time rights. Accepts simultaneous submissions if so noted. Does NOT accept e-mail submissions. Uses up to 30 of the 2,500 submissions received each year. Please do not send abstract or amateurish rhyming verse. Interested in fiction. Annual "Editors' Awards." Details online or send SASE.

The Formalist: A Journal of Metrical Poetry

320 Hunter Drive, Evansville, Indiana, USA 47711

Editor: William Baer

| Since: 1990 | Format: Paper | Circ: 500 | Sample: $8 US |
| Time: 1-2 months | Money: No | Copies: 2 | Sub: $15 US |

Authors published: Donald Justice, Louis Simpson, Maxine Kumin & John Updike.

Send 3-5 poems, of up to 1 page each. Requests first North American serial rights. Does NOT accept simultaneous submissions, previously published work or disk submissions. Interested in translations. "We're looking for well-crafted poetry in contemporary idiom which uses meter and the full range of traditional poetic conventions in vigorous and interesting ways. We're especially interested in sonnets, couplets, tercets, ballads, the French forms, etc. Please do not send haiku (or syllabic verse of any kind) or sestinas. We have no interest in any type of erotica, blasphemy, vulgarity or racism." Runs writing contest. Send SASE for details.

Frogpond

PO Box 2461, Winchester, Virgina, USA 22604-1661

Editor: Jim Kacian

Telephone: (540) 722-2156

E-mail: redmoon@shentel.net

| Since: 1968 | Format: Paper | Circ: 1,000+ | Sample: $7 US |
| Time: 2-3 weeks | Money: No | Copies: 1 | Sub: $20 US |

Send 5-10 poems. Requests first North American serial rights. Accepts e-mail submissions. Does NOT accept simultaneous submissions. Uses 600 of the up to 10,000 submissions received each year. "We are interested only in haiku and haiku-related work." Please query regarding articles, book reviews, translations, artwork or photography.

Fuel Magazine

PO Box 408979, Chicago, Illinois, USA 60640

Editor: Ms. Andy Lowry

E-mail: alowry@chicagoreader.com

| Since: 1992 | Format: Paper | Circ: 500 | Sample: $3 US |
| Time: 2 months | Money: No | Copies: 2 | Sub: $10 US |

Authors published: Nicole Panter, Errol Miller, Ed Mycue & Kury Nimmo.

Associated with Anaconda Press. Send up to 8 poems. Requests one-time rights. Does NOT accept simultaneous submissions. Accepts e-mail submissions. Uses 200 of the 3,500 submissions received each year. Please do not send romance, sci-fi or rhyming poetry. Interested in fiction, artwork and photography. Runs theme issue once a year. Send SASE for details.

Georgetown Review

PO Box 6309, Southern Station, Hattiesburg, Mississippi, USA 39406-6309
Editor: Steve Conti Poetry Editor: Marvyn Petrucci
E-mail: steve@georgetownreview.com

| Since: 1993 | Format: Paper | Circ: 800 | Sample: $8 US |
| Time: 4 months | Money: No | Copies: 2 | Sub: $15 US |

Authors published: D.C. Berry, Sallie Bingham, Richard Garcia & Vivian Shipley.

Send any number of one page poems. Requests first North American serial rights. Accepts simultaneous submissions if so noted. Use e-mail address ONLY for correspondence NOT submissions. Uses 24 of the 300 submissions received each year. Interested in translations and fiction. Runs annual contest. Send SASE for details.

The Georgia Review

The University of Georgia, Athens, Georgia, USA 30602-9009
Editor: Stanley W. Lindberg
Telephone: (706) 542-3481 Fax: (706) 542-0047
Website: www.uga.edu/~garev

| Since: 1947 | Format: Paper | Circ: 5,500 | Sample: $6 US |
| Time: 2-3 months | Money: $3 US/line | Copies: 1+ sub. | Sub: $18 US |

Authors published: Rita Dove, Donald Hall, Maxine Kumin & Philip Levine.

Send 3-5 poems. Requests first North American serial rights. Does NOT accept simultaneous submissions. Uses up to 140 of the 14,000 submissions received each year. Reads submissions September–May. Interested in fiction, artwork and photography. Query first for book reviews. "Our journal draws its material from a wide range of cultural interest, including (but not limited to) literature, history, philosophy, anthropology, politics, film, music, and the visual arts. We look for material that engages both the intelligent reader and the specialist. We are open to all kinds of original, well-crafted poems."

Hanging Loose

231 Wyckoff Street, Brooklyn, New York, USA 11217
Editor: Robert Hershon
Telephone: (212) 206-8465 Fax: (212) 243-7499
E-mail: Print225@aol.com

| Since: 1966 | Format: Paper | Circ: 2,000 | Sample: $8.50 US |
| Time: Up to 3 months | Money: Yes | Copies: 2 | Sub: $17.50 US |

Authors published: Sherman Alexie, Kimilko Hahn, Paul Violi & Donna Brook.

Send 4-6 poems. Requests first North American serial rights. Does NOT accept e-mail submissions or simultaneous submissions. Interested in translations, and fiction. Please do not send "junk."

Hawaii Pacific Review

Hawaii Pacific University, 1060 Bishop Street, Honolulu, Hawaii, USA 96813

Poetry Editor: Patrice M. Wilson Fiction Editor: Catherine Sustana
Telephone: (808) 544-1107 Fax: (808) 544-0862
E-mail: hpreview@hpu.edu

| Since: 1986 | Format: Paper | Circ: 500 | Sample: $ 5 US |
| Time: 3-4 months | Money: No | Copies: 2 | Sub: $10 US |

Authors published: Robert Cooperman, Sheila Nickerson & Susan Clayton-Goldner.

Send 5 poems. Requests first North American serial rights. Accepts simultaneous submissions if so noted. Does NOT accept e-mail submissions. Reads submissions September–December. Uses 40 of the 800 submissions received each year. Interested in book reviews, translations and fiction.

Hawaii Review

1733 Donaghho Road, Honolulu, Hawaii, USA 96822
Editor: Jason Monauw Poetry Editor: Losa Kanue
Telephone: (808) 956-3030 Fax: (808) 956-9962

| Since: 1973 | Format: Paper | Circ: 1,000 | Sample: $10 US |
| Time: 1-4 months | Money: No | Copies: 4 | Sub: $20 US |

Send 6 poems. Requests first North American serial rights. Accepts simultaneous submissions if so noted. Uses 100 of the 1,000 submissions received each year. Interested in translations, fiction, artwork and photography. Please send only one story at a time.

Hayden's Ferry Review

Box 871502, Arizona State University, Tempe, Arizona, USA 85287-1502
Managing Editor: S. Keegan
Telephone: (602) 965-1243 Fax: (602) 965-2229
E-mail: HFR@asu.edu
Website: www.news.vpsq.asu.edu/hfr/hfr.html

| Since: 1986 | Format: Paper | Circ: 1,300 | Sample: $6 US |
| Time: 1-2 months | Money: No | Copies: 2 | Sub: $10 US |

Authors published: Jean Valentine, Robert Hase, David St. John, Rita Dove & Raymond Carver.

Send 6 poems. Requests first North American serial rights. Accepts simultaneous submissions if so noted. Does NOT accept e-mail submissions. Uses 50 of 3,000 submissions received each year. Interested in translations, fiction, artwork and photography. "*Hayden's Ferry Review* promotes the work of emerging and established writers of fiction and poetry."

Heaven Bone

PO Box 486, Chester, New York, USA 10918
Editor: Steve Hirsch
Telephone: (914) 469-9018
E-mail: poetsteve@compuserve.com

| Since: 1986 | Format: Paper | Circ: 2,000 | Sample: $8 US |
| Time: 8 months | Money: No | Copies: 2 | Sub: N/A |

Authors published: Anne Waldman, Diane DiPrima & Michael McClure.

Send 3-10 poems. Requests first North American rights. Accepts simultaneous submissions if so noted. Also accepts e-mail submissions. Please get guidelines

BEFORE submitting. Uses up to 60 of the 1,500+ submissions received each year. Not interested in campy rhymed verse. Interested in book reviews, translations, fiction, artwork and photography. "Excellence is our only criteria but our sensibilities lean toward the surreal experimental, ethno-poetic, esoteric, spiritual, Buddhist/Hindu and concrete modes. No other magazine is doing what we're doing— you must see a sample to understand." Heaven Bone Press runs annual International Chapbook Competition.

The Hudson Review
684 Park Avenue, New York, New York, USA 10021
Editor: Paula Deitz
Telephone: (212) 650-0020 Fax: (212) 774-1911

Since: 1948	Format: Paper	Circ: 5,000	Sample: $8 US
Time: 3 months	Money: $.50 US/line	Copies: 2	Sub: $32 US

Authors published: Thomas M. Disch, Gary Krist, Joseph Epstein & Louis Simpson.
Send no more than 10 poems. Requests first publication rights. Does NOT accept simultaneous submissions or e-mail submissions. Uses few of the 4,000 submissions received each year. Prefers poetry submissions April–July. Interested in book reviews, translations, and fiction up to 10,000 words.

Indiana Review
465 Ballantine Hall, Bloomington, Indiana, USA 47408
Editor: Changes yearly.
Telephone: (812) 855-3439 Fax: (812) 855-4243
Website: www.Indiana.edu/~inreview

Since: 1981	Format: Paper	Circ: 2,700	Sample: $7 US
Time: 2-3 months	Money: $5 US/page	Copies: 2+sub.	Sub: $12 US

Authors published: Campbell McGrath, Jason Brown, Dan Chaon & Heather McHugh.
Send 4–6 poems, up to three pages each. Requests first North American rights. Accepts simultaneous submissions if so noted. Uses up to 80 of the 8,000 submissions received each year. Please do not send "explicit genre or sentimental work." Interested in book reviews, translations, fiction up to 40 pages. "We look for an intelligent sense of form and language, and admire poems of risk, ambition and scope."

International Poetry Review
PO Box 26170, Greensboro, North Carolina, USA 27402-6170
Editor: Mark Smith-Soto
Telephone: (336) 334-5655 Fax: (336) 334-5358
E-mail: smithsom@unco.edu
Website: www.uncg.edu/rom/ipr

Since: 1975	Format: Paper	Circ: 350	Sample: $5 US
Time: 3-6 months	Money: No	Copies: 1	Sub: $10 US

Authors published: Ana Istarl, Carmen Ollé & Fred Chappell.
Send 5 poems. Requests one-time rights. Accepts simultaneous submissions if so noted. Does NOT accept e-mail submissions. Uses 50 of the 500 submissions received each year. Reads submissions September 1–April 30. Interested in book reviews and b/w artwork or photos. "We publish primarily translations with the original on the facing page. We prefer contemporary work. Translators are responsible for securing publi-

cation rights. Please note, we prefer shorter works." Runs theme issues. Send SASE for details.

The Iowa Review

308 EPB, The University of Iowa, Iowa City, Iowa, USA 52242
Editors: Mary Hussman & David Hamilton
Telephone: (319) 335-0462 Fax: (319) 335-2535
E-mail: iowa-review@uiowa.edu
Website: www.uiowa.edu/~iareview

Since: 1970	Format: Paper/Web	Circ: 1,500	Sample: $6 US
Time: 2-3 months	Money: $1 US/line	Copies: 2	Sub: $18 US

Authors published: Marvin Bell, Marilyn Krysl, Frankie Paino & Reginald Shepherd.
Send 3-6 poems. Requests first North American serial rights and non-exclusive e-rights. Accepts simultaneous submissions if so noted. Does NOT accept e-mail submissions. Uses 120 of the 4,000 submissions received each year. Reads submissions from September–January. Interested in book reviews, translations and fiction.

The Kenyon Review

Kenyon College, Gambier, Ohio, USA 43022
Editor: David H. Lynn Poetry Editors: David Baker & Jennifer Clarvoe
Telephone: (740) 427-5208 Fax: (740) 427-5417
E-mail: kenyonreview@kenyon.edu
Website: www.kenyonreview.com

Since: 1939	Format: Paper	Circ: 4,500	Sample: $8 US
Time: 3 months	Money: $15 US/page	Copies: 4	Sub: $25 US

Send up to 5 poems. Requests full first publication rights including e-rights. Does NOT accept e-mail or simultaneous submissions. Reads submissions September–April. Uses 90 of the 4,000 submissions received each year. Sometimes comments on rejections. Interested in translations, fiction, artwork and photography.

Kuumba

PO Box 83912, Los Angeles, California, USA 90083-0912
Poetry Editor: Reginald Harris
Telephone: (310) 410-0808 Fax: (310) 410-9250
E-mail: reggieh@blk.com
Website: www.blk.com

X

Since: 1991	Format: Paper	Circ: Varies	Sample: $4.50 US
Time: 3 months	Money: No	Copies: 2	Sub: $7.50 US

Authors published: G. Winston James, Terri Jewel & Robert Penn.
Send 3-5 poems. Requests first North American and anthology rights. Accepts e-mail submissions, and simultaneous submissions if so noted. Two deadlines: Feb. 1 for Spring issue, Sept. 1 for Fall issue. Uses 125 of 500 submissions received each year. Interested in pen and ink line drawings. "Subject matter must relate to black lesbian and gay concerns. We are not interested in 'gay only' subjects with no black content, or 'black only' subjects with no gay content."

The Laurel Review

Department of English, Northwest Missouri State University, Maryville, Missouri, USA 64468

Editors: William Trowbridge, David Slater & Beth Richards
Telephone: (660) 562-1265

| Since: 1961 | Format: Paper | Circ: 900 | Sample: $5 US |
| Time: 1-4 months | Money: No | Copies: 2+sub. | Sub: $8 US |

Authors published: Ian MacMillan, David Citano & Albert Goldbarth.

Associated with Green Tower Press. Send 4 poems. Requests one-time rights. Does NOT accept simultaneous submissions. Uses 35 of the 3,500 submissions received each year. Please do not send genre fiction, political polemics, juvenile or religious poetry. Interested in fiction up to 4,000 words.

The Ledge Poetry Magazine
78-44 80th Street, Glendale, New York, USA 11385
Editor: Timothy Monaghan

| Since: 1988 | Format: Paper | Circ: 1,000 | Sample: $7 US |
| Time: 3-4 months | Money: No | Copies: 2 | Sub: $12 US |

Authors published: Sherman Alexie, David Kirby, Elliot Richman & Brooke Wiese.

Send 3-5 poems. Requests first-time rights. Accepts simultaneous submissions if so noted. Uses 150 of the 3,000 submissions received each year. Reads submissions September-May. Interested in translations. "Excellence is the only criterion." Runs annual poetry chapbook contest and annual poetry award competition. Send SASE for details.

The Literary Review
285 Madison Avenue, Madison, New Jersey, USA 07940
Editor: Walter Cummins
Telephone: (973) 443-8564 Fax: (973) 443-8564
E-mail: tlr@fdu.edu
Website: www.webdelsol.com/tlr

| Since: 1957 | Format: Paper | Circ: 2,100 | Sample: $6 US |
| Time: 2-3 months | Money: No | Copies: 2+ | Sub: $21 US |

Authors published: Maureen O'Neill & Todd Pierce.

Send 6-8 poems. Requests first US rights. Accepts simultaneous submissions if so noted. Does NOT accept e-mail submissions. Reads submissions September-June. Uses 30 of the 1,500 submissions received each year. Please send only contemporary work. Interested in book reviews, translations, and fiction. Runs two theme issues, two general issues each year.

Louisiana Literature
Southeastern Louisiana University, SLU 792, Hammond, Louisiana, USA 70402
Editor: Jack B. Bedell
Telephone: (504) 549-5022 Fax: (504) 549-5021
E-mail: jbedell@selu.edu
Website: www.selu.edu/lalit

| Since: 1978 | Format: Paper/Web | Circ: 700 | Sample: $6 US |
| Time: 2 months | Money: No | Copies: 2+sub. | Sub: $12 US |

Authors published: Walter MacDonald, Elton Glaser & Charles Rafferty.

Associated with Louisiana Literature Press. Send 3-5 poems. Requests first North American serial rights. Does NOT accept e-mail or simultaneous submissions. Uses

100 of the 2,000 submissions received each year. Often comments on rejections. Please do not send hermetic, "post-modern," or L=A=N=G=U=A=G=E poetry. Interested in fiction. Query regarding book reviews. Runs theme issue once each year. Runs annual Louisiana Literature Poetry Prize. Details online or send SASE.

Lullwater Review

Emory University, Box 22036, Atlanta, Georgia, USA 30322

Editor: Becky Brooks Poetry Editors: Ryan Caster & Leah Wolfson

Telephone: (404) 727-6184

Since: 1990	Format: Paper	Circ: 2,000	Sample: $5 US
Time: 3 months	Money: No	Copies: 3	Sub: $12 US

Authors published: Randall Garrison, Lyn Lifshin, Ruth Moose & Geri Rosenzweig

Send up to 6 poems. Requests first-time rights. Accepts simultaneous submissions if so noted. Uses the work of up to 50 contributors each year. Reads submissions August-May. Interested in translations, fiction up to 5,000 words, artwork and photography. Runs annual Lullwater Prize for Poetry Competition. Send SASE for details.

The MacGuffin

Schoolcraft College, 18600 Haggerty Road, Livonia, Michigan, USA 48152

Editor: Arthur J. Lindenberg Poetry Editor: Carol Was

Telephone: (734) 462-4400 ext.5292

E-mail: alindenb@schoolcraft.cc.mi.us

Website: www.schoolcraft.cc.mi.us

Since: 1983	Format: Paper	Circ: 600	Sample: $5 US
Time: 10-12 weeks	Money: No	Copies: 2	Sub: $15 US

Authors published: Jack Ridl, CB Follett & Diane Pinkley.

Send 5 poems, up to 300 lines each. Requests first-time rights. Does NOT accept simultaneous submissions or e-mail submissions. Uses 80 or more of the 800 or more submissions received each year. Not interested in pornography, trite or sloppy poetry. Please do not send haiku, concrete poetry or light verse. Interested in translations, fiction, artwork and photography. Runs theme issue in June. Runs annual National Poet Hunt contest. Send SASE for details.

MĀNOA: A Pacific Journal of International Writing

University of Hawaii, English Department, 1733 Donaghho Road, Honolulu, Hawaii, USA 96822

Editor: Frank Stewart

Telephone: (808) 956-3070 Fax: (808) 956-7808

E-mail: mjournal-l@hawaii.edu

Website: www2.hawaii.edu/mjournal

Since: 1989	Format: Paper	Circ: 2,000	Sample: $10 US
Time: 6 weeks	Money: $25 US/page	Copies: 2	Sub: $22 US

Authors published: bpNichol, Sid Marty, Jan Zwicky & Don Gayton.

Send 5-6 poems. Requests first North American serial rights and one-time reprint rights. Accepts simultaneous submissions if so noted. Does NOT accept e-mail submissions. Uses only some of the 3,000 submissions received each year. Interested in fiction, artwork and photography. Translations are usually handled by guest editor but feel free to query. "Ordinarily we are not interested in genre writing, Pacific exotica or picturesque impressions of the region."

The Massachusetts Review

South College, University of Massachusetts, Amherst, Massachusetts, USA 01003
Editors: Mary Heath & Jules Chametzky Poetry Editors: Paul Jenkins, Anne Halley & Martín Espada
Telephone: (413) 545-2689 Fax: (413) 577-0740
E-mail: massrev@external.umass.edu
Website: www.litline.org/html/massreview.html

| Since: 1959 | Format: Paper | Circ: 1,600 | Sample: $7 US |
| Time: 1-2 months | Money: $.35 US/line | Copies: 2 | Sub: $18 US |

Authors published: Jean Valentine, Adrienne Rich, Stephen Dobyns & Julia Alvarez.

Send 5-7 poems, up to 100 lines each. Requests first publication rights, reissue rights, and e-rights. Copyright returned to author upon request. Accepts simultaneous submissions if so noted. Does NOT accept e-mail submissions. Reads poetry submissions all year, fiction submissions October-May. Uses 50 of the 2,500 submissions received each year. Encourages submission of translations. Interested in fiction up to 30 pages. May be interested in artwork or photography. Query. Occasionally runs theme issues. Details online or send SASE.

Mayfly

4634 Hale Drive, Decatur, Illinois, USA 62526
Editors: Randy Brooks & Shirley Brooks
Telephone: (217) 877-2966
E-mail: brooksbooks@q-com.com
Website: www.family-net.net/~brooksbooks

| Since: 1986 | Format: Paper | Circ: 300 | Sample: $4 US |
| Time: 3 months | Money: $5 US/poem | Copies: Nil | Sub: $8 US |

Authors published: George Swede, Michael Dudley & Leroy Gorman.

Send 5 poems. Requests first North American serial rights and e-posting. Accepts e-mail submissions. Does NOT accept simultaneous submissions. Reads submissions January–March and August–October. Uses 28 of the 800 submissions received each year. Interested in haiku ONLY. "We feature individual haiku, one per page."

Michigan Quarterly Review

University of Michigan, 3032 Rackham Building, 915 East Washington Street, Ann Arbor, Michigan, USA 48109-1070
Editor: Laurence Goldstein
Telephone: (734) 764-9265
E-mail: MQR@umich.edu
Website: www.umich.edu/~mqr

| Since: 1962 | Format: Paper | Circ: 1,300 | Sample: $2.50 US |
| Time: 6 weeks | Money: $10 US/page | Copies: 2 | Sub: $18 US |

Authors published: Joyce Carol Oates, Arthur Miller, Charles H. Webb & David Lehman.

Send 1-3 poems. Requests first rights only. Does NOT accept e-mail or simultaneous submissions. Uses 80 of the 1,000 submissions received each year. Interested in book reviews, translations, and fiction up to 5,000 words. Artwork or photography may be requested at the time of manuscript acceptance. Query. Lawrence Foundation Prize of $1,000 US awarded to the author of the best short story published in *MQR* the previous year.

Mid-American Review

English Department, Bowling Green State University, Bowling Green, Ohio, USA 43403
Editor: George Looney Poetry Editor: David Hawkins
Telephone: (419) 372-2725

Since: 1980	Format: Paper	Circ: 1,000	Sample: $5 US
Time: 1-4 months	Money: $10 US/poem	Copies: 2+disc.	Sub: $12 US

Authors published: Michael Martone, David Foster Wallace, Albert Goldbarth & Chase Twichell.

Send 3-5 poems. Requests first rights. Accepts simultaneous submissions if so noted. Reads submissions September-May. Uses up to 60 of the up to 3,000 submissions received each year. Please do not send genre work or juvenilia. Interested in book reviews, translations, fiction up to 5,000 words, artwork and photography. "*Mid-American Review* seeks the best contemporary poetry, fiction and non-fiction with the understanding that contemporary implies an awareness of both the nature of literature and the nature of the world in which that literature exists."

Minnesota Review

Department of English, University of Missouri, Columbia, Missouri, USA 65211
Editor: Jeffrey Williams

Since: 1960	Format: Paper	Circ: 1,500	Sample: $7.50 US
Time: 2 months	Money: No	Copies: 2-3	Sub: $12 US

Authors published: Warren Leher, Amitara Kumar, S.K. Duff & Maggie Jaffe.

Send 1-6 poems. Requests first publications rights. Accepts simultaneous submissions if so noted. Uses 20 of the 1,000 submissions received each year. Interested in book reviews, translations, and fiction. "We prefer submissions which have political significance."

Modern Haiku

PO Box 1752, Madison, Wisconsin, USA 53701-1752
Editor: Robert Spiess
Telephone: (608) 133-1738

Since: 1969	Format: Paper	Circ: 630	Sample: $5.75 US
Time: 2 weeks	Money: Yes	Copies: Nil	Sub: $17 US

Authors published: LeRoy Gorman, Anne McKay & George Swede.

Send any number of poems. Requests first North American serial rights. Does NOT accept simultaneous submissions. Uses 850 of the 12,000 submissions received each year. Please do not send tanka, lined verse, or short poems. Interested in book reviews and translations. "*Modern Haiku* is the foremost international English-language haiku journal. Not interested in 'pretty' or sentimental haiku. All 'styles' of haiku considered but must be genuine haiku, not ones that strive for novel effect." Runs annual haiku contest for high school seniors. For details send SASE.

Mississippi Mud

7119 Santa Fe Avenue, Dallas, Texas, USA 75223
Editor: Joel Weinstein

Telephone: (214) 321-8955

Since: 1973	Format: Paper	Circ: 1,500	Sample: $6 US
Time: 4-6 months	Money: $25 US/poem	Copies: 2	Sub: $12 US

Authors published: Diane Averill, Fileman Waitts & Edward Kleinschmidt.

Send up to 6 poems. Requests first North American rights. Accepts simultaneous submissions if so noted. Uses 10 of the 300 submissions received each year. Interested in translations, fiction, artwork and photography.

Murderous Intent Mystery Magazine

PO Box 5947, Vancouver, Washington, USA 98668-5947

Editor: Margo Power

Telephone: (360) 695-9004 Fax: (360) 693-3354

E-mail: madison@teleport.com

Website: www.teleport.com/~madison/mimm.htm

Since: 1994	Format: Paper	Circ: 5,000	Sample: $5.95 US
Time: 9-12 months	Money: $2 US/poem	Copies: 1	Sub: $20 US

Authors published: Jan Burke, Michael Mallory & L.L. Thrasher.

Send 6 poems of 4-8 humourous lines each. Requests one-time rights and one-time e-rights. Accepts simultaneous submissions if so noted. Does NOT accept e-mail submissions. Interested in receiving more poetry submissions. May use many if the quality is there. Interested in mystery/suspense fiction. May be interested in artwork and photography. Query with samples.

Nassau Review

English Department, Nassau College, 1 Education Drive, Garden City, New York, US 11530

Managing Editor: Dr. Paul A. Doyle Poetry Editor: Editorial Board

Telephone: (516) 272-7792

Since: 1964	Format: Paper	Circ: 1,200	Sample: Free
Time: 5-7 months	Money: No	Copies: 3	Sub: Free

Send 3 poems. Requests first-time rights. Does NOT accept simultaneous submissions. Uses only some of the 1,800 submissions received each year. Reads submissions November–March. Interested in fiction, artwork and photography. If submitting fiction please send only one story. Runs annual contests for best poem, best short story and best essay. Send SASE for details.

National Forum: The Phi Kappa Phi Journal

129 Quad Center, Mell Street, Auburn University, Alabama, USA 36849-5306

Editor: James P. Kaetz Poetry Editors: Lois Roma-Deeley & Randy Phillis

Telephone: (334) 844-5200 Fax: (334) 844-5994

E-mail: kaetzjp@mail.auburn.edu

Website: www.auburn.edu/academic/societies/phi_kappa_phi/natforum.html

Since: 1917	Format: Paper	Circ: 120,000	Sample:$6.25 US
Time: 3 months	Money: No	Copies: 10	Sub: $25 US

Send 3-5 poems, up to 1 page each. Requests one-time rights. Accepts simultaneous submissions if so noted as well as e-mail submissions. Uses 15 of the 500 submissions received each year. "Please do not send poems containing obscenities or overtly sexual situations. We have a conservative readership." Every issue is a theme issue and themes vary widely. Details online or send SASE.

The Nebraska Review

Writer's Workshop, University of Nebraska at Omaha, Omaha, Nebraska, USA 68108

Editor: James Reed Poetry Editor: Susan Aizenberg

Telephone: (402) 554-3159

| Since: 1972 | Format: Paper | Circ: 1,000 | Sample: $3.50 US |
| Time: 3-6 months | Money: No | Copies: 2+sub. | Sub: $11 US |

Authors published: Stewart O'Nan, Dewitt Henry, Vivian Shipley & Anne Caston.

Send 5-6 poems, totaling up to six pages. Requests first North American serial rights and e-rights. Accepts simultaneous submissions if so noted. Uses 30 of the 900 submissions received each year. Reads submissions January–April 15. Interested in fiction. Runs annual fiction and poetry contests. Send SASE for details.

Negative Capability

62 Ridgelawn Drive East, Mobile, Alabama, USA 36688

Editors: Sue Walker & James Walker

E-mail: negcap@datasync.com

| Since: 1981 | Format: Paper | Circ: 1,000 | Sample: $8 US |
| Time: 6 weeks | Money: No | Copies: 1 | Sub: $16 US |

Authors published: Diane Wakoski, Vivian Shipley & Michael Bugeja.

Associated with Negative Capability Press. Send 3-5 poems. Requests first rights. Accepts invited e-mail submissions ONLY. Does NOT accept simultaneous submissions. Reads submissions September–May. Uses 500 of the 3,000 submissions received each year. Please do not send sexually explicit material. Occasionally comments on rejections. Interested in book reviews, translations, short fiction, artwork and photography. "We wish to promote writing that serves as an axe that breaks the frozen sea within us." Runs annual Eve of St. Agnes Poetry Competition, and annual Brannan Fiction Award.

New England Review

Middlebury College, Middlebury, Vermont, USA 05753

Editor: Stephen Donadio Managing Editor: Jodee Rubins

Telephone: (802) 443-5075 Fax: (802) 443-2088

E-mail: nereview@mail.middlebury.edu

Website: /www.middlebury.edu/~nereview/index.html

| Since: 1978 | Format: Paper | Circ: 2,000 | Sample: $7 US |
| Time: 3 months | Money: $20 US | Copies: 2 | Sub: $23 US |

Send up to 6 poems. Requests first rights and reprint option in subsequent editions of the magazine in any form. Accepts simultaneous submissions if so noted. Does NOT accept e-mail submissions. Uses 90 of the thousands of submissions received each year. Reads submissions postmarked September 1–May 31 ONLY. Please do not send light verse. Interested in serious literary works only. Interested in fiction up to 7,500 words, non-fiction up to 7,500 words, and long reviews up to 1,500 words. "We are interested in translations and letters from throughout the world."

New Letters

University of Missouri-Kansas City, 5101 Rockhill Road, Kansas City, Missouri, USA 64110

Editor: James McKinley Poetry Editor: Robert Stewart

Telephone: (816) 235-1168 Fax: (816) 235-2611

Website: www.umkc.edu/newletters

| Since: 1934 | Format: Paper | Circ: 2,000 | Sample: $5 US |
| Time: 2-3 months | Money: No | Copies: 2 | Sub: $17 US |

Authors published: Janet Borroway, Alberto Rios, Carolyn Kizer & Miller Williams.

Send 3-6 poems. Requests first-time rights. Accepts simultaneous submissions if so noted. Reads submissions October 15–May 15. Uses 100 of the up to 3,000 submissions received each year. Please do not send bad writing or academic writing. Interested in translations, fiction up to 5,000 words, artwork and photography. Sometimes runs theme issues. Also runs writing contest. Details online or send SASE.

New Orleans Review
Department of English, Loyola University, New Orleans, Louisiana, USA 70118
Editor: Ralph Adamo
Telephone: (504) 865-2295 Fax: (504) 865-2294
E-mail: noreview@loyno.edu
Website: www.loyno.edu/english/programs/noreview.htm

| Since: 1968 | Format: Paper | Circ: 1,500 | Sample: $9 US |
| Time: 2 months | Money: No | Copies: 2-5 | Sub: $18 US |

Authors published: Rodney Jones, Jack Gilbert, Colette Inez & Doug Glover.

Send 3-5 poems. Requests first North American serial rights. Does NOT accept simultaneous submissions or e-mail submissions. Uses perhaps 36 of the up to 5,000 submissions received. Interested in translations and fiction. Query regarding artwork or photography.

Nexus Magazine
W016A Student Union, Wright State University, Dayton, Ohio, USA 45435
Editor: Adam Cline
Telephone: (937) 775-5533

| Since: 1967 | Format: Paper | Circ: 1,000 | Sample: $5 US |
| Time: Varies | Money: No | Copies: 2 | Sub: $25 US |

Authors published: Lawrence Ferlinghetti, Jack Micheline & Charles Henry Ford.

Send 3-5 poems. Requests first-time rights. Accepts simultaneous submissions if so noted. Interested in translations, fiction, artwork and photography. "*Nexus Magazine* strives to be as diverse as possible. We welcome any new or innovative ideas. As our editorial staff shifts yearly, so does the magazine's focus and direction shift. We challenge the artist to make us take notice, and to shift in our direction."

Northwest Review
369 PLC, University of Oregon, Eugene, Oregon, USA 97403
Editor: John Witte
Telephone: (541) 346-3957 Fax: (541) 346-1509

| Since: 1957 | Format: Paper | Circ: 1,100 | Sample: $4 US |
| Time: 10 weeks | Money: No | Copies: 3+sub. | Sub: $20 US |

Authors published: Doris Dorrie, Mark Levine, David Kirby & Madeline DeFrees.

Send 5-6 poems. Requests first North American serial rights. Does NOT accept simultaneous submissions. Uses 60 of the 4,000 submissions received each year. Author may request additional discounted copies. Please do not send small-hearted work. Interested in book reviews and fiction. Special interest in translations. Artwork and photography should be preceded by query and samples.

Paintbrush: A Journal of Poetry and Translation

Truman State University, Kirksville, Missouri, USA 63501

Editor: Ben Bennani

Telephone: (660) 785-4185 Fax: (660) 785-7486

E-mail: pbrush@truman.edu

Website: www.paintbrush.org

Since: 1974	Format: Paper	Circ: 500	Sample: $15 US
Time: 3-5 weeks	Money: No	Copies: 2	Sub: $20 US

Authors published: B'ruchac Momaday, X.J. Kennedy & Naomi Shihab Nye.

Send 3-5 poems. Requests first-time rights. Does NOT accept simultaneous submissions. Uses up to 100 of the 2,000 submissions received each year. Reads submissions in the fall and spring. Interested in book reviews, translations, artwork and photography. Runs theme issues. Send SASE for details. Runs annual Ezra Pound Poetry Award. Winners receive $2,000 US and publication of their full-length manuscript. Details online or send SASE.

Painted Bride Quarterly

230 Vine Street, Philadephia, Pennsylvania, USA 19106

Poetry Editor: Marion Wrenn Fiction Editor: Kathy Volk-Miller

Since: 1974	Format: Paper	Circ: 1,200	Sample: $6 US
Time: 4 months	Money: $5 US/poem	Copies: 1	Sub: $16 US

Authors published: Yusef Komonyakaa, Sonia Sanchez, Henry Brown & Tina Barr.

Send 3-5 poems. Requests first publications rights. Accepts simultaneous submissions if so noted. Uses up to 200 of the 2,000 submissions received each year. Interested in book reviews, translations and fiction.

The Paris Review

541 East 72nd Street, New York, New York, USA 10021

Editor: George Plimpton Poetry Editor: Richard Howard

Telephone: (212) 861-0016 Fax: (212) 861-4504

Since: 1953	Format: Paper	Circ: 15,000	Sample: $14 US
Time: 3 months	Money: Varies	Copies: 2	Sub: $44 US

Authors published: Charles Wright, Anthony Hecht & Jorie Graham.

Send 1-5 poems. Requests first serial rights. Accepts simultaneous submissions if so noted. Does NOT accept e-mail submissions. Uses 80 of the 20,000 submissions received each year. Interested in translations, fiction, artwork and photography. Runs theme issues. Send SASE for details.

Parnassus: Poetry in Review

205 West 89th Street, #8-F, New York, New York, USA 10024-1835

Editor: Herbert Leibowitz

Telephone: (212) 362-3492 Fax: (212) 875-0148

E-mail: parnew@aol.com

Since: 1972	Format: Paper	Circ: 1,500	Sample: $15 US
Time: 4-6 weeks	Money: $25-$50 US/poem	Copies: 1	Sub: $30 US

Authors published: Albert Goldbarth, Wayne Koestenbaum & Richard Howard.

Send 3-5 pages. Copyright returned upon request to author following publication. Accepts simultaneous submissions if so noted. Does NOT accept e-mail submissions.

Uses 30 of the up to 400 submissions received each year. "Most of the poetry we publish is solicited though we try to give unsolicited work close scrutiny. Our only criterion is excellence." Often comments on rejections. Please do not send academic prose. Interested in translations, some fiction, artwork and photography. Runs theme issues. Some recent themes have been on poetry and film, poetry and prose, and international poetry. Publishes in the form of a trade paperback up to 500 pages.

Parnassus Literary Journal

PO Box 1384, Forest Park, Georgia, USA 30298-1384

Editor: Denver Stull

Telephone: (404) 366-3177

Since: 1975	Format: Paper	Circ: 200+	Sample: $6 US
Time: 30 days	Money: No	Copies: 1	Sub: $18 US

Authors published: T.K. Splake, Jean Jorgensen & Ruth Schuler.

Send 3 poems, up to 24 lines each. Requests "any" rights. Accepts simultaneous submissions if so noted. Uses up to 10% of the submissions received each year. Often comments on rejections. Please do not send smut or preachy poetry. "Due to backlog, shorter pieces have a better chance for acceptance. We prefer uplifting poetry."

Passages North

Department of English, Northern Michigan University, 1401 Presque Isle Avenue, Marquette, Michigan, USA 49829

Editor: Katie Hanson Poetry Editor: Anne Ohman Youngs

Telephone: (906) 227-1203 Fax: (906) 227-1096

E-mail: ayoungs@nmu.edu

Since: 1979	Format: Paper	Circ: 500	Sample: $6 US
Time: 6-8 weeks	Money: No	Copies: 2	Sub: $13 US

Authors published: Wendy Mnookin, Jim Daniels & Jack Driscoll.

Send 3-5 poems. Requests copyright. Will return copyright to author upon request. Does NOT accept e-mail submissions or simultaneous submissions. Reads submissions September–April. Uses up to 80 of the 4,000 submissions received each year. Please do not send light verse or preachy poems. Interested in translations and fiction. Occasionally runs writing contest.

Permafrost

Department of English, University of Alaska, Fairbanks, Alaska, USA 99775

Editor: Ryan Johnson Poetry Editor: Kent Fielding

Telephone: (907) 474-5398 Fax: (907) 474-5314

E-mail: ftrmj1@uaf.edu

Since: 1977	Format: Paper	Circ: 300+	Sample: $5 US
Time: 1-2 months	Money: No	Copies: 2	Sub: $8 US

Authors published: Allen Ginsberg, Peter Orlovsky & Ethelbert Miller.

Send up to 5 poems. Requests one-time rights. Accepts simultaneous submissions if so noted. Does NOT accept e-mail submissions. Reads submissions September–March. Uses 30 or more of the 500 submissions received each year. Please do not send sci-fi or genre fiction. Interested in book reviews, translations, fiction, artwork and photography. "Please don't submit Alzskznz poetry— especially if you've never been to Alaska." Runs chapbook contest. Send SASE for details.

Phoebe: A Journal of Literary Arts

George Mason University, 4400 University Drive, MSN 2D6, Fairfax, Virgina, USA 22030

Editor: Mehera Dennison

Telephone: (703) 993-2915

E-mail: phoebe@gmu.edu

Website: www.gmu.edu/pubs/phoebe

Since: 1971	Format: Paper	Circ: 1,500	Sample: $6 US
Time: 3 months	Money: No	Copies: 2	Sub: $12 US

Authors published: Amy Gerstler & Russell Edson.

Send up 4-6 poems. Requests first time North American rights. Does NOT accept simultaneous submissions or e-mail submissions. Uses up to 75 of the 2,000 submissions received each year. Reads submissions August-May. Please do not send juvenilia, romance, worn-out forms or cliches. Interested in fiction up to 2,500 words, artwork and photography. "We prefer poetry that is experimental, vibrant, and new, new, new!" Runs annual Greg Grummer Poetry Contest, and separate annual fiction contest.

Pig Iron Series

26 North Phelps Street, PO Box 237, Youngstown, Ohio, USA 44501

Editor: Jim Villani

Telephone: (330) 747-6932 Fax: (330) 747-0599

Since: 1975	Format: Paper	Circ: 1,000	Sample: $6 US
Time: 6 months	Money: No	Copies: 2	Sub: $12 US

Authors published: Judith Hemschemeyer, Jim Sanderson & Andrena Zawinski.

Send up to 10 poems. Requests one-time rights. Accepts simultaneous submissions if so noted. Uses up to 60 poems, 15 stories, 50 drawings in any one year. Interested in fiction up to 6,000 words, artwork and photography. Every issue a theme issue. Send SASE for details. Runs full-manuscript poetry or fiction contest in alternating years.

The Pittsburgh Quarterly

36 Haberman Avenue, Pittsburgh, Pennsylvania, USA 15211-2144

Editor: Frank Correnti

Telephone: (412) 431-8885

E-mail: tpq@city-net.com

Website: www.city-net.com/~tpq

Since: 1991	Format: Paper/Web	Circ: 600	Sample: $5 US
Time: 4-6 months	Money: No	Copies: 2	Sub: $12 US

Authors published: Margaret Almon, Dennis Brutus, Joe Blades & Susan Terris.

Send 3-5 poems. Requests first-time rights. Accepts e-mail submissions. Does NOT accept simultaneous submissions. Uses 100 of the 1,000 submissions received each year. Please do not send doggerel. Interested in book reviews, translations and fiction. "Regarding artwork: line drawing is preferred; may be transmitted as scan electronically; can work with EPSF. *The Pittsburgh Quarterly* is a small press publication that seeks to publish experienced and new writers to our international community. Bruce Hoffman edits our separate electronic magazine *TPQ Online*." The print magazine runs a poetry competition: the Sara Henderson Hay Prize. Details online or send SASE.

Poem

c/o English Department, University of Alabama in Huntsville, Huntsville, Alabama, USA 35899
Poetry Editor: Nancy Frey Dillard
Telephone: (256) 890-6320

| Since: 1967 | Format: Paper | Circ: 400 | Sample: $5 US |
| Time: 1 month | Money: No | Copies: 2 | Sub: $15 US |

Send 3–5 poems. Requests first serial rights. Does NOT accept simultaneous submissions. Uses the work of up to 25 poets in each issue, often with more than one poem. Please do not send light verse, religious, confessional or prose poems. Prefers short poems. "We are interested in new as well as established poets who have a high degree of verbal precision and poetic ability."

Poetry Flash

1450 Fourth Street, #4, Berkeley, California, USA 94710
Editor: Joyce Jenkins
Telephone: (510) 525-5476 Fax: (510) 525-6752

| Since: 1972 | Format: Paper | Circ: 21,000 | Sample: Free |
| Time: 2-3 month | Money: Varies | Copies: 5+2yr/sub. | Sub: $16 US |

Send 5–6 poems. Requests first serial rights. May request anthology rights. Accepts simultaneous submissions if so noted. Uses the work of up to 10 poets in each issue. "We are very selective. Only the best, highest-quality submissions are selected."

Poetry Magazine

60 West Walton Street, Chicago, Illinois, USA 60610
Editor: Joseph Parisi
Telephone: (312) 255-3703
E-mail: poetry@poetrymagazine.org
Website: www.poetrymagazine.org

| Since: 1912 | Format: Paper | Circ: 7,700 | Sample: $5 US |
| Time: 3 months | Money: $2 US/line | Copies: 2 | Sub: $30 US |

Authors published: A.R. Ammons, John Ashberry, Rita Dove & Seamus Heaney.
Send 4 poems. Requests all rights. Does NOT accept simultaneous or e-mail submissions. Uses 200 of the 80,000 submissions received each year. Interested in book reviews and translations.

Prairie Schooner

201 Andrews Hall, Lincoln, Nebraska, USA 68588-0334
Editor: Hilda Raz
Telephone: (402) 472-0911 Fax: (402) 472-9771
E-mail: lrandolp@unlinfo.unl.edu
Website: www.unl.edu/schooner/psmain.htm

| Since: 1926 | Format: Paper | Circ: 3,500 | Sample: $5 US |
| Time: 4 months | Money: No | Copies: 3 | Sub: $22 US |

Associated with University of Nebraska Press. Send 6–10 poems. Requests first North American and electronic rights. Does NOT accept e-mail or simultaneous submissions. Uses up to 80 of the 500 submissions received each month. Reads submissions September–May. Please do not send scholarly articles. Interested in book reviews, translations and fiction. Occasionally runs special issues. Usually these are devoted to a region or a country.

Puerto Del Sol

Box 30001, Department 3E, New Mexico State University, Las Cences, New Mexico, USA 88003-8001

Editor: Kevin McIlvoy Poetry Editor: Kathleene West

Telephone: (505)646-2345 Fax: (505) 646-7725

E-mail: kwest@nmsu.edu (poetry queries only)

Since: 1975	Format: Paper	Circ: 2,000	Sample: $8 US
Time: 4-6 months	Money: No	Copies: 2	Sub: $10 US

Authors published: Tony Hoagland, Bill Ransom, Julie King & Luis Urrea.

Send up to 6 poems. Requests one-time rights. Accepts simultaneous submissions if so noted. Does NOT accept e-mail submissions. Uses up to 55 of the 700 submissions received each year. Reads submissions from September 1–March 1. Often comments on rejections. Interested in translations, fiction, artwork and photography.

Radiance: The Magazine for Large Women

PO Box 30246, Oakland, California, USA 94604

Editor: Alice Ansfield

Telephone: (510) 482-0680

E-mail: info@radiancemagazine.com

Website: www.radiancemagazine.com

Since: 1984	Format: Paper	Circ: 17,000+	Sample: $3.50 US
Time: 2-3 months	Money: $15 US/poem	Copies: 1	Sub: $26 US

Send any number of poems. Requests one-time rights and may request e-rights. Accepts simultaneous submissions if so noted. Does NOT accept e-mail submissions. Uses 180 of the 1,800 poems received each year. Sometimes comments on rejections. Interested in book reviews, fiction, artwork and photography. "Our magazine is one of the leading resources in the worldwide size–acceptance movement. We document and celebrate women all sizes of large, of all ages, lifestyles, and ethnicities."

RE:AL, The Journal of Liberal Arts

PO Box 13007-SFA, Nacogdoches, Texas, USA 75962-3007

Editor: W. Dale Hearell

Telephone: (409) 468-2059 Fax: (409) 468-2190

E-mail: REAL@sfasu.edu

Website: www.libarts.sfasu.edu/real/index.html

Since: 1968	Format: Paper/Web	Circ: 500	Sample: $5 US
Time: 2-3 months	Money: No	Copies: 2	Sub: $25 US

Send 1–5 poems. Requests first publications rights. Does NOT accept simultaneous or e-mail submissions. Uses over 200 of the thousands of submissions received each year. Editor notes it is best to send two copies of any submission to speed consideration process. Disk copy of work will be requested if accepted. Please do not send any drama. Interested in translations, fiction or criticism up to 5,000 words. Often comments on rejections. May be interested in line drawings. Query.

Response: A Contemporary Jewish Review

114 West 26th Street, Suite 1004, New York, New York, USA 10001-6812

Editor: Chanita Baumhaft

Telephone: (212) 620-0350 Fax: (212) 929-3459

E-mail: response@panix.com
Website: www.responseweb.org

Since: 1967	Format: Paper	Circ: 6,000	Sample: $6 US
Time: 6 weeks	Money: No	Copies: 3	Sub: $20 US

Authors published: Yerah Gover, Naomi Hetherington & Pamela Brown.

Send 3 poems. Requests varying rights. Accepts e-mail submissions. Does not accept simultaneous submissions. Uses 20 of the 200 submissions received each year. Interested in book reviews, translations, fiction, artwork and photography. "Submissions should be on a Jewish theme, but avoid the trite or predictable."

RHINO

PO Box 554, Winnetka, Illinois, USA 60093
Editor: Alice George Poetry Editor: Deborah Nodler Rosen
Website: www.artic.edu/~ageorge/RHINO

Since: 1976	Format: Paper	Circ: 500	Sample: $7 US
Time: 2-3 months	Money: No	Copies: 2	Sub: $7 US

Authors published: Roger Mitchell, Anne Calcagno & Maureen Seaton.

Send 3-5 poems, up to two pages each. Requests first North American rights. Accepts simultaneous submissions if so noted. Uses up to 80 of the 1,000 submissions received each year. Please do not send political, religious or superficial poems. Occasionally comments on rejections. Interested in translations, short-shorts, artwork and photography.

River City

Department of English, The University of Memphis, Memphis, Tennessee, USA 38152
Editor: Thomas Russell
Telephone: (901) 678-4591 Fax: (901) 678-2226

Since: 1970	Format: Paper	Circ: 1,200	Sample: $7 US
Time: 1 month	Money: No	Copies: 2	Sub: $12 US

Authors published: Stephen Dobyns, Seamus Heaney & Adrienne Rich.

Send no more than 20 pages. Requests first North American serial rights and e-rights. Does NOT accept simultaneous submissions. Reads submissions September–April. Uses up to 40 of the 800 submissions received each year. Please do not send children's stories, pornography, sci-fi, or romance. Interested in book reviews, translations, fiction up to 7,500 words, artwork and photography. Runs theme issues. Runs fiction contest. Send SASE for details.

River Styx Magazine

3207 Washington, St. Louis, Missouri, USA 63103
Editor: Richard Newman
Telephone: (314) 533-4541

Since: 1974	Format: Paper	Circ: 2,000	Sample: $7 US
Time: 3-5 months	Money: No	Copies: 2	Sub: $20 US

Authors published: Andrew Hodgins, Yusef Komunyakaa, Julia Alvarez & Marilyn Hacker.

Send 3-5 poems. Requests either first-time rights or one-time rights. Accepts simultaneous submissions if so noted. Reads submissions May–November. Uses perhaps 50 of the 5,000 submissions received each year. Occasionally comments on rejections. Please do not send poems about poetry or poets, or being a poet. Interested in translations, fiction, artwork and photography. "We want poems that are clear and musical, energetic poems, poems that are about something, poems that compel the reader on the first read yet reward with subsequent readings." Runs a theme issue once a year. Annually runs a short-short story contest and a poetry contest. Send SASE for details.

Sanskrit Literary Arts Magazine

Student Media Offices, The Cone University Center, University of North
Carolina-Charlotte, Charlotte, North Carolina, USA 28223-001
Editors: Courtney Norris & Mariah Cowan Literary Editor: Kevin Croussore
Telephone: (704) 547-2326
E-mail: sanskrit@E-mail.uncc.edu
Website: www.uncc.edu (Student organizations directory)

| Since: 1969 | Format: Paper/Web | Circ: 3,500 | Sample: $10 US |
| Time: Varies | Money: No | Copies: 1 | Sub: N/A |

Authors published: Jason Lane Byrd & Juston Gray.

Send up to 15 poems. Requests first serial rights. Accepts e-mail submissions, and simultaneous submissions if so noted. Uses up to 24 of the 500+ submissions received each year. Notification of accepted work occurs November-January ONLY. Interested in translations, fiction up to 3,500 words, artwork and photography. Please send 75 word author bio.

Sing Heavenly Muse!

PO Box 13320, Minneapolis, Minnesota, USA 55414
Editor: Collective

| Since: 1977 | Format: Paper | Circ: 300 | Sample: $4 US |
| Time: 9 months | Money: Varies | Copies: 2 | Sub: $21 US |

Authors published: Vers Jensen, Ana L. Ortiz de Montellino & Barbara Helfgott-Hyett.

Send up to 6 poems. Requests first North American serial rights. Does NOT accept simultaneous submissions. Interested in fiction. "*Sing Heavenly Muse!* offers readers insights into women's lives." Runs theme issues. Send SASE for details.

Slipstream

PO Box 2071, Niagara Falls, New York, USA 14301
Editors: Dan Sicoli, Livio Farallo & Robert Borgatti
Website: www.wings.buffalo.edu/libraries/units/pl/slipstream

| Since: 1980 | Format: Paper | Circ: 500 | Sample: $7 US |
| Time: 1-2 months | Money: No | Copies: 1-2 | Sub: $20 US |

Authors published: A.D. Winans, Jeff Parsons, Joan Jobe Smith & Gerald Locklin.

Send 3-6 poems. Requests first North American rights. Accepts simultaneous submissions if so noted. Uses up to 100 of the 2,000 submissions received each year. Please do not send religious, rhyming, pastoral verse. Interested in fiction up to 15 pages, as well as artwork and photography which display contemporary urban themes. Runs theme issues. Runs chapbook contest. Details online or send SASE.

Sojourners

2401 15th Street North West, Washington, D.C., USA 20009
Editor: Jim Wallis Poetry Editor: Rose Berger
Telephone: (202) 328-8842

E-mail: sojourners@sojourners.com
Website: www.sojourners.com

| Since: 1971 | Format: Paper | Circ: 40,000 | Sample: $3.95 US |
| Time: 6 weeks | Money: $25 US/poem | Copies: 5 | Sub: $30 US |

Send 3 poems, up to 25 lines each. Requests first publication rights. Does not accept e-mail or simultaneous submissions. Uses 12 of the 300 submissions received each year. Please do not send poems which contain exclusive language, sexist or racist images. Interested in translations. "We look for poetry that reflects simple celebrations of life and beauty. We often try to use poetry geared toward a particular season. Send us your best."

Sonora Review

English Department, University of Arizona, Tucson, Arizona, USA 85721

Editor: Charles Yearly

Telephone: (520) 626-2555

| Since: 1980 | Format: Paper | Circ: 1,000 | Sample: $6 US |
| Time: 2-3 months | Money: No | Copies: 2 | Sub: $12 US |

Authors published: James Tate, Ira Sadoff, Jane Mead & Lee Gutkind.

Send up to 12 pages of poetry. Requests first publication rights. Accepts simultaneous submissions if so noted. Does NOT accept e-mail submissions. Please do not send genre work. Interested in book reviews, translations, and fiction up to 8,000 words. "We look for work that stays with you, lingers, incites revelation." May run theme issues. Runs annual writing contests for fiction, non-fiction and poetry. Send SASE for details.

The Sounds of Poetry

2076 Vinewood, Detroit, Michigan, USA 48216-5506

Editor: Jacqueline Rae Rawlson Sanchez

Telephone: (313) 843-2352

| Since: 1983 | Format: Paper | Circ: 200 | Sample: $5 US |
| Time: 1-6 months | Money: No | Copies: 1 | Sub: $12. 50 US |

Authors published: Gil Saenz, Ruben de la Vega, Denice Childers & Ann Sams.

Send 5 poems, up to 38 lines each. Requests one-time rights. Does NOT accept e-mail or simultaneous submissions. Uses up to 600 of the 800 submissions received each year. Please do not send rhyme or pornography, though light erotica is acceptable. Interested in very brief book reviews, as well as translations. "We want people to write what they feel and take that emotion to its highest state."

The South Carolina Review

English Department, Clemson University, Strode Tower, Box 341503, Clemson, South Carolina, USA 29634-1503

Editor: Wayne Chapman

| Since: 1968 | Format: Paper | Circ: 600 | Sample: $10 US |
| Time: 6-9 months | Money: No | Copies: 2 | Sub: N/A |

Authors published: Sharon Olds, Robert Pinsky, Joyce Carol Oates & Garrison Keillor.

Send 5 poems. Requests first publication rights. Does NOT accept simultaneous submissions. Interested in book reviews, fiction, essays, scholarly articles and criticism. Runs theme issues. Send SASE for details.

South Dakota Review

Box 111, University Exchange, University of South Dakota, Vermillion, South Dakota, USA 57069

Editor: Brian Bedard Poetry Editors: Marcella Remund & Ed Allen

Telephone: (605) 677-5184 Fax: (605) 677-7298

Website: www.usd.edu/engl/SDR/index.html

Since: 1963	Format: Paper	Circ: 600	Sample: $6 US
Time: 5-8 weeks	Money: No	Copies: 2-3	Sub: $18 US

Authors published: H.E. Francis, Dan O'Brien, Dianna Henning & S.K. Kelen.

Send 4-6 poems. Requests first North American serial rights and reprint rights. Accepts simultaneous submissions if so noted. Uses up to 120 of the up to 1,200 submissions received each year. Please do not send light verse, self-indulgent confessional poetry. Interested in translations, and a wide variety of fiction from short-shorts to novellas.

Southern Humanities Review

9088 Haley Center, Auburn University, Alabama, USA 36849

Editors: Dan Latimer & Virginia M. Kouidis Poetry Editor: Virginia M. Kouidis

Telephone: (334) 844-9088 Fax: (334) 844-9027

E-mail: shrengl@mail.auburn.edu

Since: 1967	Format: Paper	Circ: 700	Sample: $7 US
Time: 1-3 months	Money: No	Copies: 2	Sub: $20 US

Authors published: Andrew Hudgins, Bin Ramke, David Citino & Eamon Grennan.

Send 3-5 poems up to two pages long each. Requests all rights until publication. Does NOT accept e-mail or simultaneous submissions. Uses perhaps 70 of the 2,200 submissions received each year. Do not send vulgarity, profanity or jargon. Interested in book reviews, translations, critical essays and fiction of 3,500–15,000 words. Submit only one story at a time. "Please do not assume from our name that we are interested in Southern topics only; any subject matter in the liberal arts is acceptable. Hoepfner Award presented annually for the best essay, story and poem published in *Southern Humanities Review* the previous year."

Southern Poetry Review

Advancement Studies-CPCC, Charlotte, North Carolina, USA 28235

Editor: Ken McLaurin

Telephone: (704) 330-6002 Fax: (704) 330-6455

Since: 1958	Format: Paper	Circ: 1,000	Sample: $3 US
Time: 3-6 months	Money: No	Copies: 1	Sub: $10 US

Send 3-5 poems. Requests first rights. Accepts simultaneous submissions if so noted. Uses up to 150 of the 2,000 submissions received each year. Reads submissions September–May. Please do not send religious or didactic poetry. May be interested in translations. Query. Runs the Guy Owen Poetry Prize Contest. Send SASE for details.

Southwest Review

Box 750374, Southern Methodist University, Dallas, Texas, USA 75275

Editor: Willard Spiegelman

Telephone: (214) 768-1036 Fax: (214) 268-1408

E-mail: swr@mail.smu.edu

Since: 1983	Format: Paper	Circ: 1,500	Sample: $6 US
Time: 1 month	Money: Varies	Copies: 5-15	Sub: $24 US

Authors published: Henri Cole, Albert Goldbarth, Adrienne Rich & Joanie Mackowski.
Send 5 poems. Requests first North American serial rights. Accepts simultaneous submissions if so noted. Does NOT accept e-mail submissions. Reads submissions September–May. Uses 50 of the 3,000 submissions received each year. Interested in fiction. Runs theme issues. "We accept both traditional and experimental writing and we have no specific limitations as to theme." The Elizabeth Matchett Stover Memorial Award is given to the author of the best poem or groups of poems published in the magazine during the previous year.

Sou'wester
Box 1438, Southern Illinois University, Edwardsville, Illinois, USA 62026
Editor: Fred W. Robbins Poetry Editor: Leigh Ramsey
Telephone: (618) 650-3190

| Since: 1960 | Format: Paper | Circ: 300 | Sample: $5 US |
| Time: 3 months | Money: No | Copies: 2 | Sub: $10 US |

Authors published: Robert Wexelblatt, Dallas Wiebe, Jennifer Atkinson & Ellen Slezak.
Send 4–5 poems. Requests all rights. Releases them upon request. Accepts simultaneous submissions if so noted. Reads submissions September–July. Uses 35 poetry submissions each year. Please do not send sci-fi or fantasy. Interested in fiction. "We look for the best work we can find. It must stand on its own internal merits. We try to be very selective."

Spitball: The Literary Baseball Magazine
5560 Fox Road, Cincinnati, Ohio, USA 45239
Editor: Mike Shannon Poetry Editor: Bill McGill

| Since: 1981 | Format: Paper | Circ: 1,000 | Sample: $6 US |
| Time: 1 month | Money: No | Copies: 2 | Sub: $12 US |

Send any number of poems. Requests one-time rights. Does NOT accept simultaneous submissions. Uses only some of the 250 submissions received each year. Please do not send anything but baseball poetry. Interested in fiction, artwork and photography. Query first regarding book reviews. Occasionally runs theme issues. Send SASE for details. "All first-time submitters must purchase a sample copy or we don't read your material. This income helps defray our costs and is a one-time charge. Spitball sponsors the CASEY Award for best baseball book of the year. Every new baseball book will automatically be considered for nomination assuming we receive a review copy from the publisher."

Sweet Annie & Sweet Pea Review
7750 Highway F-24 West, Baxter, Indiana, USA 50028
Editor: B. A. Clark
Telephone: (515) 792-3578 Fax: (515) 792-1310
E-mail: anniespl@netins.net

| Since: 1995 | Format: Paper | Circ: 100+ | Sample: $6 US |
| Time: 4-6 months | Money: No | Copies: 1 | Sub: $24 US |

Authors published: L. Robiner, C. Bowman, R. Reynolds & U. Wehler.
Send 6 poems. Requests first rights. Accepts simultaneous submissions if so noted. Does NOT accept e-mail submissions. Uses 50 of the 200+ submissions received each year. Please do not send violence or graphic sex. Interested in fiction of 500–3,000

words, artwork and photography. "Each issue has a general theme. We prefer strong writing on outdoor themes, men and women issues and spirituality (not religion). All submissions must fit our 5x8 inch format."

Sycamore Review

English Department, 1356 Heavilon Hall, Purdue University, West Lafayette, Indiana, USA 47907-1356

Editor: Sarah Griffiths Poetry Editors: Carolyn LaMontagne & Michelle Murphy

Telephone: (765) 494-3783 Fax: (765) 494-3780

E-mail: sycamore@expert.cc.purdue.edu

Website: www.sla.purdue.edu/academic/engl/sycamore

Since: 1988	Format: Paper	Circ: 1,000	Sample: $7 US
Time: 2 months	Money: No	Copies: 2	Sub: $14 US

Authors published: Mark Halliday, Joshua Clover, Brenda Coultas & David Cameron.

Send 3-5 poems. Requests first North American rights. Accepts simultaneous submissions if so noted. Does NOT accept e-mail submissions. Reads submissions September–March. Uses 40 of the 600 submissions received each year. Interested in translations, and fiction. "We are interested in experimental and innovative poetry."

Talisman: A Journal of Contemporary Poetry and Poetics

PO Box 3157, Jersey City, New Jersey, USA 07303-3157

Editor: Edward Foster

Telephone: (201) 938-0698 Fax: (201) 938-1693

Since: 1988	Format: Paper	Circ: 2,000	Sample: $9 US
Time: Varies	Money: No	Copies: 1	Sub: $14 US

Authors published: William Bronk, Armand Schwerner & Eileen Myles.

Send 3-4 poems. Requests first North American rights. Does NOT accept simultaneous submissions. Uses very few of the 2,000 submissions received each year. Interested in book reviews and translations.

Taproot Literary Review

Box 204, Ambridge, Pennsylvania, USA 15003

Editor: Tikvah Feinstein

Telephone: (724) 266-8476

E-mail: taproot10@aol.com

Since: 1986	Format: Paper	Circ: 500+	Sample: $5 US
Time: 1-2 months	Money: No	Copies: 2	Sub: $6.95 US

Authors published: Joyce Nower, Dennis Must & T. Anders Carson.

Send 5 poems, up to 35 lines each. Requests first serial rights. Does NOT accept simultaneous submissions. Reads submissions September–December. Uses 70 of the 120 submissions received each year. Please do not send porn, religious or political poetry. Interested in translations and fiction. "We leave the subject and style up to the writers. We encourage fresh voices and established writers to submit their quality writing."

Tar River Poetry

English Department, East Carolina University, Greenville, North Carolina, USA 27858

Editor: Peter Makuck

Telephone: (919) 252-6046 Fax: (919) 252-4889

| Since: 1978 | Format: Paper | Circ: 750 | Sample: $5.50 US |
| Time: 4-6 weeks | Money: No | Copies: 3 | Sub: $10 US |

Authors published: A.R. Amnons, Louis Simpson, Betty Adcock & Carolyn Kizer.
Send 3-5 poems. Requests first rights. Does not accept simultaneous submissions. Reads submissions September–April. Uses 100 of the 5,000 submissions received each year. Interested only in poetry.

tight
PO Box 1591, Guerneville, California, USA 95446
Editor: Ann Erickson

| Since: 1990 | Format: Paper | Circ: 100 | Sample: $5 US |
| Time: 2-4 months | Money: No | Copies: 1 | Sub: $20 US |

Authors published: Greg Evason, Sheila E. Murphy, Sean Brendan-Brown & Cydney Chadwick.
Send 1-5 poems. Specifically requests NO bio be sent. Requests one-time rights. Accepts simultaneous submissions if so noted. Please do not send idea-based poetry, abstract language, full statement with "punchline," fully extended metaphor, narrative poetry, didactic poetry, intellectualization, persona or violence. Interested in translations, short prose-poems, and b/w art which can be reproduced by photocopy. "I look for work that is immediate, experimental, fragmented, concrete, vivid, attention to form, condensed, visionary."

Tricycle: The Buddhist Review
92 Vandam Street, New York, New York, USA 10013
Editor: Paul Morris
Telephone: 1-800-950-7008 Fax: (212) 645-1493
E-mail: triked@aol.com
Website: www.tricycle.com

| Since: 1991 | Format: Paper | Circ: 65,000 | Sample: $10 US |
| Time: Varies | Money: No | Copies: 1 | Sub: $29 US |

Send 3 poems. Requests one-time rights. Accepts e-mail submissions. Sometimes comments on rejections. Interested in book reviews, translations, artwork and photography. Runs theme issues. "All submissions must reflect the magazine's Buddhist orientation."

Tundra
248 Beach Park Boulevard, Foster City, California, USA 94404
Editor: Michael Dylan Welch
Telephone: (650) 571-9428
E-mail: WelchM@aol.com

| Since: 1998 | Format: Paper | Circ: 750 | Sample: $7 US |
| Time: 1-3 weeks | Money: No | Copies: 1 | Sub: $21 US |

Authors published: Ted Kooser, Tom Disch, Jane Hirshfield & Dana Gioia.
Associated with Press Here Press. Send 5-15 poems for shorter forms such as haiku. Send fewer poems if they are longer forms. Requests first serial rights. Accepts e-mail submissions, include complete name and street mailing address. Uses 270 of the 9,000 submissions received each year. Please do not send any form of fiction other than haiban. Interested in translations. Query regarding book reviews as they use very few.

May be interested in photography but please query first. "I only rarely make exceptions to my preference for poems of 13 lines or less. I prefer the imagistic to the conceptual or intellectual. Make it new, see freshly, and amaze me, but don't be gimmicky, cutesy, cliched or contrived. I welcome all short poetry, especially haiku, senryu, and tanka, but also welcome longer free-form poems. Being a Canadian, I am particularly sympathetic to Canadian poets."

Turnstile

175 5th Avenue, Suite 2348, New York, New York, USA 10010
Poetry Editor: Justine Gardner Fiction Editors: Jaira Placide & Dee Dee Zobian
Website: www.turnstilepress.com

Since: 1989	Format: Paper/Web	Circ: 1,500	Sample: $6.50 US
Time: 3-4 months	Money: No	Copies: 4	Sub: N/A

Send 5 poems. Requests one-time rights. Accepts simultaneous submissions if so noted. Please do not send satire, humour or genre fiction. Sometimes comments on rejections. Interested in fiction, artwork and photography.

Verse

English Department, Plymouth State College, Plymouth, New Hampshire, USA 03264
Editors: Brian Henry & Andrew Zawacki

Since: 1984	Format: Paper	Circ: 1,000	Sample: $6 US
Time: 1-2 months	Money: No	Copies: 2+sub.	Sub: $15 US

Authors published: James Tate, August Kleinzahler, Heather McHugh & Paul Muldoon. Send 3-5 poems. Requests first North American rights. Does NOT accept simultaneous submissions. Reads submissions September-May. Uses up to 200 of the 5,000 submissions received each year. Often comments on rejections. Please do not send fiction, doggerel, haiku, or therapeutic self-indulgence. Runs theme issues, often devoted to particular countries or as tributes to individual writers. *Verse* publishes high-quality translations and is a critical forum, with interviews, essays and book reviews. "We welcome more work from Canadian poets, critics and translators."

Weber Studies

1214 University Circle, Ogden, Utah, USA 84408-1214
Editor: Sherwin W. Howard
Telephone: (801) 626-6473
E-mail: swhoward@weber.edu
Website: weberstudies.weber.edu

Since: 1984	Format: Paper/Web	Circ: 1,000	Sample: $7 US
Time: 2 months	Money: Varies	Copies: 2	Sub: $20 US

Authors published: Ann Beattie, Mark Strand & E.L. Doctorow. Send 4 poems. Requests first serial rights and electronic rights. Does NOT accept e-mail or simultaneous submissions. Uses up to 16 of the up to 600 poetry submissions received each year. Interested in fiction. "We are particularly interested in work that informs about the environment and culture of the western United States."

West Branch

Bucknell Hall, Bucknell University, Lewisburg, Pennsylvania, USA 17837
Editors: Karl Patten & Robert Love Taylor
Telephone: (717) 524-1853 Fax: (717) 524-3760

E-mail: rtaylor@bucknell.edu

Since: 1977	Format: Paper	Circ: 500	Sample: $3 US
Time: 8 weeks	Money: No	Copies: 2	Sub: $7 US

Authors published: David Citino and others.

Send 4–6 poems. Requests first North American serial rights. Does NOT accept e-mail or simultaneous submissions. Uses 80 of the 800 submissions received each year. Interested in fiction and perhaps translations.

Whiskey Island Magazine

English Department, Cleveland State University, Cleveland, Ohio, USA 44115
Editor: Pat Stansberry Poetry Editor: Tim Deines
Telephone: (216) 687-2056 Fax: (216) 687-6943
E-mail: whiskeyisland@popmail.csuohio.edu
Website: www.csuohio.edu/whiskey_island

Since: 1972	Format: Paper	Circ: 1,500	Sample: $5 US
Time: 3-4 months	Money: No	Copies: 2+sub.	Sub: $12 US

Authors published: Robert Cooperman, Rita Grabowski & Lyn Lifshin.

Send up to 10 pages of poems. Requests one-time US publishing rights. Accepts e-mail submissions, and simultaneous submissions if so noted. Reads submissions from September–April. Uses 60 of the 1,000 submissions received each year. Please do not send light verse or inspirational poetry. Interested in book reviews, fiction, and b/w artwork and photography. "We publish serious work, which is not to say that it cannot be humourous or fun, but simply that it must use refined, controlled language to accomplish a meaningful aim." Runs annual writing contest. Details online or send SASE.

Willow Springs

c/o Eastern Washington University, Mail Stop #1, 705 West 1st Avenue, Spokane, Washington, USA 99201
Editor: Christopher Howell Poetry Editors: Randy Kromwall & Khris Christensen
Telephone: (509) 623-4349 Fax: (509) 623-4238

Since: 1977	Format: Paper	Circ: 1,200	Sample: $5.50 US
Time: 3 months	Money: No	Copies: 2+sub.	Sub: $10.50 US

Send up to 6 poems. Requests first-time rights. Does NOT accept simultaneous submissions. Reads submissions September 15–May 15. Uses 60 of the 1,300 submissions received each year. Although interested in fiction, please do not send genre work. Interested in book reviews, translations, artwork and photography. Runs annual fiction and poetry contests. Send SASE for details.

Wind Magazine

PO Box 24548, Lexington, Kentucky, USA 40524
Editor: Charlie Hughes Poetry Editor: Leatha Kendrick
E-mail: wind@lit-arts.com
Website: www.lit-arts.com/wind

Since: 1971	Format: Paper	Circ: 500	Sample: $4.50 US
Time: 2 months	Money: No	Copies: 1	Sub: $10 US

Send 3–5 poems. Requests first North American serial rights. Accepts simultaneous submissions if so noted. Does NOT accept e-mail submissions. Uses 100 of the 2,000 submissions received each year. Occasionally comments on rejections. Interested in

translations, fiction up to 5,000 words, and b/w artwork and photography. Runs annual poetry, short story and chapbook competitions. Encourages emerging writers.

Wisconsin Review

Radford Hall, Box 158, University of Wisconsin-Oshkosh, Oshkosh, Wisconsin, USA 54901

Editors: Jonathan Wittman & Aaron Ramponi

Telephone: (920) 424-2267

Since: 1966	Format: Paper	Circ: 2,000	Sample: $4 US
Time: 3-6 months	Money: No	Copies: 2	Sub: $10 US

Authors published: Laurel Speer, Julian Edney, Robert Coles & Mark Taksa.

Send 4-6 poems. Requests one-time rights. Accepts simultaneous submissions if so noted. Uses 150 of the 2,000 submissions received each year. Reads submissions September–May. Interested in translations, fiction, artwork and photography. "The poetry we publish is mostly free verse, though we have published rhymed poems. We look for strong imagery, fresh voices and new themes."

Writer's Guidelines & News

PO Box 18566, Sarasota, Florida, USA 34276

Editor: Ned Burke

Telephone: (941) 924-3201 Fax: (941) 925-4468

E-mail: ymagazette@aol.com

Since: 1988	Format: Paper	Circ: 2,500	Sample: $6 US
Time: 2 months	Money: No	Copies: 2	Sub: $21 US

Authors published: Alta McLain, Jack Alexander & Becky McClure.

Send 1-3 poems, up to 24 lines each. Requests first North American serial rights. Does NOT accept e-mail or simultaneous submissions. Uses 30 of the 3,000 submissions received each year. Sometimes comments on rejections. Interested in book reviews, fiction up to 2,000 words, artwork and photography. "We are always seeking new and innovative writers. Please note all submissions must have a writing slant."

XCP: Cross Cultural Poetics

c/o College of St. Catherine-Minneapolis, 601 25th Avenue South, Minneapolis, Minnesota, USA 55454

Editor: Mark Nowak

Fax: (612) 690-7849

Website: www.stkate.edu/xcp

Since: 1997	Format: Paper/Web	Circ: 1,000	Sample: $10 US
Time: 1 month	Money: No	Copies: 2	Sub: $30 US

Authors published: Amiri Baraka, Fred Wah, Diane Glancy & Edwin Torres.

Send 5-7 poems. Requests first-time rights. Does NOT accept e-mail or simultaneous submissions. Uses 10 of the 500 submissions received each year. Interested in book reviews and translations. "XCP is a journal of poetry, poetics, ethnography, cultural and ethnic studies." Runs theme issues. Details online or send SASE.

The Yale Review

Yale University, PO Box 208243, New Haven, Connecticut, USA 06520-8243

Editor: J.D. McClatchy

Telephone: (203) 432-0499

| Since: 1916 | Format: Paper | Circ: 6,000 | Sample: $10 US |
| Time: 2 months | Money: Varies | Copies: 2 | Sub: $27.50 US |

Authors published: W.S. Merwin & Rachel Hadas.

Send 1-10 poems. Rights negotiated with publisher. Does NOT accept simultaneous submissions. Uses 50 of the 1,000 submissions received each year. Interested in book reviews and fiction. May be interested in artwork and photography. Query.

The following US periodicals have ceased publication since the sixth edition of this book:

The Lowell Pearl, The Tennessee Quarterly, Entelechy

The following US periodicals no longer publish poetry or they have asked to be delisted:

College English, Granta, Unmuzzled Ox

The following periodicals believed to still be active, failed to respond to requests for information:

African Voices, Alaska Quarterly Review, Antioch Review, Aphrodite Gone Berserk, Ascent, Aura Literary Review, Black Lace, Blue Mesa Review, Crazyhorse, Duckburg Times, Fat Tuesday, Georgetown Review, Gettysburg Review, Greensboro Review, Haight Ashbury Literary, Kairos, Keltic Fringe, Lillipur Review, Malachite and Agate, Moonrabbit Review, Nation, Nerve Bundle Review, New Delta Review, New Orleans Review, New Virgina Review, New Yorker, North Coast Review, North Dakota Review, North Stone Review, Old Red Kimono, Onthebus, Paintbrush, Paper Boat Magazine, Place in the Woods, Ploughshares, Ranger Rick Magazine, Raritan Quarterly, Stones in My Pocket, SunDog, Threepenny Review, Unit Circle, Vietnam Generation, Visions International, Wind, Yellow Silk, Zone 3

1.8 INTERNATIONAL PERIODICAL LISTINGS

Most of the magazines listed below publish primarily in the English language. A few publish in another language and offer their readers English translations of one or more poems per issue. All offer you the opportunity to be published internationally.

The hassle and expense of International Reply Coupons (IRCs) may tempt you to fax or e-mail a submission to an editor without prior permission. This is never appropriate except where a listing states e-mail submissions are welcomed. Be considerate and keep your submission short. E-mail is not the proper venue for an epic or novella.

There are a few things to note that are particular to this section:

1. Where copyright is mentioned you will find an inordinate number of editors who request "one-time rights." This is the default used when an editor claimed "no rights" were requested. As explained earlier in this book, every time your work is published, some right has been used. Therefore, "one-time rights" is a warning to you to ask the editor what rights they really want: first rights, first British rights, one-time rights exclusive of the internet, and so on. The easiest way to do this is to state in your covering letter what rights you are offering and wait for the response. If your work is accepted and published without comment you can assume your offer was acceptable to the editor.

2. Although it is unlikely that you will subscribe to a magazine without first reading it, you may wish to request a sample copy based on what you read here. Please note the cost of a sample copy or subscription is subject to change. Refer to a recent copy of the magazine or the website to confirm the amount stated is correct for overseas subscribers.

3. There are a few listings which state no contributor's copy will be sent to overseas writers. In your cover letter let the editor know you would appreciate receipt of a contributor's copy. The publication may send one. If not, you must decide if it is important to have a record of your work and if so, you might send the editor a couple of IRCs to help pay for the magazine's return postage.

4. You can direct an editor to destroy/dispose of your submission if it does not meet their needs. If you are comfortable with this, you need only enclose a single IRC with a SAE for the editor's response to your submission.

5. Few overseas magazines (with the exception of those in Australia and New Zealand) have an online presence. For the number of magazines in the United Kingdom it is surprising how few can be researched or contacted online at the time of writing. However, more magazines will have an online presence within the next two years, many with the help of Canadians. Simon Fraser University's Master in Publishing student Carla Livingstone went to India as part of her work program. Her task? To build a website for an Indian women's magazine. Things change daily on the internet. Take the time to search the internet for those magazines which interest you. By the time you read this, they might be there.

ARGENTINA

Provincia
Libertad s/n, Casa 16, Barrio Los Olivos (5870) Villa Dolores CBA, Argentina

Editor: Rafael Mario Altamirano-Ninalquín
Telephone: 0544-21889

Since: 1967	Format: Paper	Circ: 400	Sample: $2
Time: 3 months	Money: See below.	Copies: 1	Sub: $18

Send up to 3 poems, up to 20 lines each. Associated with a literary magazine in Spain (unnamed). Publishes mainly in Spanish. There was a single translation in the June 1998 issue. However, the editor would like to publish more in the future. May be interested in reviews of international periodicals. Please note, editor conducted all communications in Spanish. Magazine is 16 pages plus cover, all printed on bond and saddle-stitched.

AUSTRALIA

Blast
PO Box 3514, Manuka, ACT 2603, Australia
Editors: Bill Tully & Craig Cormick
Telephone: (02) 6248 5027 Fax: (02) 6273 5081
E-mail: b.tully@nla.gov.au

Since: 1987	Format: Paper	Circ: 600-800	Sample: $4 Aus.
Time: 2-6 weeks	Money: $10 Aus.	Copies: 2	Sub: $30 Aus.

Send 4 poems, up to one page in length. Requests one-time rights. Accepts simultaneous submissions. Does NOT accept e-mail submissions. Uses 8-10 of the 50 submissions received each year. Interested in fiction up to 2,000 words, book reviews, translations, artwork and photography. Please do not send fascist, racist, sexist, ageist or self-absorbed pieces.

The Dawn
203 Great Ocean Road, Anglesea, Australia 3230
Editor: Veronica Schwartz
Telephone: 61 3 5263 2811 Fax: 61 3 5263 2811
E-mail: veronica@mypostbox.com
Website: redback.ne.com.au/~veronica

Since: 1994	Format: Paper	Circ: 500	Sample: $7.50 Aus.
Time: 3 weeks	Money: No	Copies: 2	Sub: $45 Aus.

Send 3 poems. Requests first Australian rights plus permission to have the work included on *The Dawn's* website if selected. Also requests that author give permission for their work to be included in the database "Gender Watch." Prefers e-mail submissions. Does NOT accept simultaneous submissions. Uses up to 35 of the 80 submissions received each year. Occasionally comments on rejections. Please do not send depressing items. Interested in book reviews, translations, artwork and photography. Has themed sections but does not run theme issues. "The Dawn seeks to encourage women writers specifically."

Going Down Swinging
PO Box 24, Clifton Hill, Victoria, Australia 3068
Editors: Lyn Boughton & Louise Craig

Since: 1980	Format: Paper	Circ: 800	Sample: $12 Aus.
Time: 3 months	Money: $20 Aus.	Copies: 1	Sub: $20 Aus.

Send 3 poems. Requests one-time rights. Does NOT accept simultaneous submissions. Uses 50 of the 1,000 poems received each year. Interested in book reviews and short fiction. Focuses on Australian writers but welcomes submissions from writers around the world.

HEAT

PO Box 752, Artarmon, New South Wales, Australia 1570
Editor: Dr. Ivor Indyk Poetry Editor: Adam Aitken
Website: www.mypostbox.com/heat

Since: 1996	Format: Paper/Web	Circ: 1,400	Sample: $20 Aus.
Time: 3 months	Money: $50-$100 Aus.	Copies: 1	Sub: $70 Aus.

Send 3-4 poems. Requests first publications rights. Does NOT accept simultaneous submissions. Uses 10 of the 500 submissions received each year. Please do not send mediocre poetry. Query regarding book reviews or translations. Interested in fiction, artwork and photography.

Hermes

c/o Publications Office, Manning House, University of Sydney, NSW, Australia 2006
Editor: Changes annually
Telephone: 61 (02) 9563 6142 or 61 (02) 9563 6104 Fax: 61 (02) 9563 6109
E-mail: hermes@netscape.com

Since: 1886	Format: Paper	Circ: 400-500	Sample: $10 Aus.
Time: 3 months	Money: No	Copies: 1	Sub: n/a

Authors published: MTC Cronin, Zan Ross, John Tranter & Coral Hull.

Hermes is the annual literary and graphic journal of the University of Sydney Union. Send any number of poems. Requests first publication rights. Accepts e-mail submissions. Does NOT accept simultaneous submissions. Uses up to 50 of 250 submissions received each year. Interested in translations, fiction up to 3,000 words, and b/w artwork and photography. Always runs theme issues.

Hobo Poetry and Haiku Magazine

PO Box 166, Hazelbrook, New South Wales, Australia 2779
Editor: Dane Thwaites

Since: 1993	Format: Paper	Circ: 720	Sample: $5.50 Aus.
Time: 6 weeks	Money: No	Copies: 1	Sub: $30 Aus.

Send 3-5 poems. Requests first-time rights and acknowledgement in any subsequent publication. Does NOT accept simultaneous submissions. Uses 10 of the 500 submissions received each year. Interested in book reviews. Runs annual haiku contest. "Overseas contributions are particularly welcome for the haiku section. Haiku experts can contribute articles to the Gum Tree Conversations, where haiku theory and philosophy are discussed."

Imago: New Writing (City of Brisbane Poetry Award)

School of Communication and Organizational Studies, Q.U.T., GPO Box 2434, Brisbane 4001, Queensland, Australia
Editor: Philip Neilson

Since: 1988	Format: Paper	Circ: 1,000	Sample: $9.50 Aus.
Time: 3-6 months	Money: $30 Aus.	Copies: 1	Sub: $25 Aus.

Send 6-8 poems, up to 50 lines each. Requests first Australian rights. Accepts simultaneous submissions if so noted. Uses up to 80 of the 500 submissions received each year. Interested in reviews of Australian books.

Linq

English Department, James Cook University, Townsville, Queensland, Australia 4811
Editor: Changes each issue

Since: 1971	Format: Paper	Circ: 350	Sample: $10 Aus.
Time: 3 months	Money: $25/poem (Aus.)	Copies: Nil	Sub: $20 Aus.

Send up to 5 poems. Requests first rights. All work must be previously unpublished. Accepts simultaneous submissions. Uses up to 60 of the 250 submissions received each year. Often comments on rejections. Interested in book reviews, and critical articles up to 3,000 words. New and established writers are welcome to submit.

Mattoid

School of Literature and Journalism, Deakin University, Geelong, Victoria, Australia 3217
Editor: Dr. Brian Edwards

Since: 1977	Format: Paper	Circ: 600	Sample: Query
Time: 3 months	Money: No	Copies: 2	Sub: Query

Send 3–5 poems. Requests first Australian rights. Accepts simultaneous submissions if so noted. Uses perhaps 95 of the 800 submissions received each year. Please do not send rhyming poems. May be interested in experimental work.

Micropress Yates

29 Brittainy Street, Petrie, Australia 4502
Editor: Gloria Yates
Telephone: (07) 3285 1462 Fax: (07) 3285 1462
E-mail: gloriabe@powerup.com.au

Since: 1992	Format: Paper	Circ: 450	Sample: $1 Aus.
Time: 2–3 weeks	Money: No	Copies: 2	Sub: $17 Aus.

Authors published: Jeff Guess, Kate O'Neill (NZ) & M. Jivani (UK).

Send 4–6 poems. Requests one-time rights. Accepts simultaneous submissions. Prefers NOT to receive submissions by e-mail but happy to respond by e-mail if requested. Accepts submissions February–November 15. Uses 480 of the 2,000 submissions received each year. Has "cloned" presses in New Zealand, and UK with plans to have one in Israel by the year 2000. Editor states "we recycle printed poems" but gives no explanation of this. Could mean accepts reprints but may offer your work to other editors without asking for rights specific to each country. Interested in translations. Publishes subscribers only.

Studio: A Journal of Christians Writing

727 Peel Street, Albury, Australia 2640
Editor: Paul Grover
Telephone: 61 2 6021 1135 Fax: 61 2 6021 1135

Since: 1980	Format: Paper	Circ: 300	Sample: $8 Aus.
Time: 4 weeks	Money: No	Copies: 1	Sub: $40 Aus.

Authors published: Les Murray, John Foulcher & Kevin Hart.

Send 2 poems, 50–70 lines each. Requests one-time rights. Accepts simultaneous submissions. Interested in translations, book reviews, fiction up to 5,000 words, artwork and photography. Uses up to 200 of the up to 2,000 submissions received each year. "Studio strives for excellence because God is excellence itself."

Ulitarra

PO Box 195, Armidale, New South Wales, Australia 2350

Editor: Michael Sharkey

Telephone: 61 2 67729135

Since: 1992	Format: Paper	Circ: 600	Sample: $15 Aus.
Time: 1 month	Money: $60 Aus.	Copies: 1	Sub: $30 Aus.

Authors published: Myron Lysenko, Peter Porter, Dorothy Hewett & Jill Jones.

Send 2-3 poems. Requests first magazine rights. Does NOT accept simultaneous submissions. Uses 60 of the 700 submissions received each year. Interested in translations, fiction, artwork and photography. Issues alternate between fiction and poetry. "We try to keep up Aboriginal content too and welcome well-written articles (non-academic format preferred) on Indigenous themes and issues. We also publish interviews with writers."

Westerly

Department of English, University of Western Australia, Nedlands, WA, Australia 6907

Editors: Delys Bird, Dennis Haskell & Ron Shapiro

Telephone: (08) 9380 3403 Fax: (08) 9380 1030

E-mail: westerly@uniwa.uwa.edu.au

Website: www.arts.uwa.edu.au/westerly

Since: 1956	Format: Paper	Circ: 1,200	Sample: $10 Aus.
Time: 2 months	Money: $40 Aus.	Copies: 1	Sub: N/A

Associated with Centre for Studies in Australian Literature. Send up to 3 poems. Requests first-time rights. Prefers e-mail submissions. Does NOT accept simultaneous submissions. Uses up to 80 of the up to 800 submissions received each year. Please do not send children's fiction, romance or fantasy work. Interested in book reviews of Australian books, translations, and fiction up to 3,000 words. December issue is always a theme issue.

AUSTRIA

The Poet's Voice

University of Salzburg, Department of English and American Studies, Akademiestr. 24, A-5050 Salzburg, Austria

Editors: Fred Beake, Wolfgang Goertschacher & James Hogg

Telephone: 662-8044-4424 Fax: 662-8044-613

E-mail: Wolfgang.Goertschacher@sbg.ac.at

Since: 1982	Format: Paper	Circ: 500	Sample: $12 Can.
Time: 6-8 weeks	Money: No	Copies: 1-2	Sub: $20 Can.

Authors published: Raymond Federman, Jon Silkin, David Miller & Robert Rehder.

Send 4-10 poems. Requests one-time rights. Accepts e-mail submissions. Does NOT accept simultaneous submissions. Uses 200 of the 6,000 submissions received each year. Interested in book reviews, translations, artwork and photography. Occasionally runs theme issues. Interested in the long poem and the avante-garde.

BELGIUM

Horizon

Stationsstraat 232 A, 1770 Liedekerke, Belgium

Editor: Johnny Haelterman

| Since: 1985 | Format: Paper | Circ: 120 | Sample: $10 US |
| Time: 2 months | Money: No | Copies: Nil | Sub: N/A |

Associated with Horizon Press. Send up to 5 poems. Requests one-time serial rights. Does NOT accept simultaneous submissions. Uses up to 50 per cent of the fiction submitted. However, only pays for fiction written in Dutch. "Poems are used as filler."

Journal Des Poétes

Chaussée de Wavre 150, B-1050, Brussels, Belgium

Editor: Jean-Luc Wauthier

Website: www.maison-int-poesie.cfwb.be

| Since: 1931 | Format: Paper | Circ: 1,000 | Sample: BF 120 |
| Time: 3 weeks | Money: No | Copies: 1-5 | Sub: BF 1,000 |

Authors published: Philippe Jaccottet (CH), Philippe Mathy (B), Jean-Jacques Celly (F) & Moire Alyn (F).

Send a minimum of 3 poems. Requests one-time rights. Accepts simultaneous submissions. Uses 5-6 poems each issue. Please do not send drama, novellas or prose. Often comments on rejections. Interested in book reviews, and translations. Runs theme issues focusing on the poets of one particular country.

ENGLAND

Acumen

6 The Mount, Higher Furzeham, Brixham, South Devon, England TQ5 8QY

Editor: Patricia Oxley

Telephone: 01803 851098

| Since: 1985 | Format: Paper | Circ: 700 | Sample: £13.50 |
| Time: Varies | Money: Varies | Copies: 1 | Sub: £13.50 |

Send up to 5 poems. Requests first British serial rights. Does NOT accept simultaneous submissions. Editor provided scant information; however this magazine is well known in the UK, and response indicates an interest in submissions from Canadian authors.

Agenda

5 Cranbourne Court, Albert Bridge Road, London, England SW11 4PE

Editor: William Cookson Assistant Editor: Anita Money

Telephone: 0171 228 0700

| Since: 1985 | Format: Paper | Circ: 1,200 | Sample: £5 |
| Time: 3 months | Money: Varies | Copies: 6 | Sub: £26 |

Send up to 6 poems. Requests one-time rights. Does NOT accept simultaneous submissions. Sometimes comments on rejections. Interested in book reviews and translations. "We believe poetry should not be affected by fashion. A great poem must remain a mystery. We look for poems written to endure, not those with immediate impact."

Aireings
24 Brudenell Road, Leeds, West York, England LS6 IBD
Editors: Jean Barker & Linda Marshall
Telephone: 0113 2785893

Since: 1980	Format: Paper	Circ: 300	Sample: £2.50
Time: 2 weeks	Money: No	Copies: 2	Sub: £15

Authors published: Pauline Kirk, Mary Sheepshanks, Valerie Blake & Brian Daldcreh.
Send up to 5 poems. Requests one-time rights. Accepts simultaneous submissions if so noted. Uses some of the many submissions received each year. Do not send racist or sexist work. Interested only in poetry. Publishes twice a year. Deadlines are January 1 and July 1.

Ambit
17 Priory Gardens, London, England N6 5QY
Editor: Martin Bax Poetry Editors: Martin Bax, Carol Ann Duffy & Henry Graham
Fiction Editors: J.G. Ballard & Geoff Nicholson
Telephone: 0181 340 3566

Since: 1959	Format: Paper	Circ: 3,000	Sample: $16 US
Time: 4 months	Money: £5/page	Copies: 2	Sub: $48 US

Authors published: Judith Kazantsis, Vernon Scannell, George Szirtes & Myra Schneider.
Send 5-6 poems. Requests one-time rights. Does NOT accept simultaneous submissions. Uses 80 of the 2,000 submissions received each year. Please do not send horror, ghost, sci-fi, fantasy or old-fashioned work. Interested in translations and fiction up to 5,000 words. Occasionally runs theme issues.

Apostrophe
41 Canute Road, Faversham, Kent, England ME13 8SH
Editor: Not named

Since: 1991	Format: Paper	Circ: 100	Sample: £1.50
Time: 1 month	Money: No	Copies: 1	Sub: £5.50

Authors published: Joanna Weston, Edmund Harwood & P.D. Wykes.
Send up to 6 poems, up to 40 lines each. Requests first-time rights. Does NOT accept simultaneous submissions. Uses 80 of the 1,000 submissions received each year. Reads submissions September-June. Please do not send poems filled with soul-searching or self-pity. An understanding of rhyme would be appreciated. Interested in book reviews and translations. Often includes the work of Canadian poets.

Blade Magazine
Maynrys, Glen Chass, Port St. Mary, Isle of Man, United Kingdom IM9 5PN
Editor: Jane Holland

Since: 1995	Format: Paper	Circ: 250	Sample: £5
Time: 3 months	Money: No	Copies: 1	Sub: £10

Authors published: Paul Violi, Robert Hershorv & Joan Jobe Smith.
Send up to 6 poems. Requests one-time rights. Does NOT accept simultaneous submissions. Uses up to 45 of the 1,500 submissions received each year. Not interested in concrete or performance poetry. Always comments on rejections if requested to do so. "*Blade* seeks to publish work which is hard, clear and purposeful. It prefers work which combines an understanding of technique with lyricism and intent. Wit is appreciated but not neccesary. An interesting but not strange covering letter is useful."

Blithe Spirit: Journal of the British Haiku Society

Hill House Farm, Knighton, Powys, England LO7 1NA

Editor: Caroline Gourlay

Telephone: 01 547528 542

| Since: 1990 | Format: Paper | Circ: 400 | Sample: £3 |
| Time: 1 month | Money: No | Copies: Nil | Sub: £12 |

Authors published: David Cobb, James Hackett, Janice Bostok & Lee Gurga.

Send up to 12 poems. Requests one-time rights. Does NOT accept simultaneous submissions. Uses 400 of 1,500 submissions received each year. Interested in haiku, tanka, haiku sequences, renga and haibun. Also interested in book reviews which relate to haiku or related material. Sponsors the James Hackett Award competition for best single haiku.

Candelabrum Poetry Magazine

1 Keyham Court, Star Mews, Peterborough, Cambridgeshire, England PE1 5NH

Poetry Editor: Michael Leonard McCarthy

| Since: 1970 | Format: Paper | Circ: 1,000 | Sample: $4 US |
| Time: 3 months | Money: No | Copies: 1 | Sub: $22 US |

Authors published: Dale Gunthorp, Philip Higson, Michael Fantina & Andrea Abraham.

Send 3–6 short poems. Requests one-time rights. Does NOT accept simultaneous submissions. Uses some of the many submissions received each year. Please do not send racism, sexism, ageism, pornography or any type of prose. Interested in translations. "*CPM* is a non-profit making fringe magazine publishing poetry only; appears twice a year. Chief interest is traditionalist rhymed and metrical poetry but good free verse is considered."

Eastern Rainbow

17 Farrow Road, Whaplode Drove, Spalding, Lincolnshire, England PE12 0TS

Editor: Paul Rance

Telephone: 01406 330242

| Since: 1985 | Format: Paper | Circ: 500 | Sample: $4 Can. |
| Time: 1 month | Money: No | Copies: 1 | Sub: $16 Can. |

Send up to 5 poems, up to 32 lines each. Requests one-time rights. Accepts simultaneous submissions if so noted. Uses up to 125 of the 500 submissions received each year. (Submissions from subscribers take precedence but considers all appropriate submissions.) Interested in translations, fiction up to 500 words, artwork and photography. "*Eastern Rainbow* includes poetry, prose and art which focuses on 20th century culture. Associated with *Peace & Freedom* magazine." Runs regular writing competitions.

Envoi

44 Rudyard Road, Biddulph Moor, Stoke-on-Trent, Staffordshire, England ST8 7JN

Editor: Roger Elkin

| Since: 1957 | Format: Paper | Circ: 1,000 | Sample: $8 US |
| Time: 4-6 weeks | Money: No | Copies: 2 | Sub: $30 US |

Send 6 poems. Requests one-time rights. Does NOT accept simultaneous submissions. Tends to run one poet's work in a single issue. Given excellent reviews by other poetry magazines. Interested in translations. Runs annual poetry contest.

Fire

Field Cottage, Old White Hill, Tackley, Kidlington, Oxfordshire, England OX5 3AB

Editor: Jeremy Hilton

Telephone: 01869 331300

Since: 1995	Format: Paper	Circ: 150	Sample: £3
Time: 7 weeks	Money: No	Copies: 2	Sub: £7

Authors published: Barry Butson, Debjani Chatterjee, Sarah Connor & Donna Hilbert.

Send 1-7 poems. If you are sending long poems, send less. Requests one-time rights. Does NOT accept simultaneous submissions. Uses less than half of the 400 submissions received each year. Please do not send rhyming verse, gratuitous violence, hatred or sexism. Comments on rejections if requested. Interested in translations, very short fiction and may be interested in b/w photography. "*Fire* is not identified with any particular school of writing but exists to enable new writers, or those who are out of fashion, or too difficult, experimental or risky for most publishers to take on, to appear alongside better known names. Left-field in orientation, willing to consider experimental, demotic or descriptive work. Inclined toward physical/nature, heart/soul emphasis. Less inclined toward neatness, cleverness, satire, domesticism or academia."

First Time

4 Burdett Place, George Street, Hastings, East Sussex, England TN34 3ED

Editor: Josephine Austin

Telephone: 01424 428855 Fax: 01424 428855

Since: 1981	Format: Paper	Circ: 1,000	Sample: £3
Time: 3 months	Money: No	Copies: Nil	Sub: £6

Send 6 poems, of up to 30 lines each. Requests first-time rights. Does NOT accept simultaneous submissions.

The Frogmore Papers

18 Nevill Road, Lewes, East Sussex, England BN7 1PF

Editor: Jeremy Page

Since: 1983	Format: Paper	Circ: 500	Sample: $5 US
Time: 3 months	Money: No	Copies: 1	Sub: $20 US

Authors published: Jane Holland, Tamar Yoseloff & Tobias Hill.

Send 4-6 poems. Requests first publication rights. Accepts simultaneous submissions if so noted. Uses 2-3% of the many submissions received each year. Please do not send work so experimental as to be incomprehensible. Interested in translations and fiction. "Because of the volume of poetry submitted to the magazine, work that does not in some way stand out from the mass is unlikely to be included."

HQ Poetry Magazine

39 Exmouth Street, Swindon, Wiltshire, England SN1 3PU

Editor: Kevin Bailey

Since: 1990	Format: Paper	Circ: 500	Sample: £2.60
Time: 6 months	Money: No	Copies: 1	Sub: £9

Authors published: Lucien Stryk, Dannie Abse, Alan Brownjohn & Alexis Lykiard.

Associated with Daydream Press. Send 6-10 poems, up to one page each. Requests one-time rights. Does NOT accept simultaneous submissions. Uses 1% of the "huge amount" of submissions received each year. Sometimes comments on rejections. Please do not send bad poetry. Interested in book reviews and translations. "We hate anything too politically correct."

HU (formerly The Honest Ulsterman)
49 Main Street, Greyabbey, County Down, England BT22 2NF
Editor: Tom Clyde

Since: 1968	Format: Paper	Circ: 1,000	Sample: £3
Time: 3 months	Money: No	Copies: 2	Sub: Varies

Authors published: Michael Longley, Brendan Kennelly & Carol Rumens.

Send 6 poems. Requests one-time rights. Does NOT accept simultaneous submissions. Uses 100 of the 700 submissions received each year. Interested in book reviews, translations and fiction. Very interested in artwork and photography.

iota
67 Hady Crescent, Chesterfield, Derbyshire, England S41 0EB
Editor: David Holliday

Since: 1988	Format: Paper	Circ: 400	Sample: $2 US
Time: 2-3 weeks	Money: No	Copies: 2	Sub: $15 US

Authors published: Bernadette Higgins, Terrance Cox & Matthew Mead.

Send up to 6 poems. Requests first British serial rights. Accepts simultaneous submissions if so noted. Uses 280 of the 5,000 submissions received each year. Please do not send concrete poetry. May comment on rejections. Interested in book reviews and translations. "We are looking for poems that have something to say, and say it concisely and effectively. Not interested in self-indulgent logorrhea. The magazine has no particular political or philosophical bias so poets are welcome to mount their hobby-horses. Light verse, to leaven the lump, is always welcome."

KRAX
63 Dixon Lane, Leeds, Yorkshire, England LS12 4RR
Editor: Andy Robson

Since: 1971	Format: Paper	Circ: 400	Sample: $5 Can.
Time: 8-10 weeks	Money: No	Copies: 1	Sub: $20 Can.

Authors published: Julia Darling, John Barlow, John Alan Douglas & Robert Dunn.

Send up to 6 poems. Requests one-time rights. Accepts simultaneous submissions if so noted. Uses 60 of the 2,500+ submissions received each year. Please do not send haiku, religious, topical, serious or sombre poetry. Interested in short fiction, b/w artwork and photography. Prefers submissions to be "witty, light-hearted work though this does not imply smutty limericks or topical satire. Further, references to mythological creatures and Shakespearian characters should be avoided. Graphic or visual poetry is acceptable, as are dialect speech and straightforward descriptive items."

Lateral Moves
5 Hamilton Street, Astley Bridge, Bolton, England BL1 6RJ
Editor: Alan White Poetry Editor: Nick Britton
Telephone: (01204) 596369

Since: 1993	Format: Paper	Circ: 250	Sample: £2.85
Time: 3 months	Money: No	Copies: 1	Sub: £12

Authors published: Steven Blyth, Patricia Pogson, Ben Wilensky & Andrew Darlington.

Send up to 6 poems. Requests one-time rights and future acknowledgement. Does

NOT accept simultaneous submissions. Uses 250 of the 1,000 submissions received each year. Please do not send new romantic poetry, uncritical praise or unchallenging work. Also no racism, sexism, genderism, or bigotry. Warmongering also unacceptable. Sometimes comments on rejections. Interested in book reviews, translations, fiction and b/w line art. Welcomes work on Mac or PC disk in plain text format. "*Lateral Moves* is a fast-paced, constantly changing magazine of new contemporary writing. The emphasis is on the writer and we will adapt the magazine on occasions where material received warrants it. Our aim is to present modern and demanding work using effective design techniques." Runs annual Aural Images Poetry Contest.

The North

The Poetry Business, The Studio, Byram Arcade, Westgate, Huddersfield, England HD1 1 ND
Poetry Editors: Peter Sanson & Janet Fisher
Telephone: 01484 434840 Fax: 01484 426566
E-mail: poetbus@pop3.poptel.org.uk

Since: 1986	Format: Paper	Circ: 500	Sample: £9
Time: 1 month	Money: £15/poem	Copies: 1	Sub: £16

Send up to 6 poems. Requests first British rights. Accepts simultaneous submissions. Does NOT accept e-mail submissions. Uses 50 of the up to 1,000 submissions received each year. Please do not send traditional, old fashioned, derivative work. Query regarding book reviews. "We are a good, well-thought-of literary journal. We welcome work from new and established writers. We like work written in contemporary idiom." Runs writing contest.

Oasis

12 Stevenage Road, London, England SW6 6ES
Poetry Editor: Ian Robinson

Since: 1969	Format: Paper	Circ: Varies	Sample: Not stated
Time: 3 months	Money: No	Copies: 2	Sub: $20

Authors published: G. Winston James, Terri Jewel & Robert Penn.

Send up to 6 poems, of up to 50 lines each. Requests one-time rights. Does NOT accept simultaneous submissions. Uses up to 10 poems of the 500 submissions received each year. Interested in translations, and fiction up to 1,800 words. Occasionally runs theme issues. "Please note: After June 1999, most of our work will be solicited. We will still welcome letters of enquiry or introduction but please do not send multi-page submissions."

Outposts Poetry Quarterly

Hippopotamus Press, 22 Whitewell Road, Frome, Somerset, England BA11 4EL
Poetry Editor: Roland John

Since: 1944	Format: Paper	Circ: 1,400	Sample: £4
Time: 2 weeks	Money: No	Copies: 1	Sub: £16

Authors published: Jared Carter, Christopher Pilling & Peter Dale.

Send up to 5 poems. Requests one-time rights. Accepts simultaneous submissions if so noted. Uses 300 of the 54,000 submissions received each year. Interested in translations. Occasionally runs theme issues. "On our pages the 'yet to be recognized' rub shoulders with the established. Our magazine does not support dogma, nor coterie."

Peace & Freedom
17 Farrow Road, Whaplode Drove, Spalding, Lincolnshire, England PE12 0TS
Editor: Paul Rance
Telephone: 01406 330242

| Since: 1985 | Format: Paper | Circ: 500 | Sample: $4 Can. |
| Time: 1 month | Money: No | Copies: 1 | Sub: $16 Can. |

Authors published: Ingrid Riley, Dorothy Bell-Hall, Bernard Shough & Maureen Watson.

Send up to 5 poems, up to 32 lines each. Requests one-time rights. Accepts simultaneous submissions if so noted. Uses up to 125 of the 500 submissions received each year. Interested in translations, fiction up to 500 words, artwork and photography. "*Peace & Freedom* is a magazine which focuses on environmental and humanitarian issues via poetry, prose and art. Work of a spiritual nature will normally be considered as well. We have produced cassette tape versions of *Peace & Freedom* and various paperback and booklet-format anthologies on subjects such as humour, the environment and dinosaurs." Also publishes *Eastern Rainbow* magazine. Runs regular writing competitions.

Pennine Platform
7 Cockley Hill Lane, Kirkheaton, Huddersfield, West Yorkshire, England HD5 0HH
Editor: Dr. K.E. Smith

| Since: 1972 | Format: Paper | Circ: 200 | Sample: £2.30 |
| Time: 3 months | Money: No | Copies: 1 | Sub: £10 |

Authors published: Pauline Kirk, Bill Headdon & Patricia Pogson.

Send up to 5 poems. Requests first-time rights. Accepts simultaneous submissions if so noted. Uses the work of up to 50 contributors each year. Interested in translations and fiction.

Poetry & Audience
School of English, University of Leeds, Leeds, England LS2 9JT
Poetry Editor: Mark Leahy
E-mail: engpanda@english.novell.leeds.ac.uk

| Since: 1950 | Format: Paper | Circ: 200 | Sample: £2 |
| Time: 2 months | Money: No | Copies: 1 | Sub: £6 |

Authors published: Bill Brody, Ian Caws, Paul Groves & Retta Bowen.

Send 1–5 poems. Requests one-time rights. Accepts e-mail submissions. Does NOT accept simultaneous submissions. Uses up to 70 of the 200 submissions received each year. Interested in book reviews and translations. "We are an eclectic but quality little magazine which welcomes submissions of any kind as our magazine has no 'angle.' Editors change every two years or so which guarantees a freshness of approach."

Poetry London Newsletter
26 Clacton Road, London, England E17 8AR
Poetry Editor: Pascale Petit
Telephone: 0181 520 6693 Fax: 0171 502 1407
E-mail: pdaniels@easynet.co.uk

| Since: 1988 | Format: Paper | Circ: 700 | Sample: £3.50 |
| Time: 1 month | Money: £20/poem | Copies: 1 | Sub: £16 |

Authors published: Kwame Dawes, Olive Senior, Anita Endiezze & Judith Barrington.

Send up to 6 poems. Requests one-time rights. Does NOT accept e-mail submissions or simultaneous submissions. Uses 65 of the 3,000 submissions received each year. Please do not send L=A=N=G=U=A=G=E poetry, bad poetry or light verse. Sometimes comments on rejections. Interested in book reviews and translations. "Send poems that are exciting, alive and fresh, poems that take risks, are ambitious. Particular interest in indigenous peoples, mixed cultures and the wilderness. Send poems that are rooted in life, juicy rather than dry." Publishes a mix of well-known writers alongside new poets.

Poetry Nottingham International
71 Saxton Avenue, Heanor, Derbyshire, England DE75 7PZ

Editor: Cathy Grindrod

Since: 1946	Format: Paper	Circ: 300	Sample: £3
Time: 6 weeks	Money: No	Copies: 1	Sub: £15

Send 4-6 poems, up to 40 lines each. Requests one-time rights. Does NOT accept simultaneous submissions or reprints. Uses up to 180 of the 1,200 submissions received each year. Comments on work that "comes close to being accepted." Editor looks for original treatment of theme, a good sense of poetic rhythm, and clear language with layers of meaning. Subtle humour, irony and upbeat poems are as welcome as more serious poetry. Runs annual poetry competition.

Poetry Review
22 Betterton Street, London, England N2 9PY

Editor: Peter Forbes

Telephone: 44 171 420 9883 Fax: 44 171 240 4818

E-mail: poetrysoc@dial.pipex.com

Website: www.poetrysoc.com

Since: 1909	Format: Paper	Circ: 4,750	Sample: Nil
Time: 3 months	Money: £40/poem	Copies: 1	Sub: £35

Authors published: Simon Armitage, Edwin Morgan & Carol Rumens.

Send 3-4 poems. Requests exclusive UK rights. Does NOT accept simultaneous submissions or e-mail submissions. Uses 125 of the 3-5,000 submissions received each year. "We are not prescriptive. We like to see the widest range of work and then choose." Runs theme issues. Details online or send SASE.

Presence
12 Grovehall Avenue, Leeds, England LS 11 7EX

Editor: Martin Lucas Poetry Editor: Stuart Quine

Since: 1996	Format: Paper	Circ: 135	Sample: $5 US
Time: 1 month	Money: No	Copies: 1	Sub: $10 US

Authors published: Michael D. Welch, Peggy W. Lyles, Brian Tasker & Annie Bachini.

Send 4-12 poems, up to 16 lines each. Requests one-time rights. Accepts e-mail submissions but please limit the number of poems submitted this way to six. Does NOT accept simultaneous submissions. Uses up to 100 of the 1,000 submissions received each year. Interested in translations and b/w artwork. Please do not send non-haiku related material. *Presence* seeks submissions of haiku, senryu, tanka, renku, haibun and related poetry. Articles, artwork and haiku books for review are welcome. The editor requested Canadians and Americans include with their subscription orders "loose bills" as *Presence* cannot cash US or Canadian cheques. (Note: this is always a bad idea. An international postal money order should be acceptable.)

Psychopoetica

Department of Psychology, University of Hull, Hull, England HU6 7RX
Editor: Geoff Lowe Poetry Editor: Trevor Millum
Telephone: 1482 465581 Fax: 1482 465599
E-mail: G.Lowe@psy.hull.ac.uk
Website: www.fernhse.demon.co.uk/eastword/psycho

Since: 1968	Format: Paper	Circ: 300	Sample: £3
Time: 5 weeks	Money: No	Copies: 1	Sub: £12

Authors published: Rod Farmer, Simon Perchik & Jennifer Bosveld.

Send up to 6 poems, under two pages each. Requests one-time rights. Accepts simultaneous submissions and e-mail submissions. Uses 100 of the 1,000 submissions received each year. May be interested in translations and artwork. Query first. Occasionally runs theme issues. "Prefer poems that are clear and lucid and draw us right into the depths of your imagination."

Purple Patch

25 Griffiths Road, West Bromwich, England B71 2EH
Editor: Geoff Stevens

Since: 1976	Format: Paper	Circ: Varies	Sample: £1.25
Time: Varies	Money: No	Copies: Nil	Sub: Not stated

Authors published: Ted Yund, M.T. Nowak and R.L. Bagula.

Send at least 2 poems, up to 40 lines each. Requests first British serial rights. Accepts simultaneous submissions if so noted. Uses up to 200 of the 2,000 submissions received each year. Please do not send rhyme or prose poetry. Interested in short book reviews, translations, very short literary fiction and artwork.

Reflections

PO Box 178, Sunderland, Tyne and Wear, England SR1 1DU
Editor: Changes annually

Since: 1991	Format: Paper	Circ: 150	Sample: £2
Time: 1 month	Money: No	Copies: 1	Sub: £5

Send any number of poems. Requests one-time rights. Accepts simultaneous submissions if so noted. Uses few of the many submissions received each year. Interested in translations, fiction up to 1,500 words, artwork and photography. Not interested in "negativity." Publishes theme issues. "*Reflections* promotes good will between people irrespective of their background."

The Rialto

PO Box 309, Aylsham, Norwich, Norfolk, England NR11 6LN
Poetry Editor: Michael Mackmin

Since: 1984	Format: Paper	Circ: 1,500	Sample: £6
Time: 3 months	Money: £20/poem	Copies: 1	Sub: £16

Authors published: Simon Armitabe, Ruth Padel & Les Murray.

Send up to 6 poems. Requests one-time rights. Accepts simultaneous submissions if so noted. Uses up to 180 of the 15,000 submissions received each year. Do not send sexist, fascist or racist rubbish. Interested in translations. Send only "excellent poems."

Rustic Rub
33 Meadow Walk, Fleet, Hampshire, England GU13 8BA
Editor: Mrs. Jay Woodman
Telephone: 01252 628538

Since: 1994	Format: Paper	Circ: 300	Sample: £5
Time: 1 month	Money: No	Copies: 1	Sub: £9

Authors published: Canadians Neil Meili & David A. Groulx, & Marc Swan from the United States.

Associated with Woodman's Press. Send up to 6 poems. Requests first British serial rights. Does NOT accept simultaneous submissions. Interested in translations and b/w artwork. Magazine has had funding difficulties but editor is optimistic they will be overcome as a result of increased subscriptions and exceptionally high quality material. Send only your best work. Does not publish same poet in consecutive issues.

SALT
Churchill College, Cambridge, England CB3 0DS*
Editor: John Kinsella
E-mail: jvk20@hermes.cam.ac.uk
Website: www.geocities.com/SoHo/Square/8574

Since: 1990	Format: Paper	Circ: 1,000	Sample: $25 Aus.
Time: 6 months	Money: Varies	Copies: 1	Sub: $60 Aus.

Authors published: Ashbery, Cixous, Hejinian, Murray, Pinsky, Hewett & Bernstein.

Send up to 12 poems. Requests first publication rights and the right to post the poems on the web for up to 12 months after publication. Accepts simultaneous submissions. Does NOT accept e-mail submissions. Uses up to 70 of the 2,000 submissions received each year. Please do not send fiction. Interested in poetry reviews and translations. Runs theme issues. "We favour the long poem and articles on poetry theory; the magazine is dedicated to breaking down the barriers between the traditional and the experimental." *The editorial offices for this magazine are in England but all production is done in Australia.

Seam
PO Box 3684, Danbury, Chelmsford, England CM3 4GP
Editors: Maggie Freeman & Frank Dullaghan

Since: 1993	Format: Paper	Circ: 250	Sample: £5
Time: 2-4 weeks	Money: No	Copies: 1	Sub: £10

Authors published: James Brockway, Anne Born & Frances Scott.

Send up to 6 poems. Requests one-time rights. Does NOT accept simultaneous submissions. New editors were unable to comment on percentage of submissions used. "We're looking for lively, interesting new poetry from established and new writers."

Sepia
Knill Cross House, Knill Cross, Millbrook, Torpoint, Cornwall, England PL10 1DX
Editor: Colin Webb

Since: 1977	Format: Paper	Circ: 100	Sample: £1
Time: 2 weeks	Money: No	Copies: 1	Sub: £5

Send up to 6 poems. Requests first publication rights. Accepts simultaneous submissions if so noted. Uses up to 120 of the 800 submissions received each year. Please do not send traditional, rhymes, strict-metre, clichés or big themes (i.e. "Why am I here?"). Interested in book reviews, translations, fiction up to 5,000 words and b/w artwork. Editor prefers an idiosyncratic approach to material, nuances not sledgehammers. Encourages writers to work from a personal or unusual angle on a topic but to be natural and original.

Smiths Knoll

49 Church Road, Little Glemham, Woodbridge, Suffolk, England IP13 0BJ
Poetry Editors: Roy Blackman & Michael Laskey

Since: 1991	Format: Paper	Circ: 450	Sample: £4
Time: 1 month	Money: £5/poem	Copies: 1	Sub: £11

Send up to 5 poems. Requests one-time rights. Does NOT accept simultaneous submissions. Uses 150 of the up to 8,000 submissions received each year. Please do not send anything but "new poetry." Interested in translations.

Smoke

Windows Project, First Floor, Liver House, 96 Bold Street, Liverpool, England L1 4HY
Editors: David Calder & Dave Ward
Telephone: 0151 709 3688

Since: 1974	Format: Paper	Circ: 500-1,000	Sample: £1
Time: 2 weeks	Money: No	Copies: 1	Sub: £5

Authors published: Simon Armitage & Carol Ann Duffy.

Send up to 6 poems, up to one page long each. Requests one-time rights. Accepts simultaneous submissions if so noted. Uses about 40 of the 3,000 submissions received each year. Interested in translations, short prose and b/w graphics.

Southfields

8 Richmond Road, Staines, Middlesex, England TW18 2AB
Editors: Raymond Friel, David Kinloch & Richard Price.

Since: 1994	Format: Paper	Circ: 100	Sample: £3
Time: 1 month	Money: No	Copies: 1	Sub: £6

Send up to 6 poems. Requests first serial rights. Uses about 40 of the 300 poems received each year. Please do not send work that doesn't engage with contemporary poetry. Interested in book reviews, translations and occasionally, fiction. Articles may be up to 1,500 words. "*Southfields* publishes a range of modern poetry from Scotland and other countries. Be sure your submission is genuinely modern."

Staple New Writing

Tor Cottage, 81 Cavendish Road, Matlock, Derbyshire, England DE4 3HD
Editor: Donald Measham Poetry Editor: Bob Windsor

Since: 1982	Format: Paper	Circ: 600	Sample: £3
Time: 6 weeks	Money: Yes*	Copies: 1	Sub: £17.50

Send up to 6 poems. Requests first-time worldwide print publication rights. Does NOT accept simultaneous submissions. Uses up to 300 of 12,000 submissions received each year. Do not send minimalism, concrete poetry, or genre fiction. May be interested in translations. Welcomes fiction submissions up to 5,000 words. *Editor states, "A small fee is paid to writers upon publication." Runs annual writing competition

Super Trooper

35 Kearsley Road, Sheffield, England S2 4TE

Editor: Andrew Savage

Since: 1985	Format: Paper	Circ: 100	Sample: £3
Time: 1 months	Money: No	Copies: 1	Sub: £11

Authors published: Andy Darlington, Jon Sumners & Wil Walker.

Send up to 3 poems. Requests one-time rights. Accepts simultaneous submissions if so noted. Interested in book reviews, translations, and fiction. All submissions must be on cassette tape, up to 5 minutes maximum. Editor prefers music with poetry as well as "strange and silly noises." Tries to use something from all taped submissions, depending on quality of work.

Tears in the Fence

38 Hod View, Stourpaine, Blandford Forum, Dorset, England DT11 8TN

Editor: David Caddy

Telephone: 00 44 1258 456803

E-mail: poets@inzit.co.uk

Since: 1985	Format: Paper	Circ: 600	Sample: £5
Time: 2-3 months	Money: No	Copies: 1	Sub: £15

Authors published: Lee Harwood, Donna Hilbert, K.V. Skene & Edward Field.

Send up to 6 poems. Requests one-time rights. Does NOT accept simultaneous submissions or e-mail submissions. Uses 200 of the 2,000 submissions received each year. Occasionally comments on rejections. Interested in book reviews, translations, fiction, artwork and photography. "We are an independent literary magazine looking for the unusual, perceptive, risk-taking as well as the imagistic and visionary. Please include a short bio with your work. We have an international readership. Our purpose is to provide a forum for lively writing and debate." Runs writing competition.

Terrible Work

21 Overton Gardens, Mannamead, Plymouth, England PL3 5BX

Editor: Tim Allen

Telephone: 01752 661339

Since: 1994	Format: Paper	Circ: 250	Sample: £3.50
Time: 1 month	Money: No	Copies: 1	Sub: £9

Authors published: Bruce Andrews, Tina Darragh & Sheila E. Murphy.

Send 7-8 poems. Requests one-time rights. Accepts simultaneous submissions if they have not been submitted elsewhere in the UK. Uses 100 of the 1,000 submissions received each year. Interested in translations, artwork and photography. "We are left-field eclectic. Particularly interested in introducing new innovative and modern (post-modern) writers."

Thumbscrew

PO Box 657, Oxford, England OX2 6PH

Editor: Tim Kendall

E-mail: tim.kendall@bristol.ac.uk

Since: 1994	Format: Paper	Circ: 500	Sample: £5
Time: 2 months	Money: No	Copies: 2	Sub: £27

Authors published: Heaney, Raine, Sherenson & Simic.

Send up to 6 poems. Requests one-time rights only. Uses up to 25 of the 1,000 submissions received each year. Does NOT accept e-mail submissions or simultaneous submissions. Interested in book reviews, translations and b/w portrait photos. "*Thumbscrew* is an international poetry magazine, publishing works by well-known writers alongside new names. We are particularly interested in high-quality, lucid prose submissions on any aspect of the contemporary poetry scene. We also welcome all kinds of poetry."

Time Haiku

105 Kings Head Hill, London, England E4 7JG

Editor: Mrs.E. Facey

Since: 1994	Format: Paper	Circ: 100	Sample: £5
Time: 6 months	Money: No	Copies: Nil	Sub: £10

Authors published: C. Sykes, D. Pugh, D. Ammons & A. Movcoff.

Send up to 18 haiku or 6 short poems no more than 30 lines each. Requests one-time rights. Uses 400 of the 1,000 poetry submissions received each year. Accepts simultaneous submissions if so noted. Interested in book reviews and translations. Will consider short essays, up to 350 words, on haiku.

The Third Half Magazine

16 Fane Close, Stamford, Lincolnshire, England PE9 1H9

Editor: Kevin Troop

Since: 1987	Format: Paper	Circ: Varies	Sample: £8
Time: 2 weeks	Money: No	Copies: 1	Sub: £8

Send up to 10 poems. Requests one-time rights. Uses some of the many poems received each year. Does NOT accept simultaneous submissions or reprints. Please do not send filth, obscene or stupid work. Interested in fiction and artwork. Often runs theme issues. Editor stresses the need for an SASE with every submission.

Upstart!

19 Cawarden, Statonbury, Milton Keynes, England MK14 6AH

Editor: Carol Barac Poetry Editor: Neil Beardmore

Telephone: 01908 317535 Fax: 01908 317535

E-mail: carol-barac@mkcn.org.uk

Since: 1995	Format: Paper	Circ: 300+	Sample: £4
Time: 6 months	Money: No	Copies: No	Sub: £6.95

Authors published: John Figuerda, David Dabydeen, Idris Caffrey & Pat Coombes.

Send up to 5 poems. Requests first-time rights. Accepts simultaneous submissions. May accept short e-mail submissions. Uses 50 of the 400 submissions received each year. Reads submissions September–March. Please do not send violence, sexual deviance, any repression or war-related material. Interested in translations, fiction up to 5,000 words, artwork and photography. "We prefer work which is unusual, quirky or off-beat." Developing a writing competition.

Weyfarers

1 Mountside, Guildford, Surrey, England GU2 5JD

Editor: Martin Jones

Telephone: 01483 504556

Since: 1970	Format: Paper	Circ: 300	Sample: £2

Time: 1-2 months   Money: No   Copies: 1   Sub: £5

Send up to 6 poems, up to 45 lines each. Requests one-time rights. Accepts simultaneous submissions if so noted. Uses 100 of the 1,000 submissions received each year. Usually comments on rejections. Interested in book reviews and translations. "Poems are chosen according to merit. Editors takes turns editing an issue. Magazine likes to be up-to-date so slight preference is given to poems which reflect the contemporary world and make a fresh comment." Associated with the Surrey Poetry Competition run by Wey Poets of Guildford.

The Zone

13 Hazely Combe, Arreton, Isle of Wight, England P030 3AJ

Editor: Tony Lee

Since: 1994   Format: Paper   Circ: 500   Sample: £5.50
Time: 4-6 weeks   Money: No   Copies: 1   Sub: £22

Authors published: Steve Sneyd, Ann Keith & Mark McLaughlin.

Associated with Pigasus Press. Send up to 6 poems. Requests first British serial rights. Uses up to 20 of the few submissions received each year. Usually comments on rejections. Does NOT accept simultaneous submissions. Interested in fiction 1,000–5,000 words, translations, book reviews of UK-based books up to 400 words, camera-ready artwork and photography. Please do not send supernatural fantasy or contemporary horror material. "*The Zone* publishes original fiction, interviews with prominent sci-fi authors, critical articles and incisive media reviews." Genre artwork (b/w, ink only) is also a feature of the magazine on covers and in "graphic poems" (i.e. verse with sequential illustrations). Enclose sufficient postage for return of your manuscript or it will be considered disposable. Guidelines or press catalogue available for SASE.

FRANCE

Breakfast All Day (BAD)

4 rue Bonne Nouvelle, Dieppe, France 76200

Editor: Philip Boxall

Telephone: 0033(0)2 35 40 33 26 Fax: 0033(0)2 35 40 33 26

Since: 1995   Format: Paper   Circ: 300   Sample: 6 IRCs
Time: 2-3 months   Money: No   Copies: 1   Sub: $24 US

Authors published: Elizabeth Howkins, Mike Lipstock, Andrew Pachuta & B.Z. Niditch.

Send 5 poems, up to 50 lines each. Requests first British serial rights. Accepts simultaneous submissions if so noted. Uses 120 of the 300 submissions received each year. Sometimes comments on rejections if requested. Interested in translations, fiction up to 4,000 words, artwork and photography. "Contributions can be on any subject, and in any style, should reflect an original or insightful point of view, and where appropriate, a sense of humour."

FRANK: An International Journal of Contemporary Writing

32 rue Edouard Vaillant, 93100 Montreuil, France

Editor: David Applefield

Telephone: (33) 1 48 59 66 58 Fax: (33) 1 48 59 66 68

E-mail: david@paris-anglo.com
Website: www.frankonline.org

| Since: 1983 | Format: Paper/Web | Circ: 3,000 | Sample: $10 US |
| Time: 2 months | Money: Query | Copies: 2 | Sub: $38 US |

Send 2-10 poems. Requests first worldwide serial rights in all forms. Accepts e-mail submissions and simultaneous submissions if so noted. Uses 20 of the 1,000 submissions received each year. Not interested in sentimental poetry. Sometimes comments on rejections. Interested in translations, fiction, artwork and photography.

Handshake Editions/Cassette Gazette

Atelier A2, 83 rue de la Tombe Issoire, Paris, France 75014
Editor: Jim Haynes
Telephone: 33-1 4327 1767 Fax: 33-1 4320 4195
E-mail: jim_haynes@wanadoo.fr

| Since: 1981 | Format: Paper/Cassette | Circ: Varies | Sample: $10 Can. |
| Time: See below. | Money: No | Copies: Varies | Sub: N/A |

Authors published: David Day is the only Canadian published so far.

Send 5-10 poems. Requests for rights varies. Please discuss with editor. Accepts e-mail submissions. Does NOT accept simultaneous submissions. Uses very few of the "too many" submissions received each year. Editor cautions his is an extremely small one-man operation and prefers to meet contributors. Encourages writers to call him when in Paris. "If I can help in any way I will be pleased to do so." Runs theme issues.

Paris/Atlantic: International Journal of Creative Work

The American University of Paris, 31 avenue Bosquet, Paris, France 75007
Editor: Elise Manley Poetry Editors: Elise Manley & Lisa Damon
Telephone: 33 1 40 62 05 89 Fax: 33 1 45 51 89 13
E-mail: auplantic@hotmail.com

| Since: 1982 | Format: Paper | Circ: 1,500 | Sample: Free |
| Time: Varies | Money: No | Copies: 2 | Sub: Not stated |

Authors published: Ben Wilensky, Steve Sneyd & T. Anders Carson.

Send 3-4 poems, under 100 lines each. Requests first rights only. Accepts e-mail submissions and simultaneous submissions. Uses 180 of the 400 submissions received each year. Interested in book reviews, translations, plays, essays, excerpts of works-in-progress and short fiction. Special interest in artwork and photography. Paris/Atlantic's editorial board is comprised of students of the American University of Paris and advisory Comparative Literature professors.

GERMANY

Rind & Schlegel: Zeitschrift für Poesie

Ursulastrasse 10, 80802 München, Germany
Editor: Klaus Friedrich
Telephone: 089 34 25 50

| Since: 1977 | Format: Paper | Circ: 1,500 | Sample: $5 US |
| Time: 3 months | Money: No | Copies: 2 | Sub: N/A |

Authors published: Carl Amery, Ernst Jünger, Karl Krolow & Ulla Hahn.

Send 5-10 poems, up to one page each. Requests one-time rights. Accepts simultaneous submissions if so noted. Please do not send racism or fanaticism of any kind. Interested in translations, and fiction up to 7,000 words. Very interested in photos of colourful realistic paintings. Runs theme issues.

PIPS: Magazine for Uncommerce

PIPS-DADA-Corporation, Prinz-Albert Str. 31, D-53113, Bonn, Germany
Editor: Claudia Pütz Poetry Editor: Katharina Eckart
Website: www.artgate.de/groups/pips

Since: 1986	Format: Paper	Circ: 100	Sample: Not stated
Time: 1 week	Money: No	Copies: 1	Sub: Not stated

Authors published: Canadians Anna Banana & Lois Klassen.

This is a visual poetry magazine. Send 3 visual poems. Requests one-time rights. Accepts only unpublished work and original artwork. Uses 120 of the 300 submissions received each year. Interested in fiction, artwork and photography. Runs specific themes each year. Contact for details. "*PIPS* is a compilation of original mail art works by networkers, mail artists and experimental poets."

HONG KONG

Renditions

Research Centre for Translation, Rm 117, Chinese University of Hong Kong, New Territories, Hong Kong SAR
Editor: Eva Hung
Telephone: 852 2609 7415 Fax: 852 2603 5110
E-mail: rct@cuhk.edu.hk or renditions@cuhk.edu.hk
Website: www.cuhk.edu.hk/renditions

Since: 1973	Format: Paper	Circ: 1,000	Sample: Free
Time: 3 months	Money: No	Copies: 2	Sub: $25 US

Authors published: Gu Cheng & Shu Ting.

Send any number of poems, but shorter is better. Negotiates rights. Accepts simultaneous submissions and e-mail submissions. Uses 5 of the 30 submissions received each year. Interested in translations from Chinese to English. Must be familiar with the proper use of the Pinyin System. Spelling and usage should be in accordance with the Shorter Oxford English Dictionary. Though not stated outright, editor implied translations are the ONLY poetry desired.

INDIA

Prakalpana Sahitya/Prakalpana Literature

P40 Nandana Park, Calcutta, W.B., India 700034
Editor: Vattacharja Chandan
Telephone: 003-478-2347

Since: 1977	Format: Paper	Circ: 1,000	Sample: 6 IRCs
Time: Varies	Money: No	Copies: 1	Sub: 6 IRCs

Authors published: Dilip Gupta, Norman Olson, Susan Smith Nash & Nark Das.

Send up to 4 poems. Requests one-time rights. Does NOT accept simultaneous submissions. Uses 10 percent of the many submissions received each year. Please do not send religious, political or conventional poetry or stories. Interested in fiction and experimental artwork and photography. Editor warns the response time can be very long and writers should provide a permanent address as opposed to a post office box number for response. Does not respond if your work has not been accepted. "Submissions should be limited to experimental poetry with visual touch which is called Sarbangin poetry and prakalpana." Published irregularly.

Kavya Bharati

Scilet, American College, PO Box 63, Madurai, India 625 002

Editor: R.P. Nair

Telephone: 91-452-533609 Fax: 91-452-531056

E-mail: scilet@md2.vsnl.net.in

Since: 1988	Format: Paper	Circ: 800	Sample: Free
Time: 1 month	Money: No	Copies: 2	Sub: $12 US

Authors published: Jayanta Mahapatra, Kamala Das, Meena Alexander & Nissim Ezekiel.

Send any number of poems. Requests one-time rights. Accepts simultaneous submissions if so noted. Accepts e-mail submissions. Uses 25 of the 100 submissions received each year. Please do not send any previously published work, fiction or drama. Interested in book reviews and translations. "Submissions are welcomed from resident and non-resident Indians and from citizens of other countries who have developed a first-hand interest in India."

Poetcrit

Poetcrit, Maranda, India 176 102

Managing Editor: Dr. D.C. Chambial

Telephone: 01894-31407

Since: 1988	Format: Paper	Circ: 5,000	Sample: 2 IRCs
Time: 3 weeks	Money: No	Copies: 1	Sub: $15 US

Send 2–3 poems, up to 25 lines each. Requests one-time publication rights. Accepts simultaneous submissions. Uses 300 of the 500 submissions received each year. Please do not send fiction. Interested in book reviews up to 1,000 words and translations. Please include a brief bio.

IRELAND

Metre

English Department, Trinity College, Dublin 2, Ireland

Editors: David Wheatley & Justin Quinn

E-mail: dwhetley@tcd.ie or quinn@ff.cuni.cz

Since: 1996	Format: Paper	Circ: 750	Sample: £6 Ir.
Time: 3 weeks	Money: No	Copies: 2	Sub: £20 Ir.

Authors published: Samuel Beckett, Seamus Heaney & Paul Muldoon.

Send up to 6 poems. Requests first publication rights and subsequent acknowledgement. Does NOT accept simultaneous submissions or e-mail submissions. Uses 30 of the 500 submissions received each year. Please do not send fiction. Interested in book reviews and translations. "Editors particularly appreciate an accompanying disk when work is of a longer nature."

Flaming Arrows

County Sligo VEC, Riverside, Sligo, Ireland

Editors: Leo Regan

Telephone: 353 71 45844 Fax: 353 71 43093

E-mail: leoregan@tinet.ie

| Since: 1989 | Format: Paper | Circ: 500 | Sample: £2.65 Ir. |
| Time: 2 weeks | Money: No | Copies: 1 | Sub: Not stated |

Authors published: Barry Butson, Ben Wilensky & Floyd Skloot.

Send 5 poems. Requests one-time rights plus permission to reprint. Accepts simultaneous submissions if so noted. Does NOT accept e-mail submissions. Reads submissions January–October. Uses 20 of the 500 submissions received each year. Interested in fiction. "New writers sought with distinctive style; polished prose, coherent, lucid, direct and strong poetry. Contemplative, metaphysical, mystical, spiritual themes are sought which are well grounded. Also interested in close relationship of character with sacred landscape in narrative or personal poetry. Could describe where the sacred is found in contemporary life, and how it is identified and sustained."

Fortnight Magazine

1 Lower Crescent, Belfast, Northern Ireland BT7 1NR

Editor: John O'Farrell Poetry Editor: Mairtin Crawford

Telephone: 44-1232-232393 Fax: 44-1232-232650

E-mail: mairtin@fortnite.dnet.co.uk

| Since: 1971 | Format: Paper | Circ: 4,500 | Sample: £3 |
| Time: 2-3 months | Money: No | Copies: 2 | Sub: Varies |

Send 3-6 poems. Requests one-time rights. Accepts e-mail submissions. Does NOT accept simultaneous submissions. Uses 10 of the 100 submissions received each year. Occasionally comments on rejections. Please do not send short stories. Interested in book reviews, translations, artwork and photography. "*Fortnight* is an independent review of politics and the arts in Ireland, especially Northern Ireland. We are non-sectarian and non-party aligned politically. We are a liberal magazine which seeks to offer a voice to all those concerned with finding a political solution to political problems. Balance is 60% politics and current affairs, 40% arts and books. All submissions must be relevant to the aims of the magazine." Publishes only 1 page of poetry per issue.

The Brobdingnagian Times

96 Albert Road, Cork, Ireland

Editor: Giovanni Malito

Telephone: (21) 311 227

| Since: 1996 | Format: Paper | Circ: 250 | Sample: 2 IRCs |
| Time: 1 month | Money: No | Copies: 2 | Sub: $5 Can. |

Authors published: Miroslau Holub, Richard Kostelanetz, Leonard Cirino & Steve Sneyd.

Send 4-6 poems, up to 40 lines each. Requests first-time rights in Ireland and the UK. Accepts simultaneous submissions if so noted. Uses up to 60 of the up to 400 submissions received each year. Please do not send long or rhyming poems. Comments on rejections if requested. Interested in translations, fiction up to 1,000 words, artwork and photography. "*The Brobdingnagian Times* is a broadsheet which when folded yields 8 panels. It does not use biographical notes for contributors. We are interested in poetry-related essays and translations for an annual we also publish. The annual does include bio notes for contributors." Requests short cover letter.

Cyphers
3 Selskar Terrace, Ranelagh, Dublin 6, Ireland
Editors: Leland Barowell, Pearse Hutchinson & Macdona Woods.
Fax: 01-4978866
E-mail: enchllm@tcd.ie

| Since: 1975 | Format: Paper | Circ: 500 | Sample: $5 US |
| Time: 6 months | Money: £10 Ir./pg | Copies: 1 | Sub: $20 US |

Send 6 poems. Requests first serial rights. Does NOT accept simultaneous submissions or e-mail submissions. Uses 60 of the up to 700 submissions received each year. Sometimes comments on rejections. Interested in translations, fiction, artwork and photography. Has run issues focused on translations from one language. "Shorter work is more likely to fit in."

Poetry Ireland Review
Bermingham Tower, Upper Yard, Dublin Castle, Dublin 2, Ireland
Editor: Changes annually
Telephone: 353 1 671 4632 Fax: 353 1 6714634
E-mail: poetry@iol.ie

| Since: 1981 | Format: Paper | Circ: 1,100 | Sample: Free |
| Time: 3 months | Money: £10+sub. | Copies: 1 | Sub: £44 |

Authors published: Michael Longley, Ciaran Carson, Theo Dorgan & Kerry Hardie.
Send 5 poems. Requests one-time rights. Accepts e-mail submissions. Does NOT accept simultaneous submissions. Interested in translations. Uses 250 of the 1,000 submissions received each year. Editor stresses poems must not be previously published anywhere.

ITALY

Semicerchio: Revista di poesia comparata
via Lorenzo il Magnifico 64, Firenze, Italy I-50129
Editor: Francesco Stella
Telephone: 390 55 495398 Fax: 390 55 495398
E-mail: stella@unisi.it
Website: www.unisi.it/semicerchio

| Since: 1990 | Format: Paper/Web | Circ: 800 | Sample: $15 |
| Time: 2 months | Money: No | Copies: 1 | Sub: $30 |

Authors published: Vesna Parun, Mario Luzi, Paul Wuhr & Charles Simic.
Send 5 poems. Requests one-time rights. Accepts e-mail submissions and simultaneous submissions. Uses 10 of the 100 submissions received each year. Please do not send novels or fiction. Often comments on rejections. Interested in book reviews and translations. Editor states, "Only a small section of the magazine is dedicated to poems. Most of the magazine is occupied by essays and reviews." Runs "thematic" sections. Details online or send SASE.

JAPAN

The Abiko Quarterly with the James Joyce Studies

8-1-8 Namiki, Abiko-shi, Chiba-ken 270-1165 Japan

Editor: Laurel Sicks

Telephone: 011-81-471-84-7904

E-mail: alp@db3.so-net.or.jp

Website: www.02.u-page.so-net.or.jp/jb3/hce

| Since: 1988 | Format: Paper | Circ: 500 | Sample: $35 |
| Time: 1 month | Money: No | Copies: 1 | Sub: $100 |

Authors published: Joan Peternel, Jesse Glass, Siobhan Fallen & Sharon Mesmer.

Send 3 poems. Requests one-time rights. Accepts e-mail submissions. Does NOT accept simultaneous submissions. Interested in book reviews, translations and fiction. Very interested in artwork and photography. "We accept only camera-ready copy on B-5 paper. B-5 paper is one size smaller than letter-size." Writers whose work is accepted must send $15 to cover the cost of shipping their complimentary copy. Please note each issue is 600–800 pages long. "All materials must relate to James Joyce." Specializes in *Finnegan's Wake*. Runs Thelma and Charlie Willis Poetry Contest and the Tsujinaka Fiction Award Contest.

Poetry Kanto Annual

Kanto Gakuin University, Kamariya-Minami 3-22-1, Kanazaw-ku, Yokohama 236-8502 Japan

Editor: William I. Elliot

Telephone: 784-8448 Fax: 784-8448

| Since: 1984 | Format: Paper | Circ: 800 | Sample: Free |
| Time: 2 weeks | Money: No | Copies: 2 | Sub: N/A |

Authors published: Nuala Ni Dhomahnail & Tanikawa Shuntarò.

Send 3-5 poems, up to 30 lines each. Requests first-time rights. Does NOT accept simultaneous submissions. Reads submissions January–March. Uses up to 25 of the 1,000 submissions received each year. Sometimes comments on rejections. Please do not send porno or Japanese poetic forms unless in Japanese. Often uses special themes.

NEW ZEALAND

Landfall

University of Otago Press, PO Box 56, Dunedin, New Zealand

Poetry Editor: Chris Price

Telephone: (64) 3 479 8807 Fax: (64) 3 479 8385

E-mail: university.press@stonebow.otago.ac.nz

| Since: 1947 | Format: Paper | Circ: 1,000 | Sample: Not stated |
| Time: 4 months | Money: NZ$12/page | Copies: 1 | Sub: $39.95 NZ |

Send up to 10 poems. Requests first New Zealand publication rights. Accepts simultaneous submissions if so noted. Accepts e-mail submissions. Made no comment on how many poems are used each year. Please do not send "popular" verse. Interested in fiction. "Work by New Zealanders, or work about New Zealand is our main priority. Send top quality contemporary poetry only."

Poetry NZ

PO Box 100-057, North Shore Mail Centre, Auckland, New Zealand
Editor: Alistair Paterson
Telephone: 649 410 6993 Fax: 649 410 6993

Since: 1990	Format: Paper	Circ: 1,000	Sample: NZ$17.95
Time: 3 weeks	Money: NZ$25	Copies: 1	Sub: NZ$30

Authors published: Paula Green, Raewyn Alexander, Koenraad Kuiper & Iain Sharp.

Send 5-6 poems. Requests first publication rights. Does NOT accept simultaneous submissions. Uses 70 of the 250 submissions received each year. Please do not send haiku or fiction. Interested in book reviews and translations. Carries the work of both new and established writers.

Southern Ocean Review

PO Box 2143, Dunedin, New Zealand 9000
Editor: Trevor Reeves Poetry Editors: Judith Wolfe & Trevor Reeves
Telephone: 03 455 3117 Fax: 03 456 1053
E-mail: treeves@es.co.nz
Website: www.book.co.nz

Since: 1996	Format: Paper/Web	Circ: 200	Sample: NZ$9.50
Time: 6 weeks	Money: No	Copies: Nil	Sub: NZ$35

Associated with Square One Press. Send up to 6 poems. Requests first publication rights. Accepts e-mail submissions. Does NOT accept simultaneous submissions. Uses up to 25% of the many submissions received each month. Please do not send scholarly essays of limited interest. Interested in book reviews, translations, and fiction up to 3,000 words. Query regarding artwork or photography. Occasionally runs theme issues.

Spin

Postal Agency, Ngakawav, Buller, New Zealand
Editor: Leicester Kyle
Telephone: 03 782 8608

Since: 1986	Format: Paper	Circ: 200	Sample: NZ$6.50
Time: 3 months	Money: No	Copies: Nil	Sub: NZ$18

Send up to 6 poems. Requests one-time rights. Does NOT accept simultaneous submissions. Uses many of the submissions received each year. Often comments on rejections. Please do not send "rubbish." Interested in book reviews, and translations. "We see ourselves as a journal that encourages aspirant poets and sets them on the way to better writing." Contributor copy sent only if you are a subscriber but all are welcome to submit.

Sport

PO Box 11-806, Wellington, New Zealand
Editor: Fergus Barrowinan Poetry Editor: James Brown
Telephone: 64-4-4966 580 Fax: 64-4-4966 581
E-mail: fergus.barrowman@vuw.ac.nz

Since: 1988	Format: Paper	Circ: 800	Sample: NZ$19.95
Time: 2-6 months	Money: No	Copies: 1	Sub: NZ$37

Authors published: Bill Marhive, Allen Curnau & Keri Hulme.

Associated with Victoria University Press. Send 2-5 poems. Requests first New Zealand serial rights. Does NOT accept simultaneous submissions. Uses 40 of the 1,000 submissions received each year. Please do not send genre work. Interested in fiction. The editor emphasizes that work sent by e-mail must be in the body of the e-mail message. All attachments are deleted unread. Runs theme issues. Prefers work with a New Zealand connection.

Takahe
PO Box 13-335, Christchurch 8001, New Zealand
Poetry Editor: Bernadette Hall
Telephone: 03 359 8133
E-mail: markj07@ibm.net

Since: 1989	Format: Paper	Circ: 320	Sample: NZ$8
Time: 4 months	Money: No	Copies: 2	Sub: NZ$32

Authors published: Sarah Quigley & Kapka Kassabova.

Send up to 6 poems, no more than 2-3 pages each. Requests first serial rights. Accepts simultaneous submissions if so noted. Does NOT accept e-mail submissions. Uses up to 45 of the 400 submissions received each year. Sometimes comments on rejections. Interested in translations and fiction. "The main intention of *Takahe* is to promote emerging New Zealand authors, poets and graphic artists, but we publish work from other countries as well to give the magazine balance and wider appeal." Occasionally runs contests.

SCOTLAND

Chapman
4 Broughton Place, Edinburgh, Scotland EH1 3RX
Editor: Joy Hendry
Telephone: 0131 557 2207 Fax: 0131 556 9565
E-mail: chapman@compura.com
Website: www.compura.com/chapman

Since: 1970	Format: Paper	Circ: 2,000	Sample: £3.50
Time: 2-3 months	Money: No	Copies: Varies	Sub: £20

Send 4-10 poems. Requests one-time rights. Does NOT accept simultaneous submissions or e-mail submissions. Uses 100 of the 600 submissions received each year. Please do not send horror or science fiction. Interested in translations, fiction up to 6,000 words, artwork and photography. Runs theme issues. "Chapman publishes established and up-and-coming writers. Focus is on Scottish issues but not exclusively. We accept work from all over the world. We are not an academic journal so essays should limit their use of footnotes. Only quality material considered."

THE VIRGIN ISLANDS

The Caribbean Writer
University of the Virgin Islands, RR#2, Box 10,000, Kingshill, St. Croix, USUI 00850
Editor: Dr. Erika J. Waters
Telephone: (340) 692-4152 Fax: (340) 692-4026

E-mail: ewaters@uvi.edu /submissions to: qmars@uvi.edu
Website: www.uvi.edu/CaribbeanWriter

| Since: 1987 | Format: Paper/Web | Circ: 1,000 | Sample: $6.50 US |
| Time: 2-3 months | Money: No | Copies: 2 | Sub: $18 US/2 yrs |

Authors published: Opal Palmer Adisa, Cecil Gray & Olive Senior.

Send up to 5 poems. Requests one-time rights. Accepts e-mail submissions and simultaneous submissions. Uses up to 75 of the up to 600 submissions received each year. Reads submissions September-February. Interested in book reviews, translations, fiction up to 3,500 words, artwork and photography. "*The Caribbean Writer* is an international magazine with a Caribbean focus. The Caribbean should be central to the work, or the work should reflect a Caribbean heritage, experience or perspective."

WALES

Borderlines

Nant Y Brithyll, Llangynyw, Near Welshpool, Powys, Wales SY21 0JS
Editor: Dave Bingham & Kevin Bamford
Telephone: 01938 810 263

| Since: 1977 | Format: Paper | Circ: Varies | Sample: £2 |
| Time: 6 weeks | Money: No | Copies: 1 | Sub: Not stated |

Send 3-6 poems, up to 40 lines each. Requests one-time rights. Does NOT accept simultaneous submissions. Uses 80 of the up to 1,000 submissions received each year. Please do not send poems about poetry or unshaped recitals of thoughts or feelings. Interested in translations.

Malfunction Press

Rose Cottage, 3 Tram Lane, Buckley, Flintshire, Wales CH7 3JB
Editor: Peter E. Presford
Telephone: 01244 543820

| Since: 1969 | Format: Paper | Circ: Varies | Sample: Not stated |
| Time: 1 month | Money: No | Copies: 1 | Sub: Not stated |

Send 3 poems. Requests one-time rights. Does NOT accept simultaneous submissions. Did not comment on number of submissions used. Please do not send "yeuky looe poetry." Interested in translations from Italian only. Also interested in fiction. Runs theme issues. "Our magazine is mainly sci-fi, fantasy, and light horror. We are also interested in poetry with an Italian theme."

New Welsh Review

Chapter Arts Centre, Market Road, Canton, Cardiff, Wales CF5 1QE
Editor: Robin Reeves
Telephone: 01222 665529 Fax: 01222 665529
E-mail: robin@nwrc.demon.co.uk

| Since: 1988 | Format: Paper | Circ: 1,000 | Sample: £5.50 |
| Time: 3 months | Money: £10-£40 | Copies: 1 | Sub: £16 |

Authors published: Peter Finch, Norman Schwenk & Robert Minhinnick.

Send 1-10 poems. States that copyright becomes jointly held between the author and the magazine. Accepts e-mail submissions. Does NOT accept simultaneous submissions. Uses 160 of the up to 2,000 submissions received each year. Please do not send music reviews. Interested in book reviews, translations, fiction of 3,000–4,000 words, artwork and photography. Sometimes runs theme issues.

Planet
PO Box 44, Aberstwyth, Ceredigion, Cymru, Wales
Editor: John Barnie
Telephone: 01970 611255 Fax: 01970 611377

Since: 1985	Format: Paper	Circ: 1,400	Sample: £2.75
Time: 2 months	Money: £40/1,000 wrds. Copies: 1		Sub: £14

Authors published: R.S. Thomas, Gillian Clarke & Gwyneth Lewis.

Send 5–6 poems. Requests one-time rights. Does NOT accept simultaneous submissions. Uses up to 25 of the 500 submissions received each year. Comments on rejections. Interested in book reviews, translations, fiction between 2,000 and 3,000 words, artwork and photography. "Submissions should preferably have a Welsh dimension if they're factual articles but there are no subject limitations on poetry or fiction."

Poetry Wales
First floor, 2 Wyndham Street, Bridgend, Wales CF31 1EF
Editor: Robert Minhinnick
Telephone: 01656 767834 Fax: 01656 767834

Since: 1965	Format: Paper	Circ: 850	Sample: £3.50
Time: 6 weeks	Money: Varies	Copies: 1	Sub: £12

Authors published: Gwyneth Lewis, Jack Mapanje, Deryn Rees-Jones & Oliver Reynolds.

Send 6 poems. Requests one-time rights. Does NOT accept simultaneous submissions. Made no comment on number of submissions used. Occasionally comments on rejections. Interested in book reviews and translations. Runs theme issues but includes a variety of work outside of theme as well. "Long poems and prose poems welcome. Main emphasis of magazine is on writing from Wales but writers from outside Wales are regularly included. Interested in work which reflects cultural diversity."

The following international periodicals have ceased publication since the sixth edition of this book:

Le Journal (France), Fatchance (England), Cobweb (Ireland), Arts Poetica (Australia), Oxford Quarterly Review (England)

The following international periodicals believed to still be active, failed to respond to requests for information:

UNITED KINGDOM: Aberdeen Leopard (formerly Leopard), Ah Pook Is Here, Ammonite, And, Angel Exhaust, Anthem, Aquarius, Artery, Beat Scene, Bradford Poetry, Braquemard, Cascando, Cencrastus, The Countryman, Delhi London Poetry Quarterly, European Judaism, Extrance, First Offence, Foolscap Magazine, Global Tapestry Journal, Grey Suit, Headlock, Hrafnhoh, Inkshed, Iron, Issue One, Joe's Soap Canoe, The Kerouac

Connection, Maelstrom, Memes, Momentum, Moonstone, Never Bury Poetry, New Hope International, New Prospects Magazine, New Spokes, New Writing Scotland, Nineties Poetry, Object Permanence, One, Orbis, Owl Magazine, Pagan America, Passion, Pause, Pen & Keyboard Magazine, The People's Poetry, Phoenix Broadsheets, Poetry Durham, Premonitions, The Reid Review, A Riot of Emotions, Skeleton Girls, Slow Dancer, Sol Magazine, South, Spectacular Diseases, Sunk Island Review, Tabla, Talus, Tandem, 10th Muse, The Third Alternative, Threads, Under Surveillance, Various Artists, Verse, West Coast Magazine, Works, Writers' Viewpoint, X-Calibrww, Zimmerframepileup

AUSTRALIA: Island, Meanjin, Otis Rush, The Phoenix Review, Poetry Australia, Quadrant, Redoubt, Scarp, Southerly, Southern Review, Womanspeak; BARBADOS: BIM Magazine; BELGIUM: Postfluxpostbooklets; EIRE: Cyphers, Eco-Runes, Limerick Poetry Broadsheet, Riverine, Strudies, Windows; FINLAND: Brio Cell, Sivullinen; FRANCE: Revue Polyphonies, Zoum-zoum; GERMANY: Miniature Obscure, Silhouette; GUYANA: Kyk-Over-al; INDIA: The Indian Writer, Manushi, Hoopoe International Poetry Review; ISRAEL: Voices Israel; ITALY: Lo Straniero, Trapani Nuova; JAMAICA: Jamaica Journal; JAPAN: Blue Jacket, The Lonsdale: international quarterly of the romantic six, Mainichi Daily News, Poetry Nippon; POLAND: Mandrake Poetry Magazine; SWITZERLAND: En Plein Air

TWO: FINDING YOUR WAY IN THE BOOK PUBLISHING BUSINESS

This section gives an overview of book publishing. At the end of the section is an extensive list of Canadian book publishers. All of those listed publish poetry in some form.

Though not listed in this edition, American publishers are interested in the work of Canadian writers. Like most publishers their main criteria is quality. You can research the needs of US book publishers through their websites or resources like *Poet's Market* (Writer's Digest Books).

The Canadian listings offer a mix of both large publishers and small press publishers. Unless noted otherwise, all welcome queries from either new or established writers.

2.1 ARE YOU READY TO WRITE A BOOK?

How will you know when you're ready to write a book? The first thing to consider is how long you have been writing poetry. A month? A year? Although Stephanie Bolster won the 1998 Governor General's Award for her first book, *White Stone: The Alice Poems*, she worked on the poems themselves for more than five years and in that time was widely published in literary journals.

Poetry books are such a financial risk for the publisher that they are unlikely to publish the ordinary and certainly won't consider the unpolished. It is only when you believe you have a body of work that is exceptional that you should consider putting together a manuscript. Publishers will be more likely to take notice of your work if it has already appeared in a number of literary magazines and/or anthologies. To be consistently published takes time.

It is your responsibility to research the needs of different publishing houses and target your work appropriately. KNOW THE MARKET. Success will come sooner if you do.

2.2 WHAT ABOUT SELF-PUBLISHING?

Self-publishing counts toward membership in the League of Canadian Poets because the League recognizes how difficult it is to find a publisher. However, the Canada Council for the Arts does not recognize the efforts of self-publishers and they are not eligible to apply for most Canada Council writer's grants.

On the bright side, as a self-publisher you have total control over how your book looks, its contents, and its cost, something you would not have control over at a publishing house.

Before committing yourself to printing a book, or even a chapbook, get the advice of a professional editor; one who has extensive experience with poetry would be best. Some poets offer such a service and again, here is where networking will pay off. Your contacts may lead you to a poet who will read your manuscript and offer some constructive criticism. Costs will vary both with the amount of time your manuscript takes to work through as well as the experience the poet brings to the job.

Once the book has been well-edited, you should consider your design plan. Examine the books which you admire. Note what you like about them and how those features might be translated for use in your book. Think out every decision carefully and never be caught up by a last minute whim. One writer's group spent months collecting and editing an anthology of members' work, having special point-of-sale display boxes made, selecting paper and cover stock only to decide at the last minute that the title of the book should be printed across the bottom third of the cover. The only part of the book showing when set in the display boxes had NOTHING on it. Even with the cooperation of area merchants, sales were dismal.

All publishing requires work on the part of the author to sell books but for obvious reasons, with self-publishing it will be entirely up to you to sell it. You will have to have sales materials, receipts, invoices, an inventory system and time to visit individual bookstores to call on the managers. National chain stores are unlikely to carry your book but may allow individual store managers some leeway to purchase books of local interest. However, few managers will be tempted by a self-published title for their traditionally slow-selling poetry section.

If you do interest a manager in your work, be aware that bookstores will request at least a forty per cent discount off the retail price and many stores will decline to carry your book even under those terms. They might agree to have you leave a small number of copies on a consignment basis. This means they agree to display your book for a set amount of time but no money changes hands until you return to collect the sales revenue (less the store's forty percent discount). If any of the books are soiled or damaged in some way, you carry the entire loss. There is no point in being naive about self-publishing; it is a risky business and the returns are generally low. Publicity is key to the success of any title and you have to be prepared to put time into promoting your book.

2.3 WHAT WILL A SUBSIDY OR VANITY PRESS DO FOR YOU?

When you contract with a vanity press you purchase the attention of a professional editor, designer, and printing company in one package. It can be expensive and though you may be left with a pretty product, it will still be your responsibility to sell it. Before you sign a contract ask to see samples of their previous work, and ask for references from at least three people who "published" with them in the past. One last note of caution: do not be fooled by contracts which state a vanity press will help you with marketing. Your title might get listed in a catalogue along with the other books they produce under contract, but it is unlikely to get any personal attention.

Some vanity presses promise to put your manuscript online for a flat fee. It will then sell your "book" to any interested party and send some portion of those proceeds on to you. At the time of writing, many of these companies did not offer editorial advice and generally presented books as plain text, an unappealing format for a book of any length. These services will become more sophisticated as consumer demand for esthetically pleasing online books grows. Even so, these companies offer no marketing support whatsoever and it will be up to you to let people know where your book is available. Money spent on an arrangement like this might be better spent printing, advertising and promoting a chapbook.

2.4 SHOULD YOU HAVE A LITERARY AGENT?

This is the only place in this book to find information on literary agents. New writers simply do not need one nor are they likely to get representation by one. As you have already noted, poetry does not pay well and 15 per cent of nothing is still nothing. In simple math 15 per cent of the author's royalties on a sold out run of 500 poetry books selling for $12.95 each is $97.13. This explains why literary agents rarely handle poetry.

Many agents charge a reading fee. This does not guarantee they will represent you. Ethical agents make the bulk of their income from the representation of particular authors. Fees are not ethical if an agent has few clients and makes the bulk of their income from reading fees charged to writers desperate to be published.

When you are ready for an agent, you will have sufficient contacts within the publishing industry to know if there are any agents you should avoid dealing with or one who will work particularly hard to place literary work. If you are determined to seek the counsel of an agent at this point, or you feel you have a project which requires representation, *The Canadian Writer's Guide* published by the Canadian Authors' Association has an excellent section listing Canadian literary agencies across the country.

2.5 CHAPBOOKS

Chapbooks can present a theme with both impact and resonance in an intimate package. The physical appearance of a chapbook can range from photocopies, saddle-stitched together, to a limited edition printed by letter press on special paper. Chapbooks are produced both by self-publishers and publishing houses. Some are published as the result of chapbook competitions. All are less than 48 pages.

There are a number of difficulties inherent in the chapbook format: they are hard to display effectively because they get "lost" between full-size books; libraries avoid them because they lack durability; and potential customers may balk at paying a reasonable retail price ($7-$12). Fortunately, there is a good following for works brought out in chapbook format.

2.6 TRADE BOOKS/LITERARY BOOKS

If you are ready to submit your work to a trade publisher, and are able to secure a contract, you can look forward to receiving excellent editorial support, the help of a dedicated design and production team as well as the efforts of a purpose-built marketing team. You may even get a small advance.

What you may not realize is how long it takes to get from the query stage to the published stage with a trade publisher. Most publishers have their lists planned anywhere from 12-24 months in advance.

Once your work is done, namely writing and rewriting to your editor's satisfaction, your book leaves your direct control and the other players on the team step in. It may surprise you to learn that depending on the publisher you deal with, you may not have much input into either the page or cover design. Even literary legends have been let down by their publisher at this step of the production process. Your editor should be able to advise you on the publisher's policy so don't be afraid to ask.

Once your book is released, and the allocated marketing budget spent, the sales force moves on to the new list. It is up to you to continue to bring attention to your book. Promotion is discussed later in this section.

You should also note that most contracts state royalties will be paid either semi-annually or annually. A full accounting of sales and returns has to take place before monies are released to you. If YOU KNOW THE MARKET you will be well-prepared to negotiate a contract that is both acceptable and fair. Publishing is a business. Take the time to learn about it.

2.7 PREPARING AND SENDING YOUR MANUSCRIPT

Did you obtain the guidelines for the publisher to which you plan to submit? Did you check the publisher's backlist and current releases to see what kinds of books they focus on? Do you know the current poetry editor's name and title? Did you prepare a cover letter and sample poems, submit them and get a positive response from the editor asking for the rest of the manuscript? If you said, "No," to any of these questions stop and do things in the right order.

FIRST CONTACT WITH THE EDITOR

Do not pitch your book over the telephone. Editors are busy and if you are going to get just one chance to impress them it's best not to try to do it while they are in the middle of their business day. Besides, poetry is like humour, unless you do a reading over the telephone, it's hard to describe. This does not mean however, that you should zip a copy of your entire manuscript off to the editor by e-mail to read at their leisure. If you do this, I can guarantee they will dump it at their pleasure. Same goes for faxed submissions. Never fax or e-mail a submission of any kind without prior permission from the editor.

You will want to get the editor's attention. Do this by sending her a sample of your work by regular mail. Choose poems that show the dimension and depth of your work. In your cover letter describe the manuscript and why you think it would fit well into their list. "It's really good and I'm sure it will sell many copies," is NOT useful information for the editor. "I note you have published a number of titles focusing on Northern Ontario. My poems explore the landscape of Sudbury and the lives of miners, from 1960 to the present day," IS information an editor would want to know.

You'll need to say something about yourself as well, but keep it brief: "As a member of a spelunking club that meets regularly, I understand the oppressive atmosphere of life underground." Add some details of your publishing history, "My poems have been published in..." and any experience you might have, "Since 1995, I have shared performance poetry with audiences from St. John's, Newfoundland to Tofino, British Columbia."

If you send sample poems out to two or more publishers at the same time you must disclose this to each editor. You do not have to mention which publishers you chose, only that your submission is a "multiple submission."

Close by thanking the editor for her time. Under your signature, be sure to include your name and any miscellaneous contact information not already contained in the letter. I put both my telephone number and my e-mail address below my name for the editor's convenience.

It's been said that the information in a query letter should be good enough for the marketing department to use as promotional copy for your book. Focus on excellence and remember to include an SASE for a reply.

2.8 PROFESSIONAL SUBMISSIONS

1. Do not illustrate your poems unless you are a professional artist or visual poetry is your aim.

2. Use only one side of plain white letter-size paper.

3. Print only one poem per page.

4. Use a common typeface like Times Roman or Courier. Never use a scripted typeface.

5. Leave wide margins of at least one inch on each side of the page.

6. Put your name and address in the upper right-hand corner of the page.

7. Poems should be single-spaced, or spaced as originally intended by the writer. (Fiction should always be double-spaced.)

8. Poems with multiple pages should have a word from the title and the page number on each consecutive page (i.e. Shallow Words, p.2).

9. Number each page of a manuscript consecutively. For full-length manuscripts there is no need to put your full name and address on each page. Use the title of the book and a page number instead.

10. Include a table of contents with poem titles and page numbers noted.

11. Keep a copy of the samples and/or manuscript.

12. To prevent yourself from making pestering telephone calls to editors to see if they received your manuscript, you can include a self-addressed stamped postcard or send your manuscript by mail with a traceable code. There is no need to insure the package because you will have kept a copy of the manuscript at home.

NO REPLY AFTER THREE MONTHS

Some editors get thousands of submissions each year so it's not surprising that it takes some time to respond. For those editors at smaller publishing houses, the crunch may not be the number of submissions but rather the number of staff. Many editors are also trying to cover the duties of publicity manager and/or production manager. If an editor is not expecting (i.e. has not made a specific request for) your manuscript, it will remain in the slush pile until it can be properly considered.

To protect yourself from waiting inordinate amounts of time (anything over six months is inordinate unless their guidelines note an even longer response time) you can advise the editor in your cover letter that if you have not heard from them by a certain date, you will assume they are not interested in your work and you will market it elsewhere.

Many writers hold their work back from the marketplace on the basis of a "maybe." This is a mistake. You cannot eat maybes. Let the editor know that you appreciate their time but you wish to submit your work elsewhere. The editor's interest is sincere but it may be that their list is full for the next year. Ask if they would be interested in reconsidering your proposal in six months if you have not found another publisher in that time. They may say yes.

2.9 IT'S REAL— THEY WANT MORE

An editor calls and asks you to send the full manuscript. Prepare the manuscript with care. At this point, you have not been offered a contract but rather an opportunity to interest the editor enough to offer one.

If you haven't already done so, you might have the manuscript looked at by a professional editor who will give you constructive criticism. The editor at the publishing house will not want to "clean up" your manuscript even if they believe your work shows great potential. Send only your best.

2.10 REJECTION IS AN UGLY WORD

Everyone faces rejection. Take it gracefully. If the editor considers your whole manuscript but decides to pass on it, you should feel comfortable asking them for specific reasons. Listen carefully to any constructive criticism offered. Do not argue with the editor. Let go of the relationship on good terms.

2.11 OR CELEBRATE— YOU'VE BEEN OFFERED A CONTRACT

Congratulations. You've done everything well up to this point. Although it might seem like an odd place to say it, KNOW YOUR MARKET. Each publisher is different and their contracts have different wording. Some contracts are more like a letter of agreement, others have pages and pages of clauses. Some demands may strike you as outrageous: one writer was asked to agree not to compete with his publisher (sell his books himself) anywhere in "the universe." I advised him to change the wording to "anywhere in the KNOWN universe." A writer should always keep his options open.

Poetry books are a risk for the publisher. Most Canadian poetry books have a print run of perhaps 500 copies and far less are actually sold. When Harbour Publishing released the anthology, *Breathing Fire: Canada's New Poets*, they had an initial and highly optimistic press run of 2,500 copies. Edited by award-winning poets, Lorna Crozier and Patrick Lane, this book has gone on to successful second and third printings. Its sales have been a pleasant anomaly. This is a long way to say you won't get a huge advance for a poetry book if you get one at all.

Excellent contract guidance is available from The Writers' Union of Canada Contracts Self-Help Package which for $25 includes three publications: "Trade Book Contract," "Help Yourself to a Better Contract," and "Writers' Guide to Electronic Publishing Rights." (More detail can be found in Section 5.3, "Building A Writer's Bookshelf.")

2.12 ONCE YOUR BOOK HAS BEEN RELEASED

Your book is finally in your hands but your job is not done. You have to help sell the book and that means getting publicity.

A standard part of your contract will be at least 10 free copies. Don't send these out to media yourself. Ask your publisher to whom review copies will be sent. If you have additional suggestions provide your publisher with all the neccesary contact information.

Community newspapers love to cover local authors and most local radio stations will welcome you as well. A relaxed friendly approach is a must when building a network of media contacts. Always be ready to listen, and don't interrupt.

To prepare for media interviews, role-play an with a friend (or the mirror) playing the interviewer. You'll soon discover whether or not you have a natural talent for adlibbing or if you need to work on a loosely structured set of answers. Do you babble? Get off track? Laugh nervously? Try to work out some of the bugs in your presentation before getting on-air or in print.

Your publisher will expect you to promote your book. All writers do readings in small settings for small audiences. The worst thing you can do is back away from publicity. One writer sold a book aimed at an undiscovered niche market but refused to do any publicity outside of handshakes and signings. She was afraid she wouldn't be able to answer audience questions well. Her book was mildly successful and it inspired a wave of books from other publishers. It was the ideal time for her publisher to offer her another contract. Instead, her publisher dropped her. They couldn't afford the risk.

Take publicity into your own hands. Apply for travel grants. Ask the League of Canadian Poets for information and support while planning a reading tour. (Information on reading venues appears in Chapter Four.) Put up a website, link it to your publisher's website. Where appropriate announce the release of your book on listservs you may belong to and share it with newsgroups as well. (Be sure the guidelines for either of these allow for such announcements.)

Be resourceful. Be creative.

2.13 CANADIAN BOOK PUBLISHER LISTINGS

above/ground press

RR#1, Maxville, Ontario K0C 1T0

Editor: rob mclennan

E-mail: az421@freenet.carleton.ca

Website: www.nonlinear.ca/aboveground

Since: 1993	Pages: 4-36	Press Run: 200-300	TWUC Contract: No
Royalties: See below.	Poetry titles: Varies	Fiction: No	Drama: No
Art: No	Children's: No	Anthologies: Few	Literary Criticism: Not yet
Non-fiction: No	Biographies: No	Textbooks: No	Time: 6-8 months

Authors recently published: Joe Blades, Michael Holmes, Anne Stone & Ellen Field.

Publishes single poem broadsides, poetry chapbooks and *Stanzas* magazine. Send SASE for catalogue. "Willing to read your work but you must include SASE for return." Authors receive one quarter of all print copies and a discount of 50% on additional copies.

Alter Ego Editions

Did not offer street address. Refers writers to their website.

E-mail: alterego@alterego.montreal.qc.ca

Website: www.alterego.montreal.qc.ca

Since: 1996	Pages: Varies	Press Run: Varies	TWUC Contract: No
Royalties: Varies	Poetry titles: 1	Fiction: Yes	Drama: No
Art: No	Children's: No	Anthologies: No	Literary Criticism: No
Non-fiction: No	Biographies: No	Textbooks: No	Time: 6 months

Authors recently published: Louky Bersianik & Régine Robin.

"We are a micro publisher and have published two full-size fiction titles but are willing to consider publishing a poetry title in the future."

Anvil Press

#204-A, 175 East Broadway, Vancouver, British Columbia V5T 1W2

Poetry Editors: Paul Pitre & Hilary Green

Telephone: (604) 876-8710 Fax: (604) 879-2667

E-mail: subter@pinc.com

Website: www.anvilpress.com

Since: 1990	Pages: 64-120	Press Run: 500-1,000	TWUC Contract: No
Royalties: 15% of net	Poetry titles: 1-2	Fiction: Yes	Drama: Yes
Art: No	Children's: No	Anthologies: Yes	Literary Criticism: Maybe
Non-fiction: Maybe	Biographies: Maybe	Textbooks: Maybe	Time: 3-6 months

Authors recently published: Lyle Neff, Bud Osborn, Heidi Greco & Isabella Mori.

"The publishing philosophy remains constant: the discovery, nurturing, and promotion of new and established Canadian literary talent. If you want be sure your manuscript has been received, include a self-addressed stamped postcard." Send query with sample (for novel send 30-40 pages, for a collection send 2-3 pieces) plus a one to two page synopsis of proposed book. Recommends you familiarize yourself with current and backlist titles before submitting. Issues a small advance, usually between $200-$400. Manuscripts without an appropriate SASE will not be responded to or returned.

Arsenal Pulp Press

103-1014 Homer Street, Vancouver, British Columbia V6B 2W9

Poetry Editor: Editorial Board

Telephone: (604) 687-4233 Fax: (604) 669-8250

E-mail: contact@arsenalpulp.com

Website: www.arsenalpulp.com

Since: 1971	Pages: 100-200	Press Run: 1,500	TWUC Contract: No
Royalties: 10% of gross	Poetry titles: 1-2	Fiction: Yes	Drama: No
Art: Yes	Children's: No	Anthologies: Yes	Literary Criticism: No
Non-fiction: Yes	Biographies: Yes	Textbooks: No	Time: 3 months

Authors recently published: Dorothy Livesay, Sheri-D Wilson, Michael Turner & Wade Compton.

Arsenal Pulp Press considers manuscripts in the following subject areas: literary fiction; literary and art studies including critical analyses; cultural studies; political/sociological studies, including historical analyses; aboriginal/First Nations studies, including historical analyses; regional studies, including BC and the Pacific Northwest; irreverent cookbooks; satiric humour. Publishes only the work of Canadian writers. Suggests queries should include a cover letter, synopsis of the work, and 50-60 sample pages. Will NOT accept submissions by either e-mail or fax. Arsenal Pulp was not considering poetry manuscripts at the time of writing but editor stated, "We hope this will change soon." Check their website for details.

Black Moss Press

2450 Byng Road, Windsor, Ontario N8W 3E8

Telephone: (519) 252-2551 Fax: (519) 253-7809

E-mail: bmoss@mnsi.net

Website: www.blackmosspress.on.ca

Since: 1972	Pages: 80	Press Run: 500	TWUC Contract: No
Royalties: 10% of gross	Poetry titles: 12	Fiction: Yes	Drama: No
Art: No	Children's: No	Anthologies: Yes	Literary Criticism: No
Non-fiction: No	Biographies: No	Textbooks: No	Time: 3 months

Accepts unsolicited manuscripts. Publishes mostly chapbooks but has published full-length novels as well. Prefers to receive a cover letter, synopsis and one sample chapter for novels. For poetry collections please send a ten–poem sample.

Borealis Press Limited

9 Ashburn Drive, Ottawa, Ontario K2E 6N4

Poetry Editors: W. Glenn Clever & Frank M. Tierney

Telephone: (613) 224-6837 or (613) 829-0150 Fax: (613) 829-7783

E-mail: borealis@istar.ca

Website: www.borealispress.com

Since: 1972	Pages: 110	Press Run: 500	TWUC Contract: No
Royalties: 10% of net	Poetry titles: 2-3	Fiction: Yes	Drama: Yes
Art: No	Children's: Yes	Anthologies: Yes	Literary Criticism: Yes
Non-fiction: Yes	Biographies: Yes	Textbooks: Yes	Time: 4 weeks

Authors recently published: Fred Cogswell, Carol Shields, Liliane Welch & Larry Rowdon. Publishes full-size poetry books.

Breakwater Books

100 Water Street, PO Box 2188, St. John's, Newfoundland A1C 6E6

Poetry Editors: Clyde Rose & Shannon M. Lewis

Telephone: (709) 722-6680 Fax: (709) 753-0708
E-mail: breakwater@nfld.com
Website: www.breakwater.nf.net

Since: 1973	Pages: 64	Press Run: 1,000	TWUC Contract: No
Royalties: 10%	Poetry titles: 2	Fiction: Yes	Drama: Yes
Art: Yes	Children's: Yes	Anthologies: Yes	Literary Criticism: Yes
Non-fiction: Yes	Biographies: Yes	Textbooks: No	Time: 3 months

Authors recently published: Roberta Buchanan, Susan Ingersoll & Boyd Chubbs.

"We normally do not accept unsolicited manuscripts. However, they do turn up and some have been accepted for publishing. If you are familiar with our list and plan to submit, send a hard copy with a diskette and SASE."

Brick Books

Box 20081, 431 Boler Road, London, Ontario N6K 4G6
Poetry Editors: Don McKay, Stan Dragland, Jan Zwicky, Marnie Parsons, John Donlan, Gary Draper & Sheila Deane.
Telephone: (519) 657-8579
E-mail: brick.books@sympatico.ca

Since: 1975	Pages: 80-96	Press Run: 500	TWUC Contract: No
Royalties: See below.	Poetry titles: 6	Fiction: No	Drama: No
Art: No	Children's: No	Anthologies: No	Literary Criticism: No
Non-fiction: No	Biographies: No	Textbooks: No	Time: 3 months

Authors recently published: Michael Crummey, Janice Kulyk Keefer, Robyn Sarah & Patrick Friesen.

"Please send a query first. We read manuscripts from January 1st to April 30th every year. Please send samples of 8-10 poems rather than a full manuscript. We publish full-size books of one author's work. Authors receive 10% of print run in books."

BuschekBooks

PO Box 74053, 35 Beechwood Avenue, Ottawa, Ontario K1M 2H9
Poetry Editor: John Buschek
Telephone: (613) 744-2589 Fax: (613) 744-2967
E-mail: buschek.books@sympatico.ca
Website: www3.sympatico.ca/buschek.books/home.html

Since: 1965	Pages: 50-250	Press Run: 500-600	TWUC Contract: No
Royalties: 10% of gross	Poetry titles: 0-2	Fiction: Yes	Drama: No
Art: No	Children's: No	Anthologies: Yes	Literary Criticism: No
Non-fiction: No	Biographies: No	Textbooks: No	Time: 1-3 months

Authors recently published: E.D. Blodgett, Tomas Tranströmer, Rita Donovan & Betsy Warland.

Interested in work of the highest quality. Query with samples first. Publishes full-size books.

Canadian Poetry Association: London Chapter

PO Box 340, Station B, London, Ontario N6A 4W1
Poetry Editor: Wayne Ray
Telephone: (519) 660-0548
E-mail: cpa@wwdc.com
Website: www.communityexpress.org or www.mirror.org/cpa

Since: 1985	Pages: Varies	Press Run: 300-1,000	TWUC Contract: No
Royalties: Varies	Poetry titles: 1	Fiction: No	Drama: No

Art: No	Children's: No	Anthologies: Yes	Literary Criticism: No
Non-fiction: No	Biographies: No	Textbooks: No	Time: N/A

Authors recently published: James Deahl.

Does not accept unsolicited manuscripts. Publishes chapbooks, anthologies and has a special interest in poetry on tape.

Coach House Books

401 Huron Street (rear) on bpNichol Lane, Toronto, Ontario M5S 2G5
Poetry Editor: Darren Wershler-Henry
Telephone: (416) 979-2217 or 1-800-367-6360 Fax: (416) 977-1158
E-mail: mail@chbooks.com
Website: www.chbooks.com

Since: 1965	Pages: 64-128	Press Run: 400-500	TWUC Contract: No
Royalties: 10% of gross	Poetry titles: 3-9	Fiction: Yes	Drama: Yes
Art: Yes	Children's: No	Anthologies: Yes	Literary Criticism: No
Non-fiction: Some	Biographies: No	Textbooks: No	Time: 1 month

Authors recently published: George Bowering, Michael Matthews, David Bromige & Karen MacCormack.

Does NOT accept unsolicited manuscripts. Publishes both chapbooks and full-size books as well as online editions. Accepts brief e-mail queries. Once contract has been negotiated, the editor prefers to receive manuscripts as "digital files of some sort. Quark-ready, plus HTML files and all graphics included."

Colombo & Company

42 Dell Park Avenue, Toronto, Ontario M6B 2T6
Telephone: (416) 782-6853 Fax: (416) 782-0285
E-mail: jrc@inforamp.net
Website: www.inforamp.net/~jrc

Since: 1994	Pages: Varies	Press Run: Varies	TWUC Contract: No
Royalties: 10% of gross	Poetry titles: 4	Fiction: Yes	Drama: Yes
Art: No	Children's: No	Anthologies: Yes	Literary Criticism: Yes
Non-fiction: Yes	Biographies: No	Textbooks: No	Time: N/A

Authors recently published: Roger Burford Mason, Gustav A. Richar, Donna Dunlop & Ed Butts.

Does NOT accept unsolicited manuscripts. "An attempt to deal with 'publisher's block,' the Colombo & Company imprint is reserved for serious works of scholarship and literature by the publisher's compeers." Publishes both chapbooks and full-size books.

Coteau Books

401-2206 Dewdney Avenue, Regina, Saskatchewan S4R 1H3
Editor: Geoffrey Ursell
Frequent Book Editor: Liz Philips
Telephone: (306) 777-0170 Fax: (306) 522-5152
E-mail: coteau@coteau.unibase.com
Website: coteau.unibase.com

Since: 1975	Pages: 64-224	Press Run: 750-1,000	TWUC Contract: No
Royalties: 10% of gross	Poetry titles: 2-4	Fiction: Yes	Drama: Yes
Art: Yes	Children's: Yes	Anthologies: Yes	Literary Criticism: Yes
Non-fiction: Yes	Biographies: Yes	Textbooks: No	Time: 3-6 months

Authors recently published: Anne Szumigalski, Barbara Nickel, Jim Smith & Susan Andrews Grace.

Accepts unsolicited manuscripts. Do NOT send multiple submissions. Publishes only the work of Canadian writers in full-size books. Not interested in chapbooks. "Coteau aims to publish the very best poetry produced in this country, in quality, affordable, attractive and popular editions. We are always looking for new and exciting poetic voices, and have just launched a new poetry book series, "Open-Eye", to reach and encourage a younger, hungrier, brasher poetry market. We are looking for manuscripts for this series in particular, young, hip, tough poetry for the new millennium."

DC Books

Box 662, 950 Decane, Ville St. Laurent, Québec H4L 4V9

Poetry Editors: Steve Luxton & Robert Allen

Telephone: (514) 843-8130 Fax: (514) 939-0569

Since: 1970	Pages: 60-100	Press Run: 500	TWUC Contract: No
Royalties: 10% of gross	Poetry titles: 2	Fiction: Yes	Drama: Yes
Art: No	Children's: No	Anthologies: Yes	Literary Criticism: Yes
Non-fiction: Yes	Biographies: Yes	Textbooks: No	Time: 3 months

Authors recently published: Bryan Sentes & Heather O'Neill.

Please query with samples after becoming familiar with both current list and backlist. Publishes full-size books.

ECW Press

2120 Queen Street East, Suite 200, Toronto, Ontario M4E 1E2

Poetry Editor: Michael Holmes

Telephone: (416) 694-3348

E-mail: ecw@sympatico.ca

Website: www.ecw.ca/press

Since: 1979	Pages: 80-160	Press Run: 500-750	TWUC Contract: No
Royalties: 10% of gross	Poetry titles: 4	Fiction: Yes	Drama: No
Art: No	Children's: No	Anthologies: No	Literary Criticism: Yes
Non-fiction: Yes	Biographies: Yes	Textbooks: No	Time: 4-6 weeks

Authors recently published: Sky Gilbert, Margaret Christakos, John Barton & David McGimpsey.

"ECW publishes innovative poetry that is actively engaged with challenging language." Send a query letter and ten-page sample. Publishes full-size books only.

Ekstasis Editions

Box 8474, Main Postal Outlet, Victoria, British Columbia V8W 3S1

Poetry Editor: Richard Olafson

Telephone: (250) 361-9941 Fax: (250) 385-3378

E-mail: ekstasis@ampsc.com

Since: 1982	Pages: 72-96	Press Run: 500-3,000	TWUC Contract: Yes
Royalties: 10% of gross	Poetry titles: 12	Fiction: Yes	Drama: Yes
Art: Yes	Children's: Yes	Anthologies: Yes	Literary Criticism: Yes
Non-fiction: Yes	Biographies: Yes	Textbooks: No	Time: 6 months

Authors recently published: Susan McCaslin, Mike Doyle & Peter Trower.

Submit a brief cover letter detailing your background and include a synopsis of proposed book. For poetry submissions, please include ten-page sample. Publishes both chapbooks and full-size books.

fingerprinting inkoperated

PO Box 657, Station P, Toronto, Ontario M5S 2Y4

Poetry Editor: damian lopes

E-mail: dal@interlog.com

Website: www.interlog.com/~dal/fi/

Since: 1990	Pages: 8-50	Press Run: 25-100	TWUC Contract: No
Royalties: Copies	Poetry titles: 4-6	Fiction: Yes	Drama: Yes
Art: Yes	Children's: Yes	Anthologies: No	Literary Criticism: No
Non-fiction: No	Biographies: No	Textbooks: No	Time: 2-3 months

Authors recently published: Nelson Ball & jwcurry.

Authors receive payment of 10% of press run in copies. No royalties. "*fi* is a micropress specializing in innovative writing that pushes hard at boundaries and explores alternative modes of communication, using forms of production that enhance content. Therefore, submissions should be queried first, and familiarity with our publications is recommended before querying. All books are hand-made, usually hand-sewn, and vary from chapbook to full book length."

Goose Lane Editions Limited

469 King Street, Fredericton, New Brunswick E3B 1E5

Poetry Editor: Laurel Boone

Telephone: (506) 450-4251 Fax: (506) 459-4991

E-mail: gooselan@nb.sympatico.ca

Since: 1957	Pages: 100-120	Press Run: 500-750	TWUC Contract: See below.
Royalties: 10% of retail	Poetry titles: 2-3	Fiction: Yes	Drama: No
Art: Yes	Children's: No	Anthologies: Yes	Literary Criticism: No
Non-fiction: Yes	Biographies: Yes	Textbooks: No	Time: 3-4 months

Authors recently published: Douglas Lochhead, Gary Geddes, Kwame Dawes & Andrew Steeves.

"Goose Lane Editions was founded as Fiddlehead Poetry Books in 1957. Although the company has undergone several metamorphoses over the years, the company has always and still continues to publish collections of poetry by new and established Canadian poets. The company's annual poetry list generally includes one or two single-author collections as well as one major collection or anthology." The latter are 200-300 pages in length with a print of 1,000-2,000 copies. Uses adaptation of the TWUC contract. Revenue from sale of subsidiary rights, including selection and serial rights is shared with author.

Greensleeves Editions

PO Box 41164, Edmonton, Alberta T6J 6M7

Poetry Editor: Mark McCawley

E-mail: cogwheels@worldgate.com

Since: 1988	Pages: 24	Press Run: 100-200	TWUC Contract: No
Royalties: N/A	Poetry titles: 1-2	Fiction: Yes	Drama: Yes*
Art: No	Children's: No	Anthologies: Yes	Literary Criticism: No
Non-fiction: Yes**	Biographies: No	Textbooks: No	Time: 4-8 weeks

Authors recently published: Daniel Jones, Beth Jankola, Carolyn Zonailo & Stephen Morrisey.

*Interested in monologues. **Interested in creative-nonfiction. For all submissions, query first with samples or synopsis. Publishes chapbooks.

Guernica Editions

Box 117, Station P, Toronto, Ontario M5S 2S6

Poetry Editor: Antonio D'Alfonso

Telephone: (416) 658-9888 Fax: (416) 657-8885

Since: 1978	Pages: 64-200	Press Run: 1,000	TWUC Contract: See below.
Royalties: 10% of gross	Poetry titles: 2-3	Fiction: Yes	Drama: Yes
Art: No	Children's: No	Anthologies: Yes	Literary Criticism: Yes
Non-fiction: Yes	Biographies: Yes	Textbooks: No	Time: 3 months

Authors recently published: Fulvio Caccia, Claude Péloquin & Gianna Patriarca.

"Guernica is a press for the bridging of cultures. We try to promote world literatures, various styles, various voices, a variety of content. We are a truly independent press." Interested in translations. Editor describes contract as "part TWUC, Union des Écrivains and Publishers' International Standards."

Harbour Publishing

PO Box 219, Madeira Park, British Columbia V0N 2H0

Poetry Editor: Marisa Alps

Telephone: (604) 883-2730 Fax: (604) 883-9451

E-mail: harbour@sunshine.net

Since: 1972	Pages: 72-200	Press Run: 1,500	TWUC Contract: No
Royalties: 15% of net	Poetry titles: 2-3	Fiction: Yes	Drama: No
Art: No	Children's: Yes	Anthologies: Yes	Literary Criticism: No
Non-fiction: Yes	Biographies: Yes	Textbooks: No	Time: Varies

Authors recently published: Al Purdy, Patrick Lane & Tom Wayman.

Call or write for full author guidelines. Receipt of manuscript or query acknowledged promptly but processing time depends on workload.

High Ground Press

RR #1, S15, C5, Madeira Park, British Columbia V0N 2H0

Poetry Editors: John Pass & Theresa Kishkan

Telephone: (604) 883-2377

E-mail: high_ground@sunshine.net

Since: 1986	Pages: 1	Press Run: 75-100	TWUC Contract: No
Royalties: n/a	Poetry titles: n/a	Fiction: No	Drama: No
Art: No	Children's: No	Anthologies: No	Literary Criticism: No
Non-fiction: No	Biographies: No	Textbooks: No	Time: 1 month

Authors recently published: Don McKay, Charles Lillard, Kate Braid & Don Domanski.

Publishes broadsheets only. Does not accept unsolicited manuscripts but has done specialty poetry projects upon occasion. Responds to queries within a month, e-mail more quickly.

HMS Press

PO Box 340, Station B, London, Ontario N6A 4W1

Poetry Editor: Wayne Ray

Telephone: (519) 660-0548

E-mail: hmspress@mirror.org

Website: www.mirror.org/hmspress

Since: 1985	Pages: 12-76	Press Run: 300	TWUC Contract: No
Royalties: 20% of gross	Poetry titles: 3-6	Fiction: No*	Drama: No
Art: No	Children's: No	Anthologies: Yes	Literary Criticism: Yes
Non-fiction: No*	Biographies: No*	Textbooks: No	Time: 1 months

Authors recently published: Bruce Ross & R.J. McCook.

Publishes primarily chapbooks and audio tapes. Does not accept unsolicited submissions. Query with samples. *Has an electronic publishing division which publishes fiction, non-fiction and biographies.

House of Anansi Press Limited

30 Lesmill Road, Toronto, Ontario M3B 2T6

Telephone: (416) 445-3333 Fax: (416) 445-5967

Website: www.anansi.ca/anansi.htm

Since: 1967	Pages: 200	Press Run: 1,000	TWUC Contract: No
Royalties: 10% of gross	Poetry titles: 3-4	Fiction: Yes	Drama: No
Art: No	Children's: No	Anthologies: Yes	Literary Criticism: Yes
Non-fiction: Yes	Biographies: Yes	Textbooks: No	Time: 3-4 months

Authors recently published: Lynn Crosbie, Esta Spalding, Steven Heighton & Patricia Young.

Prefers to receive poetry samples from proposed book rather than full manuscript. Include a literary cv or some background information on yourself and your writing. Include an SASE for return of work. Rarely provides editorial comment on manuscripts not accepted for publication.

Jesperson Publishing

39 James Lane, St. John's, Newfoundland A1E 3H3

Poetry Editor: JoAnne Soper-Cook

Telephone: (709) 753-0633 Fax: (709) 753-5507

E-mail: mbf1051@infonet.st-johns.nf.ca

Since: 1969	Pages: 125-140	Press Run: 500	TWUC Contract: No
Royalties: Varies	Poetry titles: 1	Fiction: Yes	Drama: No
Art: No	Children's: No	Anthologies: Yes	Literary Criticism: No
Non-fiction: Yes	Biographies: No	Textbooks: Yes	Time: 1-3 months

Authors recently published: Peggy Smith Krachuon & Nellie Strowbridge.

Send query letter with outline/synopsis. Replies to queries within the week. Publishes full-size books. Not interested in religious poetry. If you submit from the US, please do not send US postage as it cannot be used in Canada.

Maritimes Arts Projects Productions

Box 596, Station A, Fredericton, New Brunswick E3B 5A6

Poetry Editor: Joe Blades

Telephone: (506) 454-5127 Fax: (506) 454-5127

E-mail: jblades@nbnet.nb.ca

Since: 1985	Pages: 80	Press Run: 500	TWUC Contract: Yes*
Royalties: 10% of gross	Poetry titles: 6-10	Fiction: Yes	Drama: No
Art: Some	Children's: No	Anthologies: Yes	Literary Criticism: Yes
Non-fiction: Yes	Biographies: Yes	Textbooks: No	Time: 6 months

Authors recently published: Kath Maclean, rob mclennan, John Weier & Allan Cooper.

All books to date are by Canadian authors, editors or translators. *Uses modified TWUC contract. Publishes general literature; poetry and fiction. Also interested in non-fiction essays, self-help/psychology and Atlantic Canadian local history/ biography. Publishes both chapbooks and full-size books. Imprints include: Broken Jaw Press; Book Rat; Dead Sea Physh Products; pOST hASTE cARDS; and Spare Time Editions. Query. Runs both New Muse Award and Poets Corner Award.

The Mercury Press
22 Prince Rupert Avenue, Toronto, Ontario M6P 2A7

Poetry Editor: Beverley Daurio

Since: 1978	Pages: 180	Press Run: 1,200	TWUC Contract: No
Royalties: 10% of list	Poetry titles: 2	Fiction: Yes	Drama: No
Art: No	Children's: No	Anthologies: Yes	Literary Criticism: Yes
Non-fiction: Yes	Biographies: Yes	Textbooks: No	Time: 4-6 months

Authors recently published: Gerry Shikatani, Anne Walker, Nelson Ball & Wayne Keon.

All submissions should include complete manuscript, CV and SASE. Fiction and non-fiction titles published generally have 200 pages. Describes contract as "similar to TWUC contract."

The Moonstone Press
167 Delaware Street, London, Ontario N5Z 2N6

Poetry Editor: Peter Baltensperger

Telephone: (519) 659-5784

E-mail: pbaltens@odyssey.on.ca

Since: 1984	Pages: 100	Press Run: 500	TWUC Contract: No
Royalties: 10% of gross	Poetry titles: 2	Fiction: Yes*	Drama: No
Art: No	Children's: No	Anthologies: Yes*	Literary Criticism: Yes*
Non-fiction: Yes	Biographies: Yes*	Textbooks: No	Time: 2-4 weeks

Authors recently published: Don Gutteridge, Martin Samuel Cohen, Barry Butson & Russell Smith.

Imprints are Moonstone Press and Gemini Editions. Publishes full-size books. Accepts unsolicited submissions but please query with samples first. *Sometimes publishes fiction, anthologies, literary criticism and biographies. States that "high quality literature of all genres considered."

Morgaine House
80 Mount Pleasant, Point Claire, Québec H9R 2T5

Poetry Editor: Mary Gurekas

Telephone: (514) 695-1624

E-mail: morgaine@videotron.ca

Since: 1994	Pages: 75	Press Run: 500	TWUC Contract: Yes
Royalties: 10% of gross	Poetry titles: 3-5	Fiction: Yes	Drama: No
Art: No	Children's: No	Anthologies: Yes	Literary Criticism: No
Non-fiction: No	Biographies: No	Textbooks: No	Time: 6-8 weeks

Authors recently published: Carolyn Zonailo & Claudia Morrison.

"We are partial to women writers, though not exclusively." Accepts unsolicited submissions. Send full manuscript for poetry and include a brief bio and SASE. Publishes both chapbooks and full-size manuscripts with chapbook payment being made in copies only with a 40% discount on additional copies.

{m}Öthêr Tøñgué Press
290 Fulford-Ganges Road, Salt Spring Island, British Columbia V8K 2K6

Poetry Editor: Mona Fertig

Telephone: (250) 537-4155 Fax: (250) 537-4725

E-mail: mothertongue@saltspring.com

Website: www.saltspring.com/art/mothertongue.htm

Since: 1990	Pages: 30	Press Run: 100	TWUC Contract: No
Royalties: n/a	Poetry titles: 4-5	Fiction: No	Drama: No

| Art: Yes* | Children's: No | Anthologies: No | Literary Criticism: No |
| Non-fiction: No | Biographies: No | Textbooks: No | Time: 1-2 months |

Authors recently published: Cathy Ford, Stephanie Bolster, Patricia Young & Lorna Crozier.

Does NOT accept unsolicited submissions. "We publish both limited edition chapbooks of both Canadian poetry and *bookart. Each is signed and numbered, letterpressed, spines, tipped in art, lino-cuts, handsewn, special endpapers, beautiful books." Query with samples but please be familiar with list first.

The Muses' Co./J. Gordon Shillingford Publishing

PO Box 86, 905 Corydon Avenue, Winnipeg, Manitoba R3M 3S3

Poetry Editor: Catherine Hunter

Telephone: (204) 779-6967 Fax: (204) 779-6970

Since: 1993	Pages: 120	Press Run: 600	TWUC Contract: No
Royalties: 10% of gross	Poetry titles: 3	Fiction: No	Drama: Yes
Art: No	Children's: No	Anthologies: Yes	Literary Criticism: No
Non-fiction: Yes	Biographies: No	Textbooks: No	Time: 8 months

Authors recently published: Patrick Friesen, Kate Bitney, Mick Burrs & Emile Martel.

The Muses' Company is the poetry imprint of the J. Gordon Shillingford Company. Shillingford was established in 1980. Welcomes unsolicited submissions. Please query with 10–25 poems. Publishes full-size books.

Natural Heritage Books

PO Box 95, Station O, Toronto, Ontario M4C 1Z3

Poetry Editor: Nancy Mayer

Telephone: (416) 694-7907 Fax: (416) 690-0819

Since: 1983	Pages: 96	Press Run: 1,000	TWUC Contract: No
Royalties: 8-10% of gross	Poetry titles: 2	Fiction: No	Drama: No
Art: No	Children's: No*	Anthologies: No	Literary Criticism: No
Non-fiction: Yes	Biographies: Yes	Textbooks: No	Time: 6 months

Authors recently published: Peter Jaillal, Linda Stitt & Robert Nero.

Accepts quality unsolicited submissions from Canadian writers. Publishes full-size books. Some may become resource/support material for schools. Has specific areas of interest: nature; contemporary feminism balanced through humour; and cross-cultural experiential. *Has published children's titles in the past but is not presently looking for manuscripts in this area.

Nightwood Editions

RR 5, S 26, C 13, Gibsons, British Columbia V0N 1V0

Poetry Editor: Marisa Alps

Telephone: (604) 885-0212 Fax: (604) 885-0212

E-mail: nightwood@sunshine.net

Since: 1991	Pages: 80	Press Run: 1,000	TWUC Contract: No
Royalties: 15% of net	Poetry titles: 2-3	Fiction: Yes	Drama: No
Art: No	Children's: Yes	Anthologies: No	Literary Criticism: No
Non-fiction: No	Biographies: No	Textbooks: No	Time: Varies

Authors recently published: Tim Bowling, Sally Ito & Diane Tucker.

Nightwood welcomes submissions from emerging poets. Receipt of manuscript is acknowledged promptly but a decision on the manuscript will depend on workload and may take up to six months. Interested in full-size book manuscripts only.

Oolichan Books

PO Box 10, Lantzville, British Columbia V0R 2H0

Poetry Editors: Ron Smith & Ursula Vaira

Telephone: (250) 390-4839 Fax: (250) 390-4839

E-mail: oolichan@mail.island.net

Website: www.island.net/~oolichan

Since: 1974	Pages: Varies	Press Run: 750	TWUC Contract: No
Royalties: 6-10% of gross	Poetry titles: 3-4	Fiction: Yes	Drama: Maybe
Art: No	Children's: Maybe	Anthologies: Maybe	Literary Criticism: Maybe
Non-fiction: No	Biographies: Maybe	Textbooks: No	Time: 6-8 weeks

Authors recently published: Mona Fertig, David Manicom, Harold Rhenisch & Timothy Brownlow.

Interested in literary fiction and poetry. Accepts unsolicited submissions. Publishes full-size books.

Outlaw Editions

2829 Dysart Road, Victoria, British Columbia V9A 2J7

Poetry Editors: Jay Ruzesky & John Harley

E-mail: ruzeskyj@mala.bc.ca

Since: 1993	Pages: 20	Press Run: 100	TWUC Contract: No
Royalties: See below.	Poetry titles: Varies	Fiction: Yes	Drama: Maybe
Art: Maybe	Children's: Maybe	Anthologies: Yes	Literary Criticism: Yes
Non-fiction: Yes	Biographies: Yes	Textbooks: No	Time: 2-3 months

Authors recently published: Beth Kope, Patrick Lane, Angus MacIntosh & Karen Schklanka.

"Our books are designed to present outstanding writing which is particularly suited to chapbook format." Instead of royalties, authors receive 10% of the print run.

Pedlar Press

PO Box 26, Station P, Toronto, Ontario M5S 2S6

Poetry Editor: Beth Follett

Telephone: (416) 926-8110 Fax: (416) 513-1805

E-mail: feralgrl@interlog.com

Since: 1996	Pages: 50-400	Press Run: 1,000	TWUC Contract: No
Royalties: 10% of gross	Poetry titles: 1-3	Fiction: Yes	Drama: Yes
Art: No	Children's: No	Anthologies: No	Literary Criticism: No
Non-fiction: No	Biographies: No	Textbooks: No	Time: 3 months

Authors recently published: Antonella Brion.

Accepts unsolicited submissions. "Seeking fresh, bold and innovative poets." Short manuscripts (up to 48 pages) will be accepted in whole. For longer manuscripts please send detailed outline. Include a short biographical statement. Send an SASE for return of material. Publisher describes contract as "a variation on the TWUC contract."

Pendas Press

C7-2163 Queen Street East, Toronto, Ontario M4L 1J1

Poetry Editor: Penn Kemp

Telephone: (416) 699-5338 Fax: (416) 699-5338

E-mail: pennk@spectranet.ca

Since: 1977	Pages: 64	Press Run: 100	TWUC Contract: No
Royalties: See below.	Poetry titles: 1-2	Fiction: No	Drama: No
Art: No	Children's: No	Anthologies: Yes*	Literary Criticism: No
Non-fiction: No	Biographies: No	Textbooks: No	Time: n/a

Authors recently published: Ontario students.

★Pendas Press publishes anthologies of student poetry that has been developed in workshops conducted by Penn Kemp. Authors receive copies. Does not accept unsolicited submissions. Publishes both chapbooks and full-size books.

Penumbra Press

PO Box 940, Manotick, Ontario K4M 1A8

Poetry Editor: John Flood

Telephone: (613) 692-5590 Fax: (613) 692-5589

Since: 1979	Pages: 104	Press Run: 500	TWUC Contract: No
Royalties: 10% of gross	Poetry titles: 2	Fiction: No	Drama: No
Art: Yes	Children's: Yes	Anthologies: No	Literary Criticism: Yes
Non-fiction: Yes	Biographies: Yes	Textbooks: No	Time: 3 months

Authors recently published: Marianne Bluger.

Accepts unsolicited submissions. Query with samples. Primarily interested in writing about the North, or written by northern and/or Native authors. Not interested in religious poetry or conventional verse forms that imitate the Canon Poets. Publishes full-size books.

The Plowman

PO Box 414, Whitby, Ontario L1N 5S4

Poetry Editor: Tony Scavetta

Telephone: (905) 668-7803

Since: 1988	Pages: 24	Press Run: 60-100	TWUC Contract: No
Royalties: 20% of gross	Poetry titles: 50	Fiction: Yes	Drama: Yes
Art: Yes	Children's: Yes	Anthologies: No	Literary Criticism: No
Non-fiction: Yes	Biographies: Yes	Textbooks: No	Time: 2-3 weeks

Authors recently published: Eric Martin & Ida-May Wegner.

Accepts unsolicited submissions. Include SASE. Publishes chapbooks only.

Polestar Book Publishers

PO Box 5238, Station B, Victoria, British Columbia V8R 6N4

Managing Editor: Lynn Henry

Telephone: (250) 361-9718 Fax: (250) 361-9738

E-mail: pstarvic@direct.ca

Website: mypage.direct.ca/p/polestar

Since: 1981	Pages: 80-144	Press Run: 1,200-2,000	TWUC Contract: No
Royalties: 10% of retail	Poetry titles: 2	Fiction: Yes	Drama: No
Art: No	Children's: Yes*	Anthologies: Yes	Literary Criticism: Yes
Non-fiction: Yes	Biographies: No	Textbooks: No	Time: 3-6 months

Authors recently published: Kate Braid, Gregory Scofield, Nadine McInnis & George Elliot Clarke.

Interested in unsolicited submissions, preferably with cover letter, synopsis and sample chapter or for poetry, sample poems. Does NOT accept submissions by e-mail or fax. Publishes full-size books. ★Publishes some children's titles but please do NOT send children's picture books. Interested in "teen novels and non-fiction for children."

Prairie Journal Press

PO Box 61203, Brentwood Post Office, Calgary, Alberta T2L 2K5

Poetry Editor: A. Burke

E-mail: prairiejournal@name.com

Web: www.geocities.com/athens/Ithaca/4336/home.htm

Since: 1983	Pages: 40-60	Press Run: 500	TWUC Contract: No
Royalties: n/a	Poetry titles: Varies	Fiction: Yes	Drama: Yes
Art: Yes	Children's: No	Anthologies: Yes	Literary Criticism: Yes
Non-fiction: Yes	Biographies: No	Textbooks: No	Time: 2 months

Authors recently published: McCandles Callaghan.

"Although we are primarily engaged in publishing a periodical, the *Prairie Journal*, we have published book-length issues as anthologies or by single-authors." Query with samples and SASE. No response to queries without SASE.

Press Gang Publishers

1723 Grant Street, Vancouver, British Columbia V5L 2Y6

Poetry Editor: Barbara Kuhne

Telephone: (604) 251-3315 Fax: (604) 251-3329

E-mail: pgangpub@portal.ca

Website: www.pressgang.bc.ca

Since: 1975	Pages: 200	Press Run: 3,500	TWUC Contract: No
Royalties: 8-10% of gross	Poetry titles: 1	Fiction: Yes	Drama: Yes
Art: Yes	Children's: No	Anthologies: Yes	Literary Criticism: No
Non-fiction: Yes	Biographies: No	Textbooks: No	Time: 2-4 months

Authors recently published: Rita Wong.

Accepts unsolicited submissions. "We give priority to Canadian women's writing which reflects a feminist perspective and we are committed to publishing writing by First Nations writers and writers of colour, books that contribute to lesbian visibility and work that reflects a wide range of class and cultural backgrounds." Publishes full-size books only.

Ragweed Press/gynergy books

PO Box 2023, Charlottetown, Prince Edward Island C1A 7N7

Managing Editor: Sibyl Frei

Telephone: (902) 566-5750 Fax: (902) 566-4473

E-mail: editor@gynergy.com

Since: 1974	Pages: 80-120	Press Run: 500-1,000	TWUC Contract: No
Royalties: 8% of gross	Poetry titles: 2	Fiction: Yes	Drama: Rarely
Art: Yes	Children's: Yes	Anthologies: Yes	Literary Criticism: No
Non-fiction: Yes	Biographies: Yes	Textbooks: No	Time: 3-4 months

Authors recently published: Aniko Galambos, Elaine Hammond, Douglas Baldwin & Dan Yashinsky.

"Ragweed Press/gynergy books publishes 6–8 books per year. We publish fiction and nonfiction, children's picture books, young adult novels, storytelling collections, regional non-fiction and under our gynergy books imprint, feminist and lesbian fiction and non-fiction." Accepts unsolicited submissions in interest areas. Publishes full-size books only.

Red Deer College Press

Box 5005, 56th Avenue & 32nd Street, Red Deer, Alberta T4N 5H5

Poetry Editor: Nicole Marcotic Fiction Editor: Aritha van Herk

Telephone: (403) 342-3321 Fax: (403) 357-3639

E-mail: vmix@admin.rdc.ab.ca

Since: 1975	Pages: 200-300	Press Run: 3,000-4,000	TWUC Contract: No
Royalties: 10% of gross	Poetry titles: 1	Fiction: Yes	Drama: Yes

Art: No	Children's: Yes	Anthologies: Yes	Literary Criticism: No
Non-fiction: Yes	Biographies: No	Textbooks: No	Time: 4-6 months

Authors recently published: Tim Wynne-Jones, Monty Reid & Ron Chambers.

Asks that writers provide a cover letter, list of writing credits, and synopsis for consideration. Has the following imprints: Writing West; Roundup Books; Discovery Books; History Along the Highway; Prairie Garden Books; Northern Lights Books for Children; Northern Lights Young Novels.

Reference West

2450 Central Avenue, Victoria, British Columbia V8S 2S8
Poetry Editor: Rhonda Batchelor
Telephone: (250) 598-0096

Since: 1990	Pages: 24-30	Press Run: 150-200	TWUC Contract: No
Royalties: n/a	Poetry titles: 8	Fiction: Yes	Drama: Yes
Art: No	Children's: No	Anthologies: No	Literary Criticism: No
Non-fiction: Yes	Biographies: No	Textbooks: No	Time: Varies

Authors recently published: P.K. Page, Don McKay, Alice Major & Michael Kenyon.

"Because we are a small, local press with no government funding and because each chapbook is "launched" with a public reading in Victoria, we are able to publish only those authors who, if accepted, are able to be here (Victoria) for the launch." The press is undergoing changes due to the deaths of Charles Lillard and Robin Skelton, but will continue to read manuscripts into the 1999–2000 season (September–May). Considers only first-rate literary material. Interested in new work and/or work-in-progress by new and/or established writers. List is mainly poetry and short fiction, always published in chapbook form. Pays author in copies.

Roseway Publishing Company Limited

RR #1, Lockeport, Nova Scotia B0T 1L0
Poetry Editor: Kathleen Tudor
Telephone: (902) 656-2223 Fax: (902) 656-2223
E-mail: ktudor@atcon.com

Since: 1989	Pages: 80-90	Press Run: 500	TWUC Contract: Yes
Royalties: 10% of gross	Poetry titles: 2	Fiction: No	Drama: No
Art: No	Children's: No	Anthologies: No	Literary Criticism: No
Non-fiction: No	Biographies: No	Textbooks: No	Time: Varies

Authors recently published: Sue McLeod & Jenni Blackmore.

Authors receive $500 on publication and 40% off books. Please send bio and samples with query. One poetry book planned for the year 2000.

Ronsdale Press

3350 West 21st Avenue, Vancouver, British Columbia V6S 1G7
Poetry Editor: Ronald B. Hatch
Telephone: (604) 738-4688 Fax: (604) 731-4548
E-mail: ronhatch@pinc.com
Website: www.ronsdalepress.com

Since: 1988	Pages: 80-150	Press Run: 750-1,000	TWUC Contract: No
Royalties: 10% of gross	Poetry titles: 2	Fiction: Yes	Drama: Some
Art: Some	Children's: Yes*	Anthologies: Some	Literary Criticism: Yes
Non-fiction: Yes	Biographies: Yes	Textbooks: No	Time: 2 months

Authors recently published: William New, Harold Rhenisch & Inge Israel.

Accepts unsolicited submissions. Send a query letter with samples and synopsis.

Publishes only Canadian writers. Poets submitting work should have a record of publishing in literary magazines. Interested in chapter books and young adult titles. *Please do not send manuscripts for picture books. Ronsdale is a literary press and is not interested in mass–market or pulp materials. Publishes full–size books only.

Rowan Books

214-21 10405 Jasper Avenue, Edmonton, Alberta T5J 3S2
Poetry Editor: Shirley Serviss
Telephone: (780) 421-1544 Fax: (780) 448-0640

Since: 1992	Pages: 64-68	Press Run: 500	TWUC Contract: No
Royalties: 9% of gross	Poetry titles: 2	Fiction: No	Drama: No
Art: No	Children's: No	Anthologies: Yes	Literary Criticism: No
Non-fiction: Yes	Biographies: No	Textbooks: No	Time: 6 months

Authors recently published: Lorie Miseck, Jannie Edwards & Alice Major.

Rowan Books publishes the Mountain Ash Poetry Series designed to introduce readers to emerging Alberta writers. Unsolicited manuscripts by Alberta poets who have not previously had a collection of their work published by a literary press will be reviewed within six months. Poets are advised to accumulate publishing credits in literary magazines prior to approaching the publisher. Self-published poets will still be considered "emerging." Also publishes anthologies of poetry and prose on various themes. Editor states their contract "is based on the Writers' Union contract."

Sober Minute Press

706 Queenston Road, Apartment C, Cambridge, Ontario N3H 3K3
Poetry Editor: Brian David Johnston
Telephone: (519) 650-4059

Since: 1988	Pages: Varies	Press Run: Varies	TWUC Contract: No
Royalties: Copies	Poetry titles: See Below.	Fiction: No	Drama: No
Art: Yes	Children's: No	Anthologies: No	Literary Criticism: No
Non-fiction: No	Biographies: No	Textbooks: No	Time: Varies

Authors recently published: Nelson Ball.

Recent efforts have been confined to publishing "concrete/visual" translations of poems by Nelson Ball. Publisher describes these as leaflets rather than books. Pays in copies. Not actively seeking submissions but may be in the future.

Sono Nis Press

PO Box 5550, Station B, Victoria, British Columbia V8R 6S4
Telephone: (250) 598-7807 Fax: (250) 598-7866
E-mail: sononis@islandnet.com
Website: www.islandnet.com/sononis/

Since: 1968	Pages: Varies	Press Run: 550+	TWUC Contract: No
Royalties: 10% of gross	Poetry titles: 2	Fiction: Yes*	Drama: No
Art: Yes	Children's: Yes	Anthologies: Yes	Literary Criticism: No
Non-fiction: Yes	Biographies: Yes	Textbooks: No	Time: 2-3 months

Authors recently published: Brian Brett, Sandy Shreve & Linda Rogers.

Does NOT accept unsolicited manuscripts. Query with cover letter and samples. *Interested in juvenile fiction only. Publishes full–size books.

Split/Quotation

L'Esplanade Postal Outlet, PO Box 71037, Ottawa, Ontario K2P 2L9
Poetry Editor: Jorge Etcheverry

Telephone: (613) 567-1567 Fax: (613) 568-1568

E-mail: jorgee@magma.ca

Since: 1986	Pages: 100-600	Press Run: 500	TWUC Contract: No
Royalties: 10% of gross	Poetry titles: 2	Fiction: Yes	Drama: No
Art: No	Children's: No	Anthologies: Yes	Literary Criticism: No
Non-fiction: No	Biographies: No	Textbooks: No	Time: Varies

Authors recently published: Anthology of contemporary Cuban poets (in Spanish).

Does not accept unsolicited submissions. Prefers to approach prospective published authors. Usually publishes "soft-covers" and has plans for a series of chapbooks.

Talon Books

#104-3100 Production Way, Burnaby, British Columbia V5A 4R4

Poetry Editor: Karl H. Siegler

Telephone: (604) 444-4889 Fax: (604) 444-1119

E-mail: talon@pinc.com

Website: www.swifty.com/talon

Since: 1967	Pages: Varies	Press Run: Varies	TWUC Contract: No
Royalties: Varies	Poetry titles: 1-4	Fiction: Yes	Drama: Yes
Art: Yes	Children's: No	Anthologies: Yes	Literary Criticism: Yes
Non-fiction: Yes	Biographies: Rarely	Textbooks: No	Time: up to 1 year

Authors recently published: bill bissett, Adeena Karasick, David McFadden & George Bowering.

Publishes full-size books only. Please send a query letter with samples and brief bio. Does NOT accept unsolicited manuscripts. Not interested in the following: drama that has not been professionally produced; mystery; romance adventure; children's fiction; how-to or self-help books.

Thistledown Press

633 Main Street, Saskatoon, Saskatchewan S7H 0J8

Poetry Editor: Patrick O'Rourke

Telephone: (306) 244-1722 Fax: (306) 244-1762

E-mail: thistle@sk.sympatico.ca

Website: www.thistledown.sk.ca

Since: 1975	Pages: 80	Press Run: 500-750	TWUC Contract: Yes
Royalties: 10% of gross	Poetry titles: 2-4	Fiction: Yes	Drama: No
Art: No	Children's: Yes*	Anthologies: Yes	Literary Criticism: Some
Non-fiction: No	Biographies: No	Textbooks: No	Time: 2-3 months

Authors recently published: Andrew Wregitt, Steven Ross Smith & John V. Hicks.

Does not accept unsolicited manuscripts. Please send query with samples and bio. Publishes only Canadian writers either residing in Canada or living outside Canada with Canadian citizenship. *Interested in young adult fiction only. Please do not send picture book manuscripts.

Trout Lily Press

87 Front Street, Stratford, Ontario N5A 4G8

Poetry Editors: Gary Draper, Charlene Diehl-Jones & Linda Kenyon

Telephone: (519) 272-0577

E-mail: dgdraper@library.uwaterloo.ca

Website: www.usjc.uwaterloo.ca/troutlily

Since: 1996	Pages: 24-52	Press Run: 500	TWUC Contract: No
Royalties: Copies	Poetry titles: 1-2	Fiction: Yes	Drama: No

Art: No	Children's: No	Anthologies: No	Literary Criticism: No
Non-fiction: No	Biographies: No	Textbooks: No	Time: 6 months

Authors recently published: April Bulmer & Charlene Diehl-Jones.

Accepts unsolicited submissions. Please send query with samples and bio. Publishes both chapbooks and full-size books. Authors are given a percentage of the books published.

Turnstone Press

607-100 Arthur Street, Winnipeg, Manitoba R3B 1H3

Poetry Editor: Manuela Dias

Telephone: (204) 947-1555 Fax: (204) 942-1555

E-mail: editor@turnstonepress.mb.ca

Website: www.turnstonepress.com

Since: 1975	Pages: 85-100	Press Run: 500	TWUC Contract: No
Royalties: 10% of gross	Poetry titles: 1-3	Fiction: Yes	Drama: No
Art: Yes	Children's: No	Anthologies: Yes	Literary Criticism: Yes
Non-fiction: Yes	Biographies: Yes	Textbooks: No	Time: 3-4 months

Authors recently published: Jan Horner & Todd Bruce.

Interested in literary fiction, non-fiction and poetry. Accepts unsolicited submissions. Please send query with samples and bio. Publishes full-size books only. Ravenstone imprint publishes mystery, gothic and speculative fiction genres.

Tyro Publishing

194 Carlbert Street, Sault Ste. Marie, Ontario P6A 5E1

Poetry Editor: George Hemingway

Telephone: (705) 253-6402 Fax: (705) 942-3625

E-mail: tyro@sympatico.ca

Since: 1984	Pages: 100	Press Run: 300	TWUC Contract: No
Royalties: 10% of gross	Poetry titles: 3	Fiction: Yes	Drama: Maybe
Art: Maybe	Children's: Maybe	Anthologies: No	Literary Criticism: No
Non-fiction: Yes	Biographies: Yes	Textbooks: Yes	Time: 3 months

Authors recently published: Gordon Stone, Lonny Boivin & Denis Robillard.

Accepts unsolicited submissions. Query with samples and bio. Queried submissions are given priority. Those submitted by e-mail even more so. Publishes full-size books.

University College of Cape Breton Press

Box 5300, Sydney, Nova Scotia B1P 6L2

Executive Director: Penny Marshall

Telephone: (902) 563-1604 Fax: (902) 563-1177

E-mail: pmarshall@uccb.ns.ca

Since: 1974	Pages: 75-100	Press Run: 500-750	TWUC Contract: No
Royalties: Varies	Poetry titles: 1	Fiction: No	Drama: Some
Art: No	Children's: Some	Anthologies: Some	Literary Criticism: No
Non-fiction: Yes	Biographies: No	Textbooks: No	Time: 1-6 months

Authors published: LeRoy Peach.

Though this press does not publish much poetry and does not have a poetry editor, it is nonetheless open to submissions. Query first with samples and bio. Once accepted for publication, text must arrive in final format, on an IBM compatible disk and in hard copy. Author's final manuscript must follow publisher's style guide.

Véhicule Press

PO Box 125, Place du Parc Station, Montréal, Québec H2W 2M9
Poetry Editor: Michael Harris
Telephone: (514) 844-6073 Fax: (514) 844-7543
E-mail: vpress@cam.org
Website: www.cam.org/~vpress

Since: 1973	Pages: 72	Press Run: 500-1,000	TWUC Contract: No
Royalties: 10% of gross	Poetry titles: 3-4	Fiction: Some	Drama: No
Art: No	Children's: No	Anthologies: Yes	Literary Criticism: No
Non-fiction: Yes	Biographies: Yes	Textbooks: No	Time: 3-6 months

Authors recently published: Stephanie Bolster, Yves Boisvert, Elizabeth Harvor & Ricardo Sternberg.

Interested in manuscripts by Canadian authors. Query with samples first. Be advised this press is booked into the year 2000. Publishes chapbooks only as part of the Véhicule Virtual Chapbook online.

Wolsak and Wynn Publishers Limited

PO Box 316, Don Mills, Ontario M3C 2S7
Poetry Editor: Maria Jacobs
Telephone: (416) 222-4690 Fax: (416) 237-0291

Since: 1983	Pages: 80-100	Press Run: 500	TWUC Contract: Yes
Royalties: 10% of gross	Poetry titles: 5-6	Fiction: No	Drama: No
Art: No	Children's: No	Anthologies: No	Literary Criticism: No
Non-fiction: No	Biographies: No	Textbooks: No	Time: 4-6 months

Authors published: Nicole Markotic & John Terpstra.

Interested in unsolicited material but please send query with 15–20 sample poems and bio. Publishes only full-size books. Editor states their contract for poetry is a "modified version" of the TWUC contract.

The following book publishers have ceased publication since the sixth edition of this book:

Black Bile Press, NC Press, pooka press, Sadhana Press

The following book publishers no longer publish poetry or they have asked to be delisted:

Cormorant Books, Fifth House Publishers, Green's Magazine Chapbooks, Hounslow Press, Insomniac Press, letters, Mekler & Deahl, Publishers

The following book publishers believed to still be active, failed to respond to requests for information:

Acorn Press, Agawa Press, Aurora Editions, Bad Moon Books, Blizzard Publishing, Borealis Press, Capers Aweigh Small Press, Childe Thursday, Cordillera Publishing, Curved H & Z, disorientation chapbooks, Empyreal Press, Exile Editions, Frei Press, ga press, Grove

Avenue Press, Gutter Press, Ice House Press, Kalamalka Press, Lowlife Publishing, McClelland & Stewart, Mosaic Press, Netherlandic Press, Nietzsche's Brolly, Nuage Editions, Oberon Press, Owl's Head Press, paperplates, Pinecone Publishing, proof press, The Porcupine's Quill, Prise de parole, Proper Tales Press, Punchpenny Press, Quarry Press, Queer Press, River City Press, Second Story Press, Seraphim Editions, Sister Vision Press, Staccato Chapbooks, Theytus Books, Third Eye, Trebarni Press, Underwhich Editions, watershedBooks

THREE: PUBLISHING ONLINE

There are thousands of websites devoted entirely to poetry on the internet. From traditional to speculative poetry, from haiku to blank verse, there is little to hold back writers from finding venues for their work.

3.1 DOING A SEARCH

Be clear about what you're searching for before employing a search engine. "Magazines" is too broad a request. Searches need to be focused. If you are a poet looking for a new market you might try "Canadian literary magazines."

Some search engines work best with quotation marks around the query, others prefer words to be joined_by_using_an_underscore_between_words. Yet others require "and" or a "+" sign be used between words. Detailed help-pages specific to individual search engines explain which method works best.

To the surprise (and consternation) of many people, search engines do not look for page content. Instead, search engines look for metatags. Metatags are "invisible" code in the background of all webpages. These "keywords" help search engines connect your query with pages which may have the type of information you are seeking.

Tanners Bookstore, for instance, would not be found if you searched for "Tanners" unless "Tanners" had been included by the webpage author as a metatag in the code for the Tanners Bookstore homepage. Instead, what you would find is a number of sites on how to cure leather.

You need to understand metatags not because you have any control over them (you don't) but to understand why even a well-executed search may fail. If it does, don't abandon it. Rethink it. If you know Tanners Bookstore is located in Sidney, British Columbia, you could try searching for the town and follow links from the townsite webpage to town retailers.

If you search for a university-based publication, it is helpful to know in advance that they are often accessible only through a subdirectory of the university's English department.

The motto for internet users is: be resourceful. Then again, if you can get the information you're looking for by picking up the telephone and dialing 411, don't bother searching online for hours.

3.2 DEAD LINKS

Undoubtedly, you will uncover numerous dead links (links which do not work) in your travels on the internet. These will annoy you but don't assume that a dead link means that what you're looking for no longer exists. Advise the webmaster of the page you're on about the bad link and then renew your search.

Dead links may be caused by a number of things including, for instance, a publisher who has changed service providers. If you think of the publisher's homepage as a file moved to another filing cabinet, it is easy to understand that although the homepage is not where you thought it was, it still exists. The information you seek may be available at a different URL. You can search for this in a number of ways:

1. Work backwards through the original URL. If the site you wanted was a subdirectory of a main site, delete the subdirectories of the URL and take a look at the main site. Often, the information you want will be on a new page attached to the main site.

2. If the site offers you a search option, use it.

3. Do a regular search using your favourite search engine. Think metatags.

If you don't find what you are looking for after trying each of these steps, remember to try searching through associated links. A small press in Toronto may not be a member of the Canadian Publishers Association but it might belong to the Literary Press Group. Be resourceful.

3.3 WEBRINGS

In an effort to collect like websites together by a series of links, a number of people have set up "webrings." Although the original idea was a good one, most webrings are now too unwieldy to be useful. Another drawback is member websites are rarely vetted for quality or even for the ability to be understood. The best webrings have strictly limited membership or have their members listed by category (speculative poetry for instance) which allows visitors to target sites in which they have a particular interest.

3.4 THE DATE CAN DO YOU IN

More than once I've been drawn into sites by headlines that blare, "COME TO THE WRITER'S FESTIVAL, OCTOBER 22 IN BIG TOWN, SOME PROVINCE," only to find out seven pages later that the event took place in 1996. Make sure the information you gather is current.

3.5 WHAT TO EXPECT ON THE PUBLISHER'S SITE

Instead of waiting weeks and perhaps months to get a copy of a publication's guidelines, you can now download them right from the publisher's site. There may be other items of interest on a publication's site as well.

Many magazines have a "web presence." That is, while they do not have a full version of their magazine online, they do offer samples of work from their print version. This allows writers a priceless opportunity to examine the kind of work an editor prefers.

You may find the biography of the editor online too. You can learn any number of things from this, including where they have been published, how long they have been with the magazine, and perhaps what inspires them in their own literary pursuits.

Many e-zines also offer biographies of contributors which in and of themselves are a good read. These bios can lead you to other magazines which might be interested in your work.

Not as common because of the work and possible expense it entails, is the inclusion online of a print magazine's back issues. However, where they are available, writers can enjoy an instant history in the evolution of the magazine's style and direction.

3.6 BEFORE YOU SUBMIT TO AN ONLINE PUBLICATION

You should become familiar with a wide variety of e-zines. Ask yourself, is the site attractive? Are the editors well qualified? Does the work on the site interest you? Is the work itself presented in a way that you appreciate? Would you visit this site again even if your work was rejected?

If the site esthetics and editorial direction match your needs, your next step is to consider the editorial policy of the e-zine. What rights do they request? Many will say they request "no rights" but this makes no sense. Before they can upload your work to their site, you have to give them permission to do so. For a clear explanation of copyright issues see Chapter One.

An often unspoken concern among writers is that their work will be more easily stolen if it appears online. This is unfounded. Once you become familiar with the internet and its opportunities, you will realize that although the number of poetry sites is huge, haiku lovers, for instance, will leap from one haiku site to another making any theft easily discovered.

E-zines are a long way from making anyone rich. Some e-zines may offer a token payment but most do not. This may change over time. If your work appears in the print version of a magazine which pays and they request the right to publish it online as well, it is appropriate to ask for an additional fee.

3.7 THE RESEARCH IS DONE AND YOU'RE READY TO SEND A SUBMISSION

NEVER submit anything by e-mail unless you know such a submission is welcome. If you have permission to submit by e-mail remember to remain professional in your approach. E-mail is business correspondence.

Much of your formatting will likely be lost when you submit by e-mail. If your work requires complicated spacing, you may wish to suggest to the editor that you fax them a hard copy of your work as well.

E-mail attachments are notorious for being a pain to deal with. Unless you've made other arrangements with the editor, copy your submission into the body of the e-mail message. It is generally best not to include graphics at the same time though you may be able to send them separately. Ask the editor what she prefers.

Your cover letter should include a brief bio of yourself and a list of the titles you submit. Your name and address should appear on the first submission page. Mark subsequent pages with your name, e-mail address and part of the title.

3.8 THEY SAID YES

Great! Getting an acceptance letter is always a thrill. If you haven't already done so, now is the time to clarify what rights the publication is requesting and how long they intend to keep your work online.

You may be surprised to find that some web publishers have little experience negotiating rights and may not clearly understand the concept. There is no doubt that if they publish your work, rights have been used. The key is to have as much control as possible over when, how, and for how long your work is used online by any publication.

It is best to have a written agreement stating the parameters under which an e-zine may publish your work. This can be a letter of agreement which includes the name of the work to be used, the length of time it may be used, whether or not it may be part of the online archive (back issues), what payment if any is expected and the date that payment will be issued. Be sure your name, address, telephone number, and that of the editor and e-zine are included. This agreement will likely not be signed but rather returned to you with the editor's approval noted.

While copyright issues were covered in Chapter One, there are a few intricacies to understand when you consider publishing in e-zines. First of all, it IS publishing. Once a work has been published online you cannot sell "first" rights to it to a print magazine. If you think the magazine may still be interested in the piece, you might offer them "first PRINT rights" but you must disclose the poem's online publication history.

Also, where writers have traditionally controlled the market for their work by specifying "first Canadian rights," or "first European rights," work published online is published "globally." Distribution (or in this case access) can be considered unlimited. Before publishing online, think about the impact it will have on reselling the piece.

Canadian writers should consider joining The Electronic Rights Licensing Agency (TERLA). As described earlier in this book, TERLA was founded to address the need to develop guidelines regarding the use of a writer's work in electronic form. According to TERLA's Executive Director, Robert Labossière, one of the advantages of dealing with electronic rights collectively is the possibility of establishing "a benchmark of fair compensation for electronic uses." For more information contact TERLA at: 1 Yonge Street, Suite 1900, Toronto, Ontario M5E 1E5, Telephone: (416) 868-0200 or 1-877-557-4616 Fax: (416) 868-0296, E-mail: rlabossiere@interlog.com

3.9 CONSIDER YOUR OWN WEBSITE

You can produce an attractive website using uncomplicated software available for any system. The question is, "Why bother?"

A website may showcase your work and allow you to be discovered by legions of fans, but take a realistic look at the competition. There are millions of writers vying for the attention of the reading public. What will make your site special? If your answer is flashy graphics, move to the back of the class.

All good writing will stand on its own merits. Ask yourself if you have the design sense it takes to produce a page which focuses the reader's attention on the words, or would you add a vampire bat that flashes its fangs every five seconds? Do you feel the need to use GREAT BIG FONT SIZES for absolutely no good reason? If so, forget about producing your own work online. Unnecessary graphics slow the download time. The average visitor will click right past your site if it takes more than ten seconds to open.

Don't be discouraged. It's fine to be inventive or outrageous if it's done with style. (See www.ubu.com which highlights visual poets in particular.) But invest some time in a web authoring course to learn the basics of HTML and spend time visiting other sites to see what does and doesn't appeal to you. This will help you organize your own site. You need to plan what the content will be, what graphic elements will be used, whether you will include a photo of yourself, and a list of your published works, etc..

The clear focus you set for yourself from the beginning can save you much time down the road. Remember to incorporate some feature that will change regularly so that people will bookmark your page and return to it again and again. This could be a weekly quote, a new poem, a book review and so on. Some websites allow visitors to join an automatic mailing list which invites them back to the site whenever a change is made. This is a handy tool for websites which incorporate multiple changes on a regular basis.

Almost every website offers a selection of links to other websites. While you might choose to include a list of your favourite sites, (i.e. the Toronto Blue Jays), links should offer some value to poetry writers or readers. You could link to writers' organizations, poetry sites that intrigue you, or your local poetry-friendly book-store. (A list of these can be found at the end of the "Reading Venues" section.)

A website is a serious time commitment and once you start one you must keep it updated. If you do a reading tour, launch a book, or help with a festival, your webpage is a great place to describe them all. As soon as the information is stale, delete it or replace it.

By the way, if you post any of your own work on your own webpage it's considered "published." It might be best to upload a small selection of your work which has been previously published, assuming of course that you retained the e-rights to your work.

Visitors may want to comment on your work or, if you have extraordinary luck, an editor may wish to invite you to submit to their magazine. Always include your e-mail address and other basic contact information on the first page of your site. Too many sites bury this information and expect visitors to search for it. Most won't. They'll get frustrated and move on to another site. It's your job to ensure your site is not only esthetically appealing, but also well organized.

3.10 LEARNING HOW TO BUILD YOUR WEBSITE

Information or courses on webpage design can be obtained through your local night school, community college, university extension department, or your internet service provider. You can also enjoy learning about webpage design online. You might prefer this as you can learn at home and choose when and for how long you work on the material. Regardless of how you choose to learn, always purchase a separate HTML manual to help you along.

A webpage introduction course should:

1. Help narrow the focus of your website.

2. Teach you to create a multi-page site.

3. Teach basic graphic design do's and don'ts, including sizing, colour and other graphic elements.

4. Explain tags and tables.

5. Explain how to link to other sites.

6. Explain how and where to locate your webpage and how to understand its limitations.

7. Explain domain names, the registration process and help you determine if a domain name is neccesary for you.

8. Provide an understanding of how to register your webpage with search engines.

9. Cost less than $150 and leave you comfortable with your skills.

You might take advanced HTML, and then go on to work with Java applets as well, but the basics are all you really need to produce an appealing site.

Online: A Beginner's Guide to HTML:
www.ncsa.uiuc.edu/General/Internet/WWW/HTMLPrimer.html

HTML 4 for the World Wide Web by Elizabeth Castro
Peachpit Press, 1249 Eighth Street, Berkeley, California, USA 94710
www.peachpit.com

3.11 BEYOND WEBSITES: E-MAIL, LISTSERVS AND NEWSGROUPS

Your e-mail signature can be a passive advertisement for your work. Just below your name, add the the website address (URL) for your personal website or the URL of a magazine where your work is displayed, or both. If you read at a writers' festival you can advertise the dates. Use your imagination and make every piece of correspondence work for you.

Generally, a listserv is a closed list of subscribers who communicate with each other by posting messages which get sent to every member. Members may then reply publicly to the group messaging system or individually to the sender. Listservs are often an offshoot of professional groups like the League of Canadian Poets.

A newsgroup is also a group of subscribers brought together by a commonality, but the focus of the newsgroup is very narrow. Instead of all members of the League of Canadian Poets choosing to share questions and general information as on a listserv, a newsgroup may have subscribers from around the world discussing the fine points of historical criticism or the origins of limericks. Newsgroups are great places to learn by listening and there are thousands to choose from.

Whether you deal with e-mail, listservs or newsgroups, avoid getting involved in "flame wars." All internet users should conduct online correspondence in the same way as any face-to-face conversation— with respect.

3.12 LEAGUES OF LITERARY LINKS

Albert Russo's Homepage
www.worldnet.net/~zapinet/links.html

Big Guide to Guidelines
www.writersdigest.com

Canadian Literature Online
canlit.st-john.umanitoba.ca/Canlitx/Framed_Version/CanlitF.html

Canadian Magazine Publishers Association
www.cmpa.ca/literary.html

Citation
www.harbour.sfu.ca/ccsp/citation

CultureNet
www.culturenet.ca/cnet/index.html

Ecola Newsstand
www.ecola.com/news/magazine

Edmonton Stroll of Poets
www.ccinet.ab.ca/stroll/slinks.htm

Electronic Poetry Centre
www.wings.buffalo.edu/epc/mags/index.html

Gila Queen's Guide to the Markets
www.members.xoom.com/GilaQueen

Inkspot
www.inkspot.com

International Poetry Webring
www.geocities.com/~poetsgalore

Internet Directory of Publications
www.publist.com/cgi-bin/search

John Labovitz's E-zine List
www.meer.net/~johnl/e-zine-list

League of Canadian Poets
www.poets.ca

Links for Writers
www.dialspace.dial.pipex.com/town/plaza/dg40/jd_links.htm

Literary Arts Webring
www.lit-arts.com/WebRing

Literary Journals
www.usd.edu/engl/journals.html

The Literary Scene
www.marebalticum.se/literature

Ozlit (Australia)
www.ozlit.org

Poetry Daily
www.poems.com

Poetry Links of the Web
www.uct.ac.za/projects/poetry/poetlink.htm

The Poetry Society (UK)
www.poetrysoc.com/index.htm

Poets & Writers
www.pw.org/lkindex.htm

The Porcupine's Quill
www.sentex.net/~pql/links.htm

Powwow Literary Magazines Links
www.geocities.com/Paris/1416/magazines.html

Publisher's Catalogues Home Page
www.lights.com/publisher/al.html

Toronto Small Press Group
www.interlog.com/~ksimons/tspg.htm

The Word on the Street
www.sympatico.ca/wots

Webdelsol
www.webdelsol.com/solhome.htm

Zuzu's Petals Literary links
www.zuzu.com/litlink.htm

FOUR: POETRY READINGS

If you make it a point to attend many readings, you will learn much about the variety of poetry written and gain some insight into how to present your own work in public.

4.1 FEELING GOOD ABOUT READING IN PUBLIC

While you don't need to be as flamboyant as performance poet Sheri-D Wilson to capture an audience, it will help both you and the audience if you take the time to practice your reading style. At my first public reading I read in a monotone one octave lower than my regular speaking voice. After I finished, the host thanked me by inviting me to read at the next funeral he attended. Most readings go better than that but a sense of humour is handy when needed. The more experienced you become, the easier it will be to quell your nerves, meet the eyes of your audience and speak clearly at a steady pace.

There is more to readings than just reading your work. Be prepared to read in a variety of atmospheres. You may be hot, cold, poorly situated in a room, have little to no audience, or have to deal with background noise. This is where your efforts to attend other readings will pay off. You'll know what to expect from your local venues. If you're going to be reading out of town you may want to ask other poets what their experiences have been at various venues. If you discover that a host is always poorly prepared, the audience always small, or the venue incredibly noisy, you may want to plan to read elsewhere.

The good news is there are few venues which fail to meet the needs of their readers. Hosts are often writers themselves. Most have volunteered to organize readings and are more than happy to work with you to make your reading a success.

4.2 OPEN-MIKE READINGS

An open-mike reading is, as the name implies, open to anyone who wants to read their work in front of an audience. Often sessions are structured around a featured reader. There may be open readings for 20-30 minutes, followed by the featured reader for another 20-30 minutes, and a final session of open readings varying from 15-45 minutes.

Signing up is the easiest part of an open-mike reading. Usually it is as easy as printing your name on a piece of paper. A general rule for open-mike sessions is no more than five minutes per reader. This allows many people to share their work in one evening.

The best way to understand how open-mike readings run is to attend them regularly before you sign up.

4.3 SCHEDULED OR FEATURED READINGS

When you have worked at your craft for some time and are a well-practiced reader it is time to consider getting a featured reading. This takes good advance planning on your part. Reading series organizers plan months in advance. Fortunately, many newspapers list a contact number with the readings announcements in their entertainment or community happenings sections. This number is usually for the series host. (A venue is WHERE you read, the host is the one who schedules WHO reads.) Call this number to ask for information on how to apply to read. Most hosts will ask you to provide them with a bio and sample poems. Before applying be sure you have enough quality work to fill 20-30 minutes of reading time.

Beyond discovering reading venues through the newspaper, there are a number of resources available to you. Readings by League of Canadian Poets (LCP) members across the country are listed on the LCP website (www.poets.ca) as well as detailed in a bimonthly brochure called "Poetry Spoken Here." For ten dollars the LCP will mail you this print resource for a full year.

A list of readings funded by the Canada Council can be found on their website (www.canadacouncil.ca/program/writing/readings.htm). Keep in mind that this list includes ONLY those venues which received Canada Council funding. Many more readings take place across the country each month.

Local and provincial writers' groups and arts councils may also offer information on where readings are taking place.

Although I've included a limited list of reading venues, the number of places which sponsor readings is endless and ever-changing: universities; colleges; public libraries; coffee houses; art galleries; community centres; writing festivals and others sponsor readings. Do not rely solely on the list provided.

4.4 GROUP READINGS

Poets often do group readings. If you are invited to take part in such an event, keep the following in mind: like the open-mike readings, there will be many readers and your allotted time will be limited. Be sure you know what the organizers expect of you: one poem? five minutes? ten? Before committing yourself ask if you will be paid, and/or whether or not your transportation, accommodation or meal expenses will be covered. Many times they are not but you may be offered a limited bar tab, a free meal, or other form of honorarium.

Arrive well in time for the reading, have your material prepared and timed and be willing to be flexible if last-minute changes need to be made.

Group readings are often a good opportunity for less-experienced poets to share the stage with well-known writers.

4.5 BOOK PROMOTION AND READING TOURS

Few poets can afford to promote their books across the country. It is an expensive proposition and publishers seldom help much due to their own financial restraints. Poets who want to promote their books must be prepared to schedule readings, plan and confirm publicity, arrange for books to be available, do the readings, sign the books, handle the cash transactions, and handle the vagaries of travel. It can be both an exhausting and exhilarating experience. Being organized can help you survive it intact.

First, plan how long a book tour you wish to do. Will it be cross-country? Only within your province? Perhaps involve only a series of day trips to other cities?

Investigate the reading venues available and make your first contact with the hosts responsible for each location where you wish to read. Try to group your readings to make your travel dollars work effectively. You might book readings in West Bank, Edmonton, St. Albert, Red Deer, and Calgary before going either east or west to continue promoting your book.

Once you have a tentative schedule, send press kits to the radio stations and newspapers in the areas you'll be visiting. These should include a one-page author's bio, a sample of your work, and a high-quality b/w photocopy of the cover of your book. Including reviews of your work, if they are available, is standard. Include a "hook" (i.e. previously held the position of Dinosaur Duster in Drumheller). This will help increase the media's interest in you and your book. Purists may object to this method of attention-getting, but the reality is most media representatives do not have the time to read everything they receive. You have to catch their attention quickly. Once you have the forum to share your work, you can concentrate on your art.

Send your press kits out two or three weeks in advance and follow up with a telephone call closer to the date you'll be in their town. Television producers will need your publicity material 8-12 weeks in advance of an appearance, if not sooner.

Before your suitcase is packed you've spent $100 on copying, postage, and telephone calls. How will you finance even a short tour? Now is the time to refer to the funding opportunities listed in Chapter Five: Resources for Writers.

There are some writers who get creative when sourcing funds for their reading tours. One LCP member contacted a number of corporations, and requested they provide something specific such as free accommodation or free meals in selected cities. He was fortunate to connect with poetry lovers at each company who helped fulfill his requests but it was his request for something concrete that really made the difference. He didn't ask for money, he asked them to fill a need and they responded to that need.

At some venues on your tour you'll be able to sell your books following your reading— but what about bookstore readings? You might expect the store to have its own stock of your book. This is not a safe assumption. To be sure your book will be available on the day of your reading, put the store in touch with your publisher or vice-versa. Also, ask the store's staff to prominently display your book the week before your scheduled reading.

Provide your publisher with your itinerary and let them know if you are able to add extra readings at a later date. Keeping them informed will help them support your efforts.

4.6 READING VENUES

Reading venues vary widely from small bookstores to large lecture halls, from art galleries to outdoor festival stages. While a long list of venues active at the time of writing is included here, more will become available over time. Keep in mind some may host only for special events and others may change hosts or even locations. It is up to you to KNOW THE MARKET.

Exciting online venues like the *Edgewise Electrolit Centre E-zine* (www.edgewisecafe.org) which offers poetry in text, Real Audio, and movie formats will proliferate over the coming years. The list below, however, is a record of reading venues which have a long history of welcoming a wide variety of poets onto a solid stage.

Please note that contact information provided here is for the host or organizer of the readings; the street address of the reading venue itself may be different from that listed in this book.

BRITISH COLUMBIA

Black Sheep Books
2740 West 4th Avenue, Vancouver, British Columbia V6K IRI
Contacts: George Koller & David Wah, (604) 688-5985 Fax: (604) 737-7685
Telephone: (604) 732-5087
E-mail: blksheep@direct.ca

The Bookstore on Bastion Street
76 Bastion Street, Nanaimo, British Columbia V9R 3A1
Contact: T. Howell
E-mail: bastion@mail.island.net
Telephone: (250) 753-2023

Burnaby Writers' Society
6584 Deer Lake Ave., Burnaby, British Columbia V5G 2J3
Contact: Pam Galloway
Telephone: (613) 435-6500

Festival of the Written Arts
Box 2299, Sechelt, British Columbia V0N 3A0
Contact: Michael Barnholden
Telephone: (604) 885-9631 Fax: (604) 885-3967

Kootenay School of Writing
112 West Hastings Street, 4th Floor, Vancouver, British Columbia V6B 1G8
Contact: Ed Varney
Telephone: (604) 266-8289 Fax: (604) 266-8289

Kootenay School-Writing Studio
606 Victoria Street, Nelson, British Columbia V1L 4K9
Contact: Tom Wayman
E-mail: ksawrite@netidea.com

Mocambo Reading Series
4596 William Head Road, Victoria, British Columbia V9B 5T7
Contact: Tanya Kern
Telephone: (250) 474-5489
E-mail: tkern@mail.sd56.bc.ca

Myles of Beans Café
7010 Kingsway, Burnaby, British Columbia V5E 1E7
Contact: Chad Norman, (604) 431-5451
Telephone: (604) 524-3700

Open Space Gallery
510 Fort Street, Victoria, British Columbia V8W 1E6
Contact: Todd Davis
Telephone: (250) 383-8833
E-mail: openarc@islandnet.com

Shadbolt Centre for the Arts
6450 Deer Lake Avenue, Burnaby, British Columbia V5G 2J3
Contact: Susan Shank
Telephone: (604) 205-3013 Fax: (604) 291-7841

Shawnigan Lake Writer's Village
PO Box #6, Shawnigan Lake, British Columbia V0R 2W0
Telephone: (250) 743-0981

Sidney and North Saanich Arts Council Readings
2319 Henry Avenue, Sidney, British Columbia V8L 2B3
Contact: Michael Cullen
Telephone: (250) 656-6870

Sunshine Coast Festival of the Written Arts
Box 2299, Sechelt, British Columbia V0N 3A0
Telephone: (604) 885-9631 Toll free 1-800-565-9631
E-mail: written_arts@sunshine.net

Vancouver International Writers Festival
1243 Cartwright Street, Vancouver, British Columbia V6H 4B7
Contact: Alma Lee
Telephone: (604) 681-6330 Fax: (604) 681-8400
E-mail: viwf@axionet.com

Vancouver Public Library
750 Burrard Street, Vancouver, British Columbia V6Z 1X5
Contact: Janice Douglas
Telephone: (604) 665-3554

Vancouver Public Library
350 West Georgia Street, Vancouver, British Columbia V6B 6B1
Contact: David Johnstone
Telephone: (604) 331-4041

Victoria Literary Arts Festival
Box 40041, 905 Gordon Street, Victoria, British Columbia V8W 3P9
Contact: Pat St. Pierre
Telephone: (250) 381-6722 Fax: (250) 381-6721
E-mail: literary@writeme.com

Victoria Read Society
720 Linden Avenue, Victoria, British Columbia V8V 4G7
Contact: Melanie Austin
Telephone: (250) 388-7225 Fax: (250) 386-8330

Victoria School of Writing
PO Box 8152, Victoria, BC V8W 3R8
Contact: Magaret Dyment
Telephone: (250) 598-5300 Fax: (250) 598-0066
E-mail: writeawy@islandnet.com

Volume One Bookstore
149 Kenneth Street
Duncan, British Columbia V9L 1N5
Contact: Betsy Nuse
(250) 748-1533
E-mail: bnuse@islandnet.com

Vortex Gallery
Salt Spring Island, British Columbia V8K 2K5

Contact: Mona Fertig
Telephone: (250) 537-4725
E-mail: mothertongue@saltspring.com

Whitby's Bookstore and Coffee House
14837 Marine Drive, White Rock, British Columbia V4B 1C1
Contact: Lynette Wilson
Telephone: (604) 536-3711

Women In Print Bookstore
76 Bastion Street, Nanaimo, British Columbia V9R 3A1
Telephone: (250) 732-4128

ALBERTA

Carole's Cafe and Bar
3106-6th Avenue South, Lethbridge, Alberta T1J 1G1
Contact: Richard Stevenson
Telephone: (403) 327-8158
E-mail: stevenr@telusplanet.net

Chapters
Brick Plaza, 9631 MacLeod Trail SW, Calgary, Alberta T2J 0P6
Telephone: (403) 212-1442

Edmonton Public Library
7 Sir Winston Churchill Square, Edmonton, Alberta
Telephone: (780) 496-7063

Latitude 53 Gallery
10137 104 Street, Edmonton, Alberta T5J 0Z9
Contact: Executive Director
Telephone: (780) 423-5353

Memorial Park Library
1221 2nd Street SW, Calgary, Alberta T2R 0W5
Contact: Aruna Marathel
Telephone: (403) 221-2007

Orlando Books
10640 Whyte Ave., Edmonton, Alberta T6E 2A7
Contact: Jacqueline Dumas
Telephone: (780) 432-7633 Fax: (780) 461-5440
E-mail: orlando@compusmart.ab.ca
Website: www.compusmart.ab.ca/orlando/

Pages Books on Kensington
1135 Kensington Road NW, Calgary, Alberta T2N 3P4
Contact: Peter Oliva
Telephone: (403) 283-6655 Fax (403) 283-6676
pagesonk@cadvision.com

Piq Niq Cafe
811-1st Street SW, Calgary, Alberta T2P 7N2
Contact: Rob Young
Telephone: (403) 263-1650

Socrates Corner Bookstore
315-555 Strathcona Blvd. SW, Calgary, Alberta T3H 2Z9
Telephone: (403) 242-8042

Stroll of Poets
53 Sundance, Edmonton, Alberta T5H 4B4
Contact: Doug Elves
Telephone: (780) 426-1751
E-mail: Elves@Oanet.com

Word Fest: Banff Calgary Writers Festival
Box 82025 1400-12 Avenue West, Calgary, Alberta T3C 3W5
Contact: Anne Green
Telephone: (403) 294-7462 Fax: (403) 294-7457

SASKATCHEWAN

A.K.A. Gallery
12-23rd Street East, Saskatoon, Saskatchewan S4R 1H3
Contact: Paul Wilson
Telephone: (306) 777-0170

Amigos
632 10th Street East, Saskatoon, Saskatchewan S7H 0G9
Telephone: (306) 652-4912

Book and Briar Patch
4065 Albert Street, Regina, Saskatchewan S4S 3R6
Contact: Paul Wilson
Telephone: (306) 757-6310

Café Browse
269B 3rd Avenue South, Saskatoon, Saskatchewan S7K 1M3
Contact: Peggy Skilnik
Telephone: (306) 664-2665

Cafe 97
1834b Scarth Street, Regina, Saskatchewan S4P 2G9

The Dunlop Art Gallery/Regina Public Library
2311-12th Avenue, Regina, Saskatchewan S4P 0N3
Telephone: (306) 777-6040

Festival of the Word
26 Crocus Road, Moose Jaw, Saskatchewan S6J 1B5
Contact: Gary Hyland
Telephone: (306) 692-8540

Lydia's
650 Broadway, Saskatoon, Saskatchewan S7N 1A9
Telephone: (306) 652-8595

Prairie Wordfest
1105 Hastings Street, Moose Jaw, Saskatchewan S6H 5S1
Contact: Brian Clemmensen
Telephone: (306) 693-9416 Fax: (306) 691-0986

St. Thomas More College
Saskatoon, Saskatchewan
Contact: Tim Lilburn, Seasonal lecturer

Sage Hill Writing Experience
Box 1731, Saskatoon, Saskatchewan S7K 3S1
Contact: Steven Smith
Telephone: (306) 652-7395 Fax: (306) 652-7395

Saskatoon Public Library, Frances Morrison Branch
311-23rd Street East, Saskatoon, Saskatchewan S7K 0J6
Contact: Patricia Pavey
Telephone: (306) 975-7566

Spring Festival Evening Readings
Station Arts Centre, 701 Railway Avenue, Rosthern, Saskatchewan S7K 5S3
Telephone: (306) 232-5332

University of Saskatchewan, English Department
Visiting Speakers Committee, Saskatoon, Saskatchewan
Contact: Anthony Harding
Telephone: (306) 966-4343
E-mail: harding@duke.usask.ca

MANITOBA

Winnipeg International Writers Festival
209-100 Arthur Street, Winnipeg, Manitoba R3B 1H3
Contact: Kathleen Darby
Telephone: (204) 956-7323
E-mail: mbwriter@escape.ca

ONTARIO

Alternative Grounds Cafe
333 Roncesvalles Avenue, Toronto, Ontario M6R 2M8
Telephone: (416) 588-1288

The Art Bar Reading Series
The Imperial Pub, 54 Dundas Street East, Toronto, Ontario M6S 3C2
Contacts: James LaTrobe and Pierre L'Abbé
Telephone: (416) 762-6356

E-mail: james_latrobe@magna.on.ca

Athena Reading Series
Mother Tongue Books Femmes de Parole, 1067 Bank Street, Ottawa, Ontario K1S 3W9
Telephone: (613) 730-2346

The Blarney Stone Café
38 Erie Street, Stratford, Ontario N5A 2M4
Contact: Jennifer Frankel
Telephone: (519) 272-0013

Centennial College Progress Campus
PO Box 631, Station A, Scarborough, Ontario M1K 5E9
Contact: John Redfern
Telephone: (416) 289-5200 ext.2523 Fax: (416) 289-5206
E-mail: dkent@cencol.on.ca

The Clay and Glass Gallery
25 Caroline Street North, Waterloo, Ontario N2L 2Y5

Comfort Zone
486 Spadina Avenue, Toronto, Ontario M5S 2H1
Telephone: (416) 250-1492

Dark City Coffee House
307 Danforth Avenue, Toronto, Ontario M5T 2E6
Telephone: (416) 461-1606

Eden Mills Festival
209 Barden Street, Eden Mills, Ontario N0B 1P0
Contact: Leon Rooke
Telephone: (519) 856-9014

Elora Writers Festival
#18— 100 Vaughan Road, Toronto, Ontario M6C 2M1
Contact: Ailsa Kay
Telephone: (416) 652-7938

Free Times Cafe
320 College Street, Toronto, Ontario M5T 1S2
Contact: Judy Perly
Telephone: (416) 967-1078

Gallery 101
319 Lisgar Street, Ottawa, Ontario K2P 0E1
Telephone: (613) 235-2783

Hamilton Poetry Centre
9 Dalewood Avenue, Hamilton, Ontario L8S 1Y6
Contact: Bernadette Rule
Telephone: (905) 529-0496

Hamilton Public Library
55 York Blvd, Box 2700, Stn LCD 1, Hamilton, Ontario L8N 4E4

Contact: Helen Benoit
Telephone: (905) 546-3420

Harbourfront Reading Series
410 Queen's Quay West, Toronto, Ontario M5V 2Z3
Contact: Greg Gatenby

The Idler Pub
225 Davenport Road, Toronto, Ontario M5R 3R2
Contact: Stan Rogal
Telephone: (416) 538-1769

Ingersoll Creative Arts Centre
245 Hall Street, Ingersoll, Ontario N5C 1V6
Telephone: (905) 485-4691

Monaco's
107 George Street, Hamilton, Ontario L9A 2W2
Contact: Linda Frank
Telephone: (905) 549-4737
E-mail: lfrank@cujo2.icom.ca

Mayworks Festival
25 Cecil Street, 2nd Floor, Toronto, Ontario M5T 1N1
Contact: Lillian Allen
Telephone: (416) 599-9096 Fax: (416) 599-8661

Metropolitan Toronto Reference Library
789 Yonge Street, Toronto, Ontario M4W 2G8
Contact: Beatriz Hausner
Telephone: (416) 393-7088

National Library of Canada
395 Wellington Street, Ottawa, Ontario K1A 0N4
Contact: Randall Ware
Telephone: (613) 992-0057 or (613) 995-9481

Nepean Public Library
101 Centrepointe Drive, Nepean, Ontario K2G SK7

North York Public Library, Black Creek Branch
2141 Jane Street, North York, Ontario M3M 1A2
Contact: Carmen La Touche
Telephone: (416) 395-5470 Fax: (416) 395-5435

Novel Idea Bookstore
156 Princess Street, Kingston, Ontario K7L 1B1
Telephone: (613) 546-9799

Readers' Ink
140 University Avenue West, Waterloo, Ontario N2L 6J3
Contact: Judith Jutzi
Telephone: (519) 746-2872

Renison College/University of Waterloo
5 Park Avenue West, Elmira, Ontario N3B IK9
Contact: Susan Bryant
Telephone: (519) 669-5321 Fax: (519) 669-1985

Runnymede Public Library
2178 Bloor Street West, Toronto, Ontario M6S IM8
Contact: Judith Jackson
Telephone: (416) 393-7697

Tree Reading Series, CLUB SAW
Contact: Stephen Harding, (613) 738-2366 Fax: (613) 738-1929
Second Contact: rob mclennan, (613) 235-2783
67 Nicholas Street, Ottawa, Ontario KIN 7B9
E-mail: az421@freenet.carleton.ca

Trinity College Readings
44 Devonshire Place, Toronto, Ontario M5S 2E2
Contact: Sylvia Przezdziecki
Telephone: (416) 599-6104

University of Toronto Bookstore
214 College Street, Toronto, Ontario M5T 3A1
Contact: Maylin Scott
Telephone: (416) 978-7908 Fax: (416) 978-7242

University of Waterloo
Conrad Grebel College, Waterloo, Ontario N2L 3G6
Contact: Hildi Froese Tiessen

Whiplash Festival
96 Rochester Street, Ottawa, Ontario KIR 7L8
Contact: rob mclennan
Telephone: (613) 235-2783
E-mail: az421@freenet.carleton.ca

Writuals Reading Series
Arbor Room, Hart House, University of Toronto
7 Hart House Circle, Toronto, Ontario M5S 3H3
Contact: Carleton Wilson Alternate Contact: Patricia Grant
Telephone: (416) 978-5362
E-mail patricia.grant@utoronto.ca

QUÉBEC

Le Bistro 4
4040 St. Laurent, Montréal, Québec
Contact: Daniel Lamoureux
Telephone: (514) 844-6246

The Devil's Voice
Montréal, Québec
Contact: thoth harris
Telephone: (514) 761-4887

Double Hook Bookshop
1235A Green Avenue, Montréal, Québec H3Z 2A4
Contact: Judith Mappin
Telephone: (514) 932-5093 Fax: (514) 932-1797
E-mail: doublehook@total.net

Language Arts Festival
257 Queen Street, Lennoxville, Québec J1M 2A5
Contact: P. Losier
Telephone: (819) 863-0770 Fax: (819) 835-5402

NEW BRUNSWICK

The Attic Owl Book Shop
885 Main Street, Moncton, New Brunswick E1C 1G5
Contact: Ed Lemond
Telephone: (506) 855-4913

Chapters Crystal Palace (Moncton)
499 rue Paul, Dieppe, New Brunswick E1A 6S5
Contact: Brigit Landry
Telephone: (506) 855-8075

Fredericton Public Library
12 Carleton Street, Fredericton, New Brunswick E3B 5P4
Telephone: (506) 460-2800

Friends Forever Bookstore
569A Main Street, Moncton, New Brunswick E1C 1C6
Telephone: (506) 389-2437

Gallery Connexion
Box 696 Stn A, Fredericton, New Brunswick E3B 5B4
Street Address: 453 Queen Street, Fredericton, New Brunswick
Contact: Sarah Maloney
Telephone: (506) 454 1433
E-mail: connex@nbnet.nb.ca
Website: www.culturenet.ca/connexion

Galerie Sans Nom
140 rue Botsford, Moncton, New Brunswick E1C 4X4
Telephone: (506) 854-5381 Fax: (506) 857-2064

Kingfisher Books
358 Queen, Fredericton, New Brunswick E3B 1B2
Contact: Eric Aubanel or Frances Giberson

Telephone: (506) 458-5531 Fax 458-5574
E-mail: kingfish@nbnet.nb.ca

Owens Art Gallery
Mount Allison University, English Department, Sackville, New Brunswick E4L 1A3
Telephone: (506) 364-2543

River Readings Series,
Box 596 Stn A, Fredericton, New Brunswick E3B 5A6.
Contact: Joe Blades
Telephone: (506) 454-5127
E-mail: jblades@nbnet.nb.ca

St. Thomas University, English Department
Box 4569, Fredericton, New Brunswick E3B 5G3
Telephone: (506) 452-0644 and/or Ron Byrne, Student Affairs Office (506) 452-0616
Fax (506) 450-9615
Website: www.stthomasu.ca

Sussex Regional Library
46 Magnolia Avenue, Sussex, New Brunswick E4E 2H2
Contact: Fennella Brewer
Telephone: (506) 432-4585

University of New Brunswick
Box 4400, Fredericton, New Brunswick E3B 5A3
Contact: Norm Ravvin (changes yearly), English Department Readings Coordinator
Telephone: (506) 453-4676 Fax: (506) 453-5069.
E-mail: nravvin@unb.ca

University of New Brunswick— Saint John
Box 5050, Saint John, New Brunswick E2L 4L5
Contact: Winnifred Bogaards
Telephone: (506) 648- 5603 Fax: (506) 648-5786.
E-mail: bogaards@unb.ca
Website: www.unb.ca

Westminster Books
445 King Street, Fredericton, New Brunswick E3B 1E5
Contact: Janet North
Telephone: (506) 454-1442.

NOVA SCOTIA

Acadia University Department of English
Contact: Gwen Davies
Telephone: (902) 585-1503

Annapolis Royal Community Arts Council
Contact: Susan Tileston
Telephone: (902) 532-7069

Chapters Bayers Lake
188 Chain Lake Dr, Halifax, Nova Scotia B3S 1C5
Telephone: (902) 450-1023

Dalhousie University Reading Series
Contact: Tina Usmiani
Telephone: (902) 494-3615

Eastern Counties Regional Library
Contact: Lorraine Fennell
Telephone: (902) 747-2597

Economy Shoe Shop
1663 Argyle Street, Halifax, Nova Scotia B3J 2B5
Coordinator: Terry Pulliam
Telephone: (902) 423-7463

Halifax City Regional Library's children's programming
Contact: Sara Brodie
Telephone: (902) 490-5887

Killam Library (MacMechan Hall)
Dalhousie University, Halifax, Nova Scotia
Telephone: (902) 429-9992

Oral Fixation Reading Series
Cafe Mokka, 1586 Granville St, Halifax, Nova Scotia B3J 1X1
Contact: Jamie Reynolds (902) 429-5396
Telephone: (902) 492-4036

Sun Room Series
St. Mary's University, Robie Street, Halifax, Nova Scotia B3H 3C3
Contact: Brian Bartlett
Telephone: (902) 420-0315
E-mail: bbartlet@shark.stmarys.ca

University College of Cape Breton
Contact: Dr. Richard Marchand
Telephone: (902) 563-1251

Windsor Children's Literature Roundtable
Contact: Jane Wamboldt
Telephone: (902) 757-1638

Word on the Street Halifax
1515 Park Street, Lord Nelson Hotel, Halifax, Nova Scotia B3J 2L2
Contact: Norene Smiley
Telephone: (902) 423-7399 Fax: (902) 423-4302
E-mail: wordhfx@istar.ca

NEWFOUNDLAND & LABRADOR

Labrador Creative Arts Festival
Box 342, Churchill Falls, Newfoundland A0R 1A0
Contact: Noreen Heighton
Telephone: (709) 925-3993 Fax: (709) 925-3488

Memorial University of Newfoundland
Sir Wilfred Grenfell College, University Drive, Corner Brook, Newfoundland A2H 6P9
Contact: John Steffler
Telephone: (709) 637-6214

Memorial University of Newfoundland
Department of English, St. John's, Newfoundland A1C 5S7
Contact: Jean Guthrie
Telephone: (709) 737-8646 Fax: (709) 737-4528

PRINCE EDWARD ISLAND

Milton Acorn Festival
115 Richmond Street #5, Charlottetown, Prince Edward Island C1A 1H7
Contact: Laurel Smyth
Telephone: (902) 894-8766 Fax: (902) 368-4418

The Winter's Tales Reading Series
Department of English, University of Prince Edward Island
Charlottetown, Prince Edward Island C1A 4P3
Contact: Richard Lemm
E-mail: rlemm@upei.ca

NORTHWEST TERRITORIES

Adult Basic Education and Literacy
Government of the Northwest Territories
Telephone: (867) 920-3482

Hay River Centennial Library
Telephone: (867) 874-6486

NWT Public Libraries Services
Telephone: (867) 874-6531

The NWT Literacy Council
Telephone: (867) 873-9262

The Yellowknife Book Cellar
Contact: Judith Drinnan
Telephone: (867) 920-2220

Yellowknife Public Library
Telephone: (867) 669-0884

NUNAVUT

Inuvik Centennial Library*
Telephone: (867) 777-2749

Iqlauit Centennial Library
Telephone (867) 979-5400

John Ayaruaq Library— Rankin Inlet
Telephone (867) 645-5034

Pond Inlet Community Library
Telephone (867) 899-8972

★There are 19 public libraries in the North West Territories and Nunavut.

YUKON

Whitehorse Public Library
Contact: Mairi MaCrae
E-mail: mairi.macrae@gov.yk.ca

SOS Second Opinion Society
708 Black Street, Whitehorse, Yukon V1A 2N8
Contact: Bruce Whittington
Telephone: (867) 667-2037

4.7 POETRY-FRIENDLY BOOKSTORES

Poetry-friendly bookstores are included here because they have made a commitment to support Canadian poets and their work. Many are reading venues and all maintain a thoughtfully selected stock of contemporary Canadian poetry and may be willing to support local poets by posting notices of new works.

BRITISH COLUMBIA

Black Sheep Books
2742 West 4th Avenue, Vancouver, British Columbia V6K 1R1
Contacts: George Koller & David Wah
Telephone: (604) 732-5087 or (604) 688-5985 Fax: (604) 737-7685
E-mail: blksheep@direct.ca

The Bookstore on Bastion Street
76 Bastion Street, Nanaimo, British Columbia V9R 3A1
Contact: T. Howell
Telephone: (250) 753-2023

Chapters
1212 Douglas Street, Victoria, British Columbia V8W 2E5
Contact: Tonja Joyce

Telephone: (250) 380-9009 Fax: (250) 380-9449
E-mail: tjoyce@pinc.com

Chapters Bookstore Inc.
1174-4700 Kingsway, Burnaby, British Columbia V5H 4M1
Contact: Eufemia Fantetti
Telephone: (604) 431-0463 Fax: (604) 431-0473
E-mail: scott@helix.net

East End Book Company
1470 Commercial Drive, Vancouver, British Columbia V5L 3X9
Contact: Jane McAslan
Telephone: (604) 251-5255 Fax: (604) 251-5660
E-mail: eastend@axionet.com

Hawthorne Bookstore
1027 Cook Street, Victoria, British Columbia V8V 3Z7
Contact: Horst Martin
Telephone: (250) 383-3215

Mosaic Books
1420 St. Paul Street, Kelowna, British Columbia V1Y 2E6
Contact: Susan Pettinger
Telephone: (250) 763-4418

Mosquito Books
1209-5th Avenue, Prince George, British Columbia V2L 3L3
Contact: George Sipos
Telephone: (250) 563-6495 Fax: (250) 563-8159
E-mail: mosquitobooks@mindlink.bc.ca

People's Co-op Bookstore
1391 Commercial Drive, Vancouver, British Columbia V5L 3X5
Contact: Ray Viaud
Telephone: (604) 253-6442

UBC Bookstore
6200 University Boulevard, Vancouver, British Columbia V6T 1Z4
Contact: Jennifer Pike
Telephone: (604) 822-2665 Fax: (604) 822-8592
E-mail: bstore@unixg.ubc.ca

Volume One Bookstore
149 Kenneth Street, Duncan, British Columbia V9L 1N5
Contact: Barb Johnson
Telephone: (250) 748-1533 Fax: (250) 748-6544

Whitby's Bookstore and Coffee House
14837 Marine Drive, White Rock, British Columbia V4B 1C1
Contact: Lynette Wilson
Telephone: (604) 536-3711

Women in Print Bookstore
3566 West 4th Avenue, Vancouver, British Columbia V6R 1N8
Contact: Dorothy Seaton
Telephone: (604) 732-4128 Fax: (604) 732-4129

Zebra Books
1095 Hornby Street, Vancouver, British Columbia V6Z 2R9
Contact: Sonya Wall
Telephone: (604) 331-0033 Fax: (604) 263-7467

ALBERTA

Audrey's Books Ltd.
10702 Jasper Avenue, Edmonton, Alberta T5J 3J5
Contact: Steve Budnarchuk
Telephone: (780) 423-3487 Fax: (780) 425-8446

B. Macabee's Booksellers
333-5th Street South, Lethbridge, Alberta T1J 2B4
Contact: Keith McArthur
Telephone: (403) 329-0771 Fax: (403) 328-5580

Books & Books
738a 17 Avenue SW, Calgary, Alberta T2S 0B7
Telephone: (403) 228-3337 Fax: (403) 262-3327

Orlando Books
10640 Whyte Avenue, Edmonton, Alberta T6E 2A7
Contact: Jacqueline Dumas
Telephone: (780) 432-7633 Fax: (780) 461-5440
E-mail: orlando@compusmart.ab.ca

Pages Books on Kensington
1135 Kensington Rd. NW, Calgary, Alberta TN2 3P4
Contact: Peter Oliva
Telephone: (403) 283-6655 Fax: (403) 283-6676
E-mail: pagesonk@cadvision.com

Socrates Corner Bookstore
315-555 Strathcona Blvd. SW, Calgary, Alberta T3H 2Z9
Contact: Lynda O'Connor
Telephone: (403) 242-8042 Fax: (403) 242-8373

University of Calgary Bookstore
2500 University Drive NW, Calgary, Alberta T2N 1N4
Contact: Colleen Reilly
Telephone: (403) 220-5170 Fax: (403) 284-4454
E-mail: creilly@aes.uclagary.ca

SASKATCHEWAN

Buzzword Books
2926B 13th Avenue, Regina, Saskatchewan S4T 1N8
Contact: Gordon Ames
Telephone: (306) 522-6562 Fax: (306) 522-6562

Saskatoon Book Store
148-2nd Avenue North, Saskatoon, Saskatchewan S7K 2B2
Contact: Beatrice Meili
Telephone: (306) 664-2572 Fax: (306) 665-5900

MANITOBA

McNally Robinson
1120 Grant Avenue, Winnipeg, Manitoba R3M 2A6
Contact: Holly McNally
Telephone: 1-800-561-1833 Fax: (204) 475-0325

QUÉBEC

Double Hook Bookshop
1235A Green Avenue, Montréal, Québec H3Z 2A4
Contact: Judith Mappin
Telephone: (514) 932-5093 Fax: (514) 932-1797
E-mail: doublehook@total.net

McGill University Bookstore
3420 McTavish, Montréal, Québec H3A 3L1
Contact: Kimberly Stephenson
Telephone: (514) 398-8352 Fax: (514) 398-7433

ONTARIO

Another Story Bookstore
164 Danforth Avenue, Toronto, Ontario M4K 1N1
Contact: S. Koffman

The Book Keeper
Northgate Plaza, 500 Exmouth Street, Sarnia, Ontario N7T 5P4
Contact: Kathy Mitchell
Telephone: (519) 337-3171

Books on the Bay
PO Box 803, 252 Main Street, Picton, Ontario K0K 2T0
Contact: David Sweet
Telephone: (613) 476-3037

Bookshelf Cafe
41 Québec Street, Guelph, Ontario N1H 2T1

Contact: Dan Evans
Telephone: (519) 821-3311
E-mail: dan@bookshelf.ca

The Book Store
120 Muskoka Road South, Gravenhurst, Ontario P1P 1V2
Contact: Bernice Murray
Telephone: (705) 687-0555 Fax: (705) 687-0555

Chapters
110 Bloor Street West, Toronto, Ontario M5S 2W7
Contact: Eric Jensen
Telephone: (416) 920-9299 Fax: (416) 920-0359

Chapters Bookstore
3175 Hwy 7, Markham, Ontario L3R 0J5
Contact: Randall Withell
Telephone: (905) 477-7217 Fax: (905) 477-1756

Chapters Oakville Town Centre
310 North Service Road West, Oakville, Ontario L6M 2R7
Contact: Sandra Neil
Telephone: (905) 815-8197 Fax: (905) 815-8204

For the Love of Books Bookstore
30 King Street, Welland, Ontario L3B 3H9
Contact: Marjory Mcpherson
Telephone: (905) 732-5742

Gulliver's Quality Books & Toys
147 Main Street West, North Bay, Ontario P1B 2T6
Contact: Suzanne Brooks
Telephone: (705) 474-7335 Fax: (705) 495-0449
E-mail: gulliver@cwconnec.ca

Indigo Books and Music
2-259 Princess Street, Kingston, Ontario K7L 1B4
Contact: Wayne Oakley
Telephone: (613) 546-4684
E-mail: ballan@indigo.ca

In the Know— A Self Discovery Emporium
901 King Street West, Hamilton, Ontario L8S 1K5
Contact: Mary or Deb
Telephone: (905) 529-3777 Fax: (905) 509-0571
E-mail: intheknow@kellkimms.com

Kent Bookstore Ltd.
32 Kent Street West, Lindsay, Ontario K9V 2Y1
Contact: Bill Jordan
Telephone: (705) 328-1600

mother tongue books/femmes de parole
1067 Bank Street, Ottawa, Ontario K1S 3W9
Contact: Evelyn Huer
Telephone: (613) 730-2346 Fax: (613) 730-2347

Northern Woman's Bookstore
65 South Court Street, Thunder Bay, Ontario P7B 2X2
Contact: Margaret Hillys
Telephone: (807) 344-7979

Pages Books and Magazines
256 Queen Street West, Toronto, Ontario M5V 1Z8
Contact: Mark Glassman
Telephone: (416) 598-1447 Fax: (416) 598-2042

South Shore Books
164 Pitt Street West, Windsor, Ontario N9A 5Z4

Tempest Books
235B Dalhousie Street South, Amherstburg, Ontario N9V 1W6
Contact: Sarah Jarvis
Telephone: (519) 736-8629 Fax: (519) 736-8620

This Ain't the Rosedale Library
483 Church Street, Toronto, Ontario M4Y 2C6
Telephone: (416) 929-9912

Toronto Women's Bookstore
73 Harbord, Toronto, Ontario M5S 1G4
Telephone: (416) 922-8744 Fax: (416) 922-1417

Toronto Women's Bookstore
248 Rhodes Avenue, Toronto, Ontario M4L 3A1
Contact: Kevin D'Souza
Telephone: (416) 778-7768

University of Toronto Bookstore
214 College Street, Toronto, Ontario M5T 3A1
Contact: Maylin Scott
Telephone: (416) 978-7908 Fax: (416) 978-7242

Writers & Company
2005 Yonge Street, Toronto, Ontario M4S 1Z8
Contact: Winston Smith
Telephone: (416) 481-8432

NEW BRUNSWICK

Kingfisher Books
358 Queen Street, Fredericton, New Brunswick E3B 1B2
Contact: Frances Giberson
Telephone: (506) 458-5531

Tidewater Books
4 Bridge Street, Sackville, New Brunswick E0A 3C0
Contact: Ellen K. Pickle
Telephone: (506) 536-0404 Fax: (506) 536-0881

University of New Brunswick Bookstore
PO Box 4400, Fredericton, New Brunswick E3B 5A3
Contact: Kim Richard
Telephone: (506) 453-4664 Fax: (506) 458-7001
E-mail: orders@sun.csd.unb.ca

NOVA SCOTIA

Frog Hollow Books
5640 Spring Garden Road, Halifax, Nova Scotia B3J 3M7
Contact: Mary Jo Anderson
Telephone: (902) 429-3318

PRINCE EDWARD ISLAND

The Reading Well
84 Great George Street, Charlottetown, Prince Edward Island C1A 4K4
Contact: Pam Martin
Telephone: (902) 566-2703 Fax: (902) 628-8437
E-mail: reji@isn.net

NEWFOUNDLAND

The Poet and Peasant Bookstore Cafe
165 Water St., St. John's, Newfoundland A1C 1B1
Contact: Steven Laird
Telephone: (709) 739-4600 Fax: (709) 739-4600
E-mail: poet.peasant@sympatico.ca

Wordplay
221 Duckworth St., St. John's, Newfoundland A1C 2C7
Contact: Jim Baird
Telephone: (709) 726-9193/800-563-9100 Fax: (709) 766-9190
E-mail: jbaird@wordplay.com

FIVE: RESOURCES FOR WRITERS

5.1 WRITERS' ASSOCIATIONS:

There is nothing better than the company of writers or the support they will give you. Joining a writers' association also offers a number of other benefits beyond a break from isolation. Most have a regular newsletter filled with market information, organization news and news of advocacy and government lobbying. Many offer workshops, retreats, mentoring opportunities, resource libraries, and active "Writers in the Schools" programs. They may help address grievances and offer opportunities for publication, and/or public readings.

Although the mandates of the many organizations which address the needs and concerns of Canadian writers differ to some extent, each one offers value to its members. The information listed below is general and meant to help you connect with organizations which may be of interest to you. Only national or provincial organizations have been listed. No attempt has been made to cover the large number of regional or municipal writers' groups.

NATIONAL

Canadian Authors Association
Box 419, Campbellford, Ontario K0L 1L0
Contact: Alec McEachern
Telephone: (705) 653-0323 Fax: (705) 653-0593
E-mail: canauth@redden.on.ca
Website: www.CanAuthors.org
Annual Fees: $115 + GST
Founded in 1921, the CAA works to "promote recognition of Canadian writers and their works, and to foster and develop a climate favourable to the creative arts." Writers Helping Writers is the motto. The association is primarily run by volunteers. There are active branches in Halifax, Montreal, Winnipeg, and Edmonton. In Ontario chapters can be found in Guelph, Hamilton, New Liskeard, Ottawa, Peterborough, Sarnia, St.Catharines/Thorold, and Toronto. In British Columbia there are branches in Kelowna, Vancouver and Victoria.

CAA publications include: *The Canadian Writer's Guide,*(Fitzhenry & Whiteside) and an online newsletter. (Print production of *Canadian Author* magazine has been suspended.)

The CAA offers or administers numerous literary awards for poetry, fiction, drama and non-fiction. The CAA also runs an annual Student Writing Contest.

Writers please note, "The Canadian Authors Association is a non-profit organization with a very limited staff and budget. Please do not send review copies of books, commercial and/or promotional e-mail or snail-mail messages to our office."

Canadian Poetry Association

PO Box 22571, St. George Postal Outlet, Toronto, Ontario M5S 1V0
Telephone: (905) 451-4528 or (416) 944-3985 Fax: (905) 312-8285
E-mail: writers@pathcom.com
Website: www.mirror.org/groups/cpa/index.html
Annual Fees: $30, $20 for seniors or students
Membership is open to all who have an interest in poetry.

The Canadian Poetry Association aims to "promote the reading, writing, publishing and preservation of poetry in Canada through the individual efforts of members; to promote communication among poets, publishers and the general public; to encourage leadership and participation from members and to encourage the formation and development of autonomous local chapters." CPA branches include: Maritimes, Moncton-New Brunswick, Hamilton, North York, Sarnia, London, Guelph, Parry Sound, and Metro Toronto.

CPA publications include: a national newsletter, *Poemata*; a series of chapbooks; and an anthology of members' work.

Canadian Society of Children's Authors, Illustrators and Performers/La Société Canadienne des Auteurs, Illustrateurs et Artistes Pour Enfants (CANSCAIP)

35 Spadina Road, Toronto, Ontario M5R 2S9
Telephone: (416) 515-1559 Fax: (416) 515-7022
E-mail: canscaip@interlog.com
Website: www.interlog.com/~canscaip
Annual Fees: $60 members, $25 friends

CANSCAIP supports creative work for children and young adults. Active participants in bringing literature and performance to schools and libraries. Full membership is available to writers and illustrators who have published in the field of children's literature.

CANSCAIP publications include: a quarterly newsletter featuring news, market information, and profiles of CANSCAIP members; *CANSCAIP Travels*, a listing of members available for workshops in children's literature, creative writing, storytelling, drawing, puppetry, clowning, mime, storytelling and drama; *The CANSCAIP Companion*, a biographical record of more than 350 CANSCAIP members; *Presenting Children's Authors, Illustrators and Performers*, profiles of the creative life; and *Behind The Story*, 22 profiles of other well-known children's authors, illustrators and performers. Titles available through Pembroke Press.

CANSCAIP's "Packaging Your Imagination" conference is held in Toronto every October.

Editors' Association of Canada

National Office, 35 Spadina Road, Toronto, Ontario M5R 2S9
Telephone: (416) 975-1379 Fax: (416) 975-1839
E-mail: eacinfo@web.net
Website: www.web.net/eac-acr
Annual Fees: $140 + GST, $95 + GST students

EAC members are both English-language and French-language editors whose experience ranges from proofreaders to copy editors, researchers to production editors, to substantive editors and desktop publishers. The goal of each member is to aid effective communication.

EAC branches are found in British Columbia, Prairie Provinces, Toronto, National

Capital Region, and Quebec/Atlantic Canada. The EAC Annual General Meeting focuses on professional development.

EAC publications include: a national newsletter for members, *Active Voice/La Voix Active*; separate branch newsletters; *EAC Directory of Editors*; *Répertoire des rédacteurs-réviseurs de l'ACR*; *Editing Canadian English*; *Meeting Editorial Standards*; *Professional Editorial Standards*; *So, You Want to Be an Editor*, and *La profession de rédacteur-réviseur vous intéresse?*

Each branch offers a hotline telephone service to put clients anywhere in Canada in touch with available editors.

EAC presents the Tom Fairley Award for Editorial Excellence in recognition of an outstanding contribution by an editor to a work published in Canada.

P.E.N. International Canadian Centre
24 Ryerson Avenue, Suite 309, Toronto, Ontario M5T 2P3
E-mail: pencan@web.net
Website: www.pencanada.ca
Annual Fees: $60

The French-speaking Centre québécois du P.E.N. is in Montréal. The two Canadian P.E.N. centres work collaboratively "on behalf of writers, at home and abroad, who have been forced into silence for writing the truth as they see it." P.E.N. also challenges legislation which violates the right to freedom of expression guaranteed in the Canadian Charter of Rights and Freedoms, protests book bannings, book seizures and censorship.

P.E.N. publications include: *Writing Home: A PEN Canada Anthology*; *Writing Away: The PEN Canada Travel Anthology*; *This Prison Where I Live— The PEN Anthology of Imprisoned Writers*; and *Freedom of Expression in the Muslim World: A Comparative Legal Study of Blasphemy and Subversive Speech in International Human Rights Law and the Laws of the Muslim World*.

The League of Canadian Poets
54 Wolseley Street, Suite 204, Toronto, Ontario M5T 1A5
Contact: Edita Petrauskaite, Executive Director
Telephone: (416) 504-1657 Fax: (416) 504-0096
E-mail: league@ican.net
Website: www.poets.ca
Annual Fees: $175 full member, $60 associate member, $25 student

The League of Canadian Poets (LCP) is a Registered National Arts Service Organization, recognized by all levels of government, and receiving government funding. It is the national voice for Canadian poets.

The LCP supports the activities of all Canadian poets through its efforts to raise the profile of Canadian poetry both at home and internationally. A detailed description of League programs appears at the beginning of this book.

LCP publications include: a national newsletter; *Poetry Spoken Here*, a monthly list of readings; *Poetry Markets for Canadians*; *Who's Who in the League of Canadian Poets*; *Poets in the Classroom*; the annual anthology, *Vintage*; the *Living Archive Series* of chapbooks; and *Siolence*, an anthology of Feminist Caucus papers presented at the LCP Annual General Meetings. All may be ordered from the LCP by mail or online.

An extensive library of books, recordings, periodicals, and biographical material can be accessed at the LCP offices.

Periodical Writers Association of Canada

54 Wolseley Street, Toronto, Ontario M5T 1A5

Telephone: (416) 504-1645 Fax: (416) 703-0059

E-mail: pwac@web.net

Website: www.web.net/~pwac

Fees: Range from $170-$195 (+GST) depending on region

PWAC promotes "the craft and livelihood of independent periodical writers."

PWAC has chapters in Victoria, Vancouver, B.C. Interior, Edmonton, Calgary, Winnipeg, London, Niagara Escarpment, Toronto, Kingston, Ottawa, Montreal, Southeastern New Brunswick and Halifax, as well as members in all regions of Canada with no chapter affiliation.

PWAC publications include: a national newsletter, *PWAContact*; separate chapter newsletters; an annual *Directory of Members*; *Copyright Information Kit*; *Freelance Writers in Canada*; and the writing guide, *Words for Sale*.

Playwrights' Union of Canada

54 Wolseley Street, 2nd Floor, Toronto, Ontario M5T 1A5

Telephone: (416) 703-0201 Fax: (416) 703-0059

Contact: Angela Rebeiro, Executive Director

E-mail: cdplays@interlog.com

Website: www.puc.ca

Annual Fees: $135+GST full member, $65+GST associate member

"The most significant service PUC provides for its full members is making their plays available as copyscripts to professional and community theatres, schools and interested members of the public."

The PUC Annual General Meeting focuses on professional development. Held in Toronto every second year.

PUC publications include: *The PUC Contracts Handbook*; *Contract Forms*; and *Theatre for Young Audiences*.

PUC offers a contract negotiation service, acts as agent for amateur productions, and handles the marketing and selling of copyscripts in addition to running a Canada Council readings program and the Ontario Playwrights in the Schools program.

PUC also runs an annual Monologue Competition. The winner and ten finalists are published in the PUC Playscript series.

The Writers' Union of Canada

24 Ryerson Avenue, Toronto, Ontario M5T 2P3

Telephone: (416) 703-8982 Fax: (416) 703-0826

Contact: Penny Dickens, Executive Director

E-mail: twuc@the-wire.com

Website: www.swifty.com/twuc

Annual Fees: $180

The Writers' Union of Canada is a national organization of Canadian writers who have published in full-length trade book form. TWUC offers many excellent low-cost publications on publishing and the publishing industry in Canada.

TWUC also offers contract evaluation service for writers considering publishing contracts ($300+GST) or agent contracts ($150+GST). A contract negotiation service is also available ($500+GST). Details available online or contact the TWUC offices.

PROVINCIAL WRITERS' ASSOCIATIONS

Writers' Guild of Alberta

3rd Floor, Percy Page Centre, 11759 Groat Road, Edmonton, Alberta T5M 3K6

Telephone: (780) 422-8174 or 1-800-665-5354 Fax: (780) 422-2663

Contact: Miki Andrejevic, Executive Director

E-mail: wga@oanet.com

Website: www.writersguild.ab.ca

Annual Fees: $60 regular member, $20 student or senior

Holds a number of annual writing competitions to recognize excellence in writing by Alberta authors.

Sponsors writer-in-residence program.

Has support offices in Calgary and Red Deer.

The Federation of British Columbia Writers

1200 West 73rd Avenue, Suite 1100, Vancouver, British Columbia V6P 6G5

Telephone: (604) 267-7087 Fax: (604) 267-7086

E-mail: fedbcwrt@pinc.com

Website: www.swifty.com/bcwa/index.html

Annual Fees: $60+GST, $30+GST for those with limited incomes

"The Federation is the voice of writers in BC— supporting, developing, and educating writers; and fostering a community for writing throughout the province."

Membership is open to professional and emerging writers, in any genre.

The FBCW co-sponsors the annual Surrey Writers Conference, and Write Out Loud at the Vancouver International Writers (and Readers) Festival.

Offers publicly accessible online membership skills database.

Their annual writing competition in short fiction is open to British Columbia writers and residents.

Manitoba Writers' Guild Inc.

206-100 Arthur Street, Winnipeg, Manitoba R3B 1H3

Telephone: (204) 947-3168 Fax: (204) 942-5754

E-mail: mbwriter@escape.ca

Website: www.mbwriter.mb.ca

Annual Fees: $40 regular membership, $20 student, senior or fixed income

A subscription to *Prairie Fire* magazine is included in membership.

"The primary aim of the Manitoba Writers' Guild is to promote and advance the art of writing, in all its forms, throughout the province of Manitoba."

The Manitoba Literary Awards Committee of the Manitoba Writers' Guild coordinates two literary awards, The McNally Robinson Book of the Year Award and The McNally Robinson Young Adult/Children's Book of the Year Award which are presented annually to Manitoba authors.

Promotes workshops, professional development meetings, Emerging Writers' Mentor Program, Café Reading Series, Audience Development Project and the Annual Conference/Annual General Meeting.

Publications include: *The Writers' Handbook*, a manual on the business of writing; and *Westwords*, the MWG newsletter.

The Writers' Federation of New Brunswick

PO Box 37, Station A, Fredericton, New Brunswick E3B 4Y2

Telephone: (506) 459-7228

E-mail: aa821@fan.nb.ca

Website: 198.164.223.2/Community_Hall/w/Writers_Federation_NB/index.html

Annual Fees: $30 per year, $20 for students or unwaged

"The Writers' Federation of New Brunswick is a non-profit organization which represents writers in all disciplines and at all levels of development. Membership in the Writers' Federation of New Brunswick is open to anyone with an interest in writers or writing in this province."

Runs annual literary competitions: Alfred G. Bailey Prize for Poetry; Richards Prize for Prose Fiction; and the Sheree Fitch Prize for Writing by Young People.

Writers' Alliance of Newfoundland & Labrador

PO Box 2681, St. John's, Newfoundland A1C 5M5

Telephone: (709) 739-5215 Fax: (709) 739-5215

E-mail Address: wanl@nfld.com

The Writers' Alliance of Newfoundland and Labrador (WANL) is a not-for-profit organization which works to serve the needs of writers in the province. Membership is open to all with an interest in writing.

Hosts monthly open readings and occasional workshops. Annual General Meeting is focused on professional development.

Publications include: Adult Basic Literacy publications, produced in cooperation with Cabot College; *Writers' Alliance Freelance Brochure*; *Writers on Tour* listing booklet; a newsletter, *WORD*; and *A Resource for Writers* manual.

Writers' Federation of Nova Scotia

Suite 901, 1809 Barrington Street, Halifax, Nova Scotia B3J 3K8

Telephone: (902) 423-8116

Annual Fees: $35, $15 for students

Runs the Atlantic Writing Competition as well as presenting three awards for published work. The Atlantic Poetry Prize is for the best book of poetry by an Atlantic Canadian; the Evelyn Richardson Non-fiction Prize is for the best non-fiction book by a Nova Scotian; the Thomas Raddall Atlantic Fiction Prize is for the best work of fiction by an Atlantic Canadian.

Annual General Meeting in May includes Writes of Spring festival. The WFNS also participates in Write of Way in Cape Breton and The Word on the Street in Halifax.

Ottawa Independent Writers/Les Écrivains Indépendents D'Ottawa

PO Box 23137, Ottawa, Ontario K2A 4E2

Telephone: (613) 841-0572

E-mail: oiw@storm.ca

Website: www.storm.ca/~oiw/news.shtml

Annual fees: $60, $30 students and seniors

"OIW focus is on the 'business' of writing and networking."

Has monthly meetings and runs occasional in-depth seminars on some aspect of the writing business.

Publications include: *OIW Internet Directory*; and a bi-monthly newsletter.

P.E.I. Writers' Guild

PO Box 2234, Charlottetown, Prince Edward Island C1A 8B9

Telephone: (902) 894 9933 Fax: (902) 961 2797

Island Writers Association (P.E.I.)

PO Box 1204, Charlottetown, Prince Edward Island C1A 7M8

Telephone: (902) 566 9748 Fax: (902) 566 9748

E-mail: creative@peinet.pe.ca

Québec Writers Federation

1200 Atwater Avenue, Montréal, Québec H3Z 1X4

Telephone: (514) 933-0878 Fax: (514) 933-0878

E-mail: qspell@total.net

Website: www.qspell.org

Two well-established organizations, The Québec Society for the Promotion of English Language Literature, and the Federation of English-language Writers, joined together in 1998 to form the Québec Writers Federation.

Saskatchewan Writers' Guild

PO Box 3986, Regina, Saskatchewan S4P 3R9

Telephone: (306) 757-6310 Fax: (306) 565-8554

E-mail: swg@sk.sympatico.ca

Website: www.skwriter.com/swghome.html

Annual fees: $50, $30 for students and seniors

"The Guild's mission is to improve the status of the writer in Saskatchewan." The Guild is the umbrella organization for several arms-length groups, including: The Saskatchewan Playwrights Centre; *Grain Magazine*; and Saskatchewan Artists/Writers Colonies.

Membership is open to Saskatchewan writers, and those interested in Saskatchewan writers and writing.

Publications include: *FreeLance*, the monthly newsmagazine of the SWG; *Saskatchewan Literary Arts Handbook*; *Saskatchewan Writes!*, a learning resource guide for educators and students; and *Saskatchewan Writers Exchange*.

The SWG hosts the Signature Reading Series (Regina); City Nights Reading Series (Regina); and the Speakeasy Reading Series (Saskatoon).

Each year the SWG presents literary awards in four categories: fiction, poetry, non-fiction, and children's literature. Their annual book-length manuscript competition rotates between fiction, poetry, non-fiction and drama. The SWG administers the City of Regina Writing Award and other awards.

The SWG offers an electronic residency program for students via the WindScript website and offers correspondence courses in a range of writing genres.

WRITERS' ORGANIZATIONS OUTSIDE CANADA

AUSTRALIA

Australia's Cultural Network
www.acn.net.au

Ozlit
www.home.vicnet.au/~ozlit/index.html

ENGLAND

The Copyright Licensing Agency
90 Tottenham Court Road, London, England WIP 0LP

The Poetry Society
22 Betterton Street, London, England WC2H 9BU
www.poetrysoc.com

The Society of Authors
84 Drayton Gardens, London, England SW10 9SB
www.thebiz.co.uk/socauth.htm

Trace International Online Writing Community
www.trace.ntu.ac.uk

US

The Academy of American Poets
548 Broadway, Suite 1208, New York, New York, USA 10012-3250
www.poets.org

The Authors' Guild
330 West 42nd Street, New York, New York, USA 10036
www.authorsguild.org

The Haiku Society of America
PO Box 1179, New York, New York 10013
www.octet.com/~hsa/member.html

Poetry Society of America
www.bookwire.com/psa/psa.html

Poets & Writers (and The Poet's House)
72 Spring Street, New York, New York, USA 10012
www.pw.org

5.2 POETRY GROUPS, WORKSHOPS AND COURSES

There is some irony in working hard to rid yourself of your inner editor, only to turn around and offer your work for public comment. Listening to feedback can help you grow as a writer and improve your chances of being published. Even the best-known poets in Canada seek the counsel of peers.

POETRY GROUPS

Poetry groups are usually small. There may be as few as three members who meet regularly in an informal setting like a home or coffee shop. Many groups develop spontaneously among friends; others, like those run by the University Womens' Club, are offshoots of organizations.

What follows are guidelines for what you might expect in a poetry group. Keep in mind each group develops its own dynamics and methods of operation.

At the beginning of the meeting, copies of members' poems are distributed. In some groups, someone other than the author reads the poem aloud followed by a reading by the author. Members listen for hiccups in the language, those hesitations and mispronunciations which can signal a difficulty in the piece. Of course, they will also have an ear for its content, patterns and themes. The essence of a poetry group is constructive criticism.

It is often difficult to separate yourself from the work on the page but you must. Your poem may have been inspired by events known to you but should not be a rigid embodiment of them. Members may suggest you strike full lines or even whole stanzas. Cliches will be pointed out and lazy phrasing dissected. Be grateful for the help while also listening to your intuitive self. The result will be a stronger poem written with a surer hand.

POETRY WORKSHOPS: WHAT TO EXPECT

Poetry workshops offer an excellent opportunity to work with the best writers in Canada. Workshops are often a part of writers' festivals or offered through the continuing education departments of colleges or universities. Most workshop courses are held evenings once a week for eight to twelve weeks, or intensively over a weekend. You may be asked to submit a sample of your work in advance but most offer open registration. There is almost always a low student-teacher ratio.

Poetry workshops are not for people looking for effusive praise. Your work will be critiqued by a group of perhaps 15 or more people. Like you, they are there to take a serious step forward with their writing. This should not intimidate you. It can be an extraordinary pleasure to be in the company of other writers.

Reading aloud to the group may be your first chance to do a "public reading," and can help you prepare for doing "real" readings in the future. Grab the opportunity.

Workshop facilitators often use writing exercises to get members writing. You may find that you cannot connect with assigned writing exercises, or that you do not want to work within a form. You may prefer to simply write what you wish and bring it to the group. Resistance is not unusual but you should allow yourself to explore the assigned exercise. It may bring surprising benefits. A sestina, for instance, may force you to invent new word combinations to meet the requirements of the form.

Your workshop may include an opportunity to have a one-on-one meeting with your workshop facilitator. Be prepared for this meeting. Select a number of your poems to discuss and prepare any questions you might have in advance.

WRITING COURSES AND CREATIVE WRITING DEGREES: THE FULL COMMITMENT

The number of poetry writing courses offered at the post-secondary level is small. At universities, budget restraints mean poetry workshop courses are often available only to Creative Writing majors. However, every school offers courses which cover poetry of a particular period or region, as well as many other English courses. Take a few minutes to explore the options open to you in your area. Even if you lack a post-secondary institution in or near your community, quality distance education courses or mentorships are offered by mail or online.

Writers-in-residence work under contract to universities, colleges, libraries and so on. They often work with the general public and their availability is worth investigating. These positions change each year, so they are not listed below.

Some writers offer independent workshops. You will find these mavericks if you network with your local writing community, contact an arts council, or check libraries and bookshops for notices of upcoming events. Other writers, like Naomi Waken, author of, *Haiku— one breath poetry*, can be found on the internet (www.islandnet.com/~prp/prp-new.htm).

If you are interested in earning a degree in Creative Writing check the Association of Universities and Colleges website at www.uacc.ca to update the list below. It offers an excellent searchable database plus links to post-secondary institutions across Canada. It is important to check the individual programs offered as most include a wide variety of creative writing classes but few focus exclusively on poetry.

The list below is broad but not comprehensive.

SOME OF CANADA'S POETRY WORKSHOPS

Banff Centre for the Arts

PO Box 1020, Station 28, 107 Tunnel Mountain Drive, Banff, Alberta T0L 0C0
Telephone: (403) 762-6180 or 1-800-565-9989 Fax: (403) 762-6345
Contact: Lorraine Schindel
E-mail: arts_info@banffcentre.ab.ca
Website: www.banffcentre.ab.ca/writing/index.html
Has several writing programs designed for writers with manuscripts in progress.

Festival of Words

88 Saskatchewan Street East, Moose Jaw, Saskatchewan S6H 0V4
Telephone: (306) 691-0557 Fax: (306) 693-2994
E-mail: word.festival@sk.sympatico.ca
Website: www3.sk.sympatico.ca/praifew
Holds a variety of writers' events and workshops. Holds separate Youth Writing Camps each August, in conjunction with the Sage Hill Writing Experience, for Saskatchewan writers 14–18 years old.

The Humber School for Writers

Humber College, Room D149, 205 Humber College Boulevard, Toronto, Ontario M9W 5L7
Telephone: (416) 675-6622 ext.4436 Fax: (416) 675-1249
Contact: Joe Kertes
E-mail: kertes@admin.humber.on.ca
Website: www.humberc.on.ca/~writers
Humber College offers an on-site week-long intensive writing workshop every summer as well as a distance education creative writing program. Both bring students in contact with top Canadian writers. Distance education students are matched with mentors who work with them to develop a completed manuscript. More than fifty students have gone on to publish their work with Canadian publishing houses. Query for application and scholarship information.

Kootenay School of the Arts

Cooperative Centre of Craft and Design, 606 Victoria Street, Nelson, British Columbia V1L 4K9
Telephone: (250) 352-2821 Fax: (250) 352-1625
E-mail: ksa@netidea.com
As part of the Kootenay School of the Arts' Writing Studio students can develop skills in poetry, scripts, fiction and/or creative non-fiction. Courses are offered at three levels, Introductory (Year I), Intermediate(Year II) and Advanced (Year III). Advanced students have the opportunity to work on their manuscripts with selected Canadian authors via the internet.

Kootenay School of Writing

112 West Hastings Street, Suite 401, Vancouver, British Columbia V6B 1G8
Telephone: (604) 688-6001
E-mail: geschwitz@intergate.bc.ca
Website: www.intergate.bc.ca/personal/geschwitz/index.html
Offers many creative writing workshops each summer in various disciplines. Low cost opportunity to attend book launches and readings, and take advantage of their writer-in-residence program.

Manitoba Writers' Guild Open Workshops

206-100 Arthur Street, Winnipeg, Manitoba R3B 1H3

Telephone: (204) 947-3168 Fax: (204) 942-5754

E-mail: mbwriter@escape.ca

Website: www.mbwriter.mb.ca

Variety of workshops offered through the year. Contact the Guild for details.

Maritime Writers' Workshop

Summer Session Department, University of New Brunswick, PO Box 4400, Fredericton, New Brunswick E3B 5A3

Telephone: (506) 454-9153 Fax: (506) 453-3572

Contact: Glenda Turner

E-mail: extensin@unb.ca

Website: www.unb.ca/web/coned/writers/marritrs.html

Runs week-long intensive writing programs each summer in many disciplines. Query for application and scholarship information.

Metchosin International Summer School of the Arts

Pearson College, 650 Pearson College Drive, Victoria, British Columbia V9C 4H7

Telephone: (250) 391-2420 Fax: (250) 391-2412

Contact: Meira Mathison

E-mail: missa@pearson-college.uwc.ca

Website: www.pearson-college.uwc.ca/pearson/summer/missa/missa.htm

Offers week-long intensive writing workshops each summer with award-winning authors. Beautiful setting. Recommends students stay in residences on site.

{m}Öthêr Tøñgué Press

290 Fulford-Ganges Road, Salt Spring Island, British Columbia V8K 2K6

Telephone: (250) 537-4155 Fax: (250) 537-4725

Contact: Mona Fertig

E-mail: mothertongue@saltspring.com

Website: www.saltspring.com/art/mothertongue.htm

Offers one- and two-day writing workshops.

Sage Hill Writing Experience

PO Box 1731, Saskatoon, Saskatchewan S7K 3S1

Telephone: (306) 652-7395

Contact: Steven Smith

E-mail: sage.hill@sk.sympatico.ca

Website: www.lights.com/sagehill

Has a variety of programs for writers of varying experience. Query for application and scholarship information.

Saltwater Writers' Workshops

RR#2, Sable River, Nova Scotia B0T 1V0

Telephone: (902) 656-3236

Contact: Kim Atwood or Kathleen Tudor

Three-day workshops open to 10 writers of fiction, literary non-fiction and poetry.

Saskatchewan Writers/Artists Colonies & Retreats

c/o PO Box 3986, Regina, Saskatchewan S4P 3R9

Telephone: (306) 757-6310 Fax: (306) 565-8554

Website: www.skwriter.com/colonies.html

Quiet time to work uninterrupted. Numerous variations on the classic writer's retreat. Query for details of their summer writers' colony or year-round individual retreats.

Sechelt Writer-in-Residence Programs

PO Box 2299, Sechelt, British Columbia V0N 3A0

Telephone: (604) 885-9631 or 1-800-565-9631 Fax: (604) 885-3967

E-mail: written_arts@sunshine.net

Workshops are led by experienced writers. Concurrent with the Sunshine Coast Festival of the Written Arts.

Surrey Writers' Conference

c/o Principal, Newton Continuing Education Centre, 12870-72nd Avenue, Surrey, British Columbia V3W 2M9

Telephone: (604) 594-2000 or July & August (604) 583-4040 Fax: (604) 590-2506 or in July & August (604) 583-5600

Website: www.vcn.bc.ca/swc

Three full days of workshops for both new and established writers. Includes opportunities to meet with editors and agents one-on-one.

Toronto Writing Workshop

PO Box 508, 264 Queen's Quay West, Toronto, Ontario M5J 1B5

Telephone: (416) 260-6621

Contact: Libby Scheier

An ongoing series of eight-week writers' workshops.

University of Toronto Creative Writing Program

School of Continuing Studies, University of Toronto, 158 St. George Street, Toronto, Ontario M5S 2V8

Telephone: (416) 978-0765 Fax: (416) 978-6666

Contact: Bruce Meyer

E-mail: bruce.meyer@utoronto.ca

Offers a variety of workshops and non-credit courses in various disciplines. Chance to work with a mentor toward completing full-length manuscript. One-day workshops also available dealing with various genres.

University of Toronto International Summer Writers' Workshop

Creative Writing Program, School of Continuing Studies, University of Toronto, 158 St. George Street, Toronto, Ontario M5S 2V8

Telephone: (416) 978-0765 Fax: (416) 978-6666

Contact: Bruce Meyer

E-mail: bruce.meyer@utoronto.ca

Courses change each year but are generally held the third week of July. Complicated fee structure. Contact school for details.

Victoria School of Writing

PO Box 8152, Victoria, British Columbia V8W 3R8
Telephone: (250) 598-5300 Fax: (250) 598-0066
Contact: Margaret Dyment
E-mail: writeawy@islandnet.com
Website: www.islandnet.com/vicwrite
Four days of writers' workshops in a variety of disciplines. Workshops are wheelchair accessible. Meals and accommodation are available onsite.

The Writing School

38 McArthur Avenue, Suite 2951, Ottawa, Ontario K1L 6R2
Telephone 1-800-267-1829 Fax: (613) 749-9551
Contact: Alex Myers
E-mail: writers@qualityofcourse.com
Website: www.qualityofcourse.com
Correspondence courses for beginners to more experienced writers.

Writers' Federation of Nova Scotia Occasional Workshop Series

Suite 901, 1809 Barrington Street, Halifax, Nova Scotia B3J 3K8
Telephone: (902) 423-8116 Fax: (902) 422-0881
E-mail: writers1@fox.nstn.ca
Website: www.chebucto.ns.ca/Culture/WFNS/workshops.html
Imaginative series of workshops covering a wide variety of topics.

CANADIAN POST-SECONDARY CREDIT COURSES AND DEGREE PROGRAMS

Concordia University

Admissions Application Centre, PO Box 2900, Montréal, Québec H3G 2S2
Website: www.concordia.ca
BA in English and Creative Writing

George Brown College

PO Box 1015, Station B, Toronto, Ontario M5T 2T9
Telephone: (416) 415-2092
Contact: Peggy Needham
Website: www.gbrownc.on.ca/GBCWEB/Marketing/conedfw/communic.html#creativewriting
Certificates offered in Creative Writing, Editing and Business Writing.

Malaspina University College Creative Writing Program

900 Fifth Street, Nanaimo, British Columbia V9R 5S5
Telephone: (250) 753-3245
Website: www.mala.bc.ca/www/crwrit/index.htm
BA, Minor in Creative Writing; BA, Liberal Studies with concentration in Creative Writing; B.Ed, BA, Concurrent Degree with Creative Writing as a Field.

York University

York Admissions Enquiry Service, 150 Atkinson College Building, 4700 Keele Street, Toronto, Ontario M3J 1P3
Telephone: (416) 736-5000
BA in Creative Writing; Certificate in Technical and Professional Writing.

University of Alberta
Office of the Registrar and Student Awards, University of Alberta, Edmonton, Alberta T6G 2M7
Telephone: (780) 492-3113
E-mail: registrar@ualberta.ca
Website: www.ualberta.ca
BA in Creative Writing.

The University of Calgary
Admissions Office, MacKimmie Library Block Room 117, University of Calgary, Calgary, Alberta T2N 1N4
Telephone: (403) 220-6645 Fax: (403) 289-1253
E-mail: applinfo@acs.ucalgary.ca
Website: www.ucalgary.ca
MA in English with Creative Writing option; PhD in English with Creative Writing option

The University of British Columbia
Undergraduate Admissions, Registrar's Office, 2016-1874 East Mall, Vancouver, British Columbia V6T 1Z1
Telephone: (604) 822-3014 Fax: (604) 822-3599
E-mail: registrar.admissions@ubc.ca
Website: www.student-services.ubc.ca/admiss
Diploma in Applied Creative Non-fiction; BFA in Creative Writing; MFA in Creative Writing.

University of Victoria
PO Box 1700, Station CSC, Victoria, British Columbia V8W 2Y2
Telephone: (250) 721-7306 Creative Writing Department
E-mail: jphillip@finearts.uvic.ca
Website: www.web.uvic.ca
Bachelor of Fine Arts in Writing; Postgraduate Diploma in Writing and Editing.

University of New Brunswick
Saint John Campus, PO Box 5050, Saint John, New Brunswick E2L 4L5
Telephone: (506)648-5695 Fax: (506)648-5528
E-mail: sjreg@unb. ca
Website: www.unb.ca
BA in Creative Writing; MA in Creative Writing.

University of PEI
550 University Avenue, Charlottetown, Prince Edward Island C1A 4P3
Telephone: (902) 566-0300
Website: www.upei.ca/~english/creative.html
Variety of creative writing courses offered on a semester basis.

University of Waterloo
200 University Avenue West, Waterloo, Ontario N2L 3G1
Telephone: (519) 885-1211 Fax (519) 884-8009
E-mail: registrar@nh1adm.uwaterloo.ca
Website: www.uwaterloo.ca
BA in Rhetoric and Professional Writing.

University of Windsor

401 Sunset Avenue, Windsor, Ontario N9B 3P4

Telephone: (519) 253-3000 Fax: (519) 973-7050

E-mail: registr@uwindsor.ca

Website: www.uwindsor.ca

BA in English Literature and Creative Writing.

5.3 BUILDING YOUR WRITER'S BOOKSHELF

There are basic resources every writer should have: an excellent dictionary, thesaurus and style manual. Don't make do with the old paperback dictionary you had in high school; take some time to look through a variety of more comprehensive dictionaries and then treat yourself to the one that suits you best. Do the same for a high-quality thesaurus. For a style manual, there's nothing better than *The Chicago Manual of Style*, although it offers only American spelling and usage.

Remember, there is no need to spend hundreds of dollars on other reference books you may only refer to occasionally. Take advantage of the selection offered by your local library system. There, you'll find books like *Literary Market Place*, an annually updated directory of the American publishing industry.

There are a variety of market guides for you to consider. Some focus on poetry markets, some on photography, and others on writing for children, etc. Some are better than others. As a Canadian writer, I tend to use market guides designed to highlight Canadian markets. However, I also use market guides and books published by Writer's Digest because they cover much of the mainstream American market. Smaller publishing companies may offer regional market guides.

Opinions vary widely regarding the benefits of using reference books available on CD-ROM or through special online services. Before subscribing to either, think about how you will use these services in your day-to-day work. How long will it take you to find the information you need compared to using a print version of the same resource?

Writers often use motivational resources; the response to such books is so deeply personal that recommending any here is a difficult task. However, I have named four.

The Artist's Way

Julia Cameron

Almost always found in bookstores beside titles on painting, this book belongs in the writers' aisle. It includes twelve weeks of exercises to help free your creative self. Take as long as you want to read through the book, and revisit the exercises. Twelve weeks is an optional structure.

Be Your Own Literary Agent: The Ultimate Insider's Guide to Getting Published
Martin P. Levin
Ten Speed Press, PO Box 7123, Berkeley, California, USA 94707
Though not targeted toward poets, from the section which deals with the hierarchy of a publishing company to the detailed description of contract intricacies, there's something to be learned here by any writer.

Canadian Guide to English Usage
Margery Fee & Janice McAlpine, Editors
Oxford University Press
www.oupcan.com

Canadian Oxford Dictionary
Katherine Barber, Editor-In-Chief
Oxford University Press
www.oupcan.com/CANOD/About/Index.html

The Canadian Writers' Contest Calendar
James Deahl, Editor
Mekler & Deahl, Publishers, 237 Prospect Street South, Hamilton, Ontario L8M 2Z6
An expanded format has been introduced for the Canadian Writers' Contest Calendar by new owners, Mekler & Deahl, Publishers. Includes more than 300 Canadian contests, prizes and awards arranged in deadline order through the year.

The Canadian Writer's Guide
Murphy O. Shewchuk, Managing Editor
Fitzhenry & Whiteside, 195 Allstate Parkway, Markham, Ontario L3R 4T8
Incredible value. More than 400 pages of short articles dealing with every aspect of publishing. Includes a broad sampling of Canadian markets.

The Canadian Writer's Market
Jem Bates, Editor
McClelland & Stewart, 481 University Avenue, Toronto, Ontario M5G 2E9
Long a staple for Canadian writers, it has a good copyright section and almost 300 pages of diverse Canadian markets including newspapers, consumer magazines and trade book publishers.

Chicago Manual of Style, 14th edition
University of Chicago Press
www.press.uchicago.edu/cgi-bin/hfs.cgi/00/12245.ctl
Not quite sure how to use dashes, commas, or semi-colons? This book is an essential reference guide for any writer. The most recent edition has 981 pages addressing everything from abbreviations to zip codes.

Creating Poetry
John Drury
Writer's Digest Books, 1507 Dana Avenue, Cincinnati, Ohio, USA 45207
www.writersdigest.com
An excellent introduction to poetry and poetics; includes more than 50 writing exercises to reinforce your understanding of what you've read.

Digital Property: Currency of the 21st Century

Lesley Ellen Harris
McGraw-Hill Ryerson, 300 Water Street, Whitby, Ontario L1N 9B6
www.copyrightlaws.com

A down-to-earth examination of copyright and the internet by a Canadian copyright and new media lawyer. Also authored *Canadian Copyright Law*.

Directory of Literary Magazines

Poets & Writers Inc., 72 Spring Street, New York, New York, USA 10012

Published by the Council of Literary Magazines and Presses. The listings are arranged in an awkward fashion but contain some good information and lesser-known markets.

Directory of Poetry Publishers

Len Fulton, Editor
Dustbooks, PO Box 100, Paradise, California, USA 95967

A fat book of address listings ranging from the obscure to the preeminent of literary magazines.

A Handbook to Literature

William Harmon and C. Hugh Holman
Prentice Hall, Upper Saddle River, New Jersey, USA 07458
www.prenticehall.ca/allbooks/hss-0132347822.html

For any writer interested in literary criticism. Over 500 pages with definitions of literary terms, many with interesting contextual examples.

The International Directory of Little Magazines and Small Presses

Len Fulton, Editor
Dustbooks, PO Box 100, Paradise, California, USA 95967

An unbelievable collection of over 6,000 markets. Most are US-based, though a good attempt is made to include foreign markets as well.

Literary Market Place

Reed Reference Publishing, 121 Chanlon Road, New Providence, New Jersey, USA 07974
www.bowker.com

An excellent resource which can help you become familiar with the US publishing industry. Look for it in your local library.

The Poet's Companion

Kim Addonizio & Dorianne Laux
WW Norton & Company

A slim volume of valuable exercises and examples to help you learn more about various forms of poetry.

Poet's Market

Chantelle Bentley, Editor
Writer's Digest Books, 1507 Dana Avenue, Cincinnati, Ohio, USA 45207
www.writersdigest.com

Published annually. If you are interested in the US market this is an excellent resource with a high rate of reliability.

Small Presses & Little Magazines of the UK and Ireland, 14th ed.,
Peter Finch, Editor
The Stationery Office Oriel Bookshop, The Friary, Cardiff, Wales, CFl 4AA
www.dialspace.dial.pipex.com/peter.finch/index.htm
Addresses only, with a maximum one-sentence editorial statement below. Some have only one word. Useful for information on UK and Ireland writing opportunities for poets.

Writers' and Artists' Yearbook
A & C Black (Publishers) Ltd., 35 Bedford Row, London, England WClR 4JH
This book is packed with information about the UK and other markets, copyright and general writing advice. Also includes contest information, interview techniques and photography tips. Touches on radio, theatre, television and film work. Good grouping of UK writer's societies and associations offered.

Webster's Compact Rhyming Dictionary
Mirriam-Webster Inc.
While you may not work with a lot of rhyme, playing with words can sometimes pull you from a tired place to a more productive place.

Writers' Market
Kristen Holm, Editor
Writers' Digest Books, 1507 Dana Avenue, Cincinnati, Ohio, USA 45207
www.writersdigest.com
Published annually. The new edition is generally available in Canada at the beginning of each October. Offers more than 8,000 book and periodical listings divided by subject. Focuses on the US market but offers some Canadian listings.

The Writers' Union of Canada Contracts Self-Help Package
Publications, The Writers' Union of Canada, 24 Ryerson Avenue, Toronto, Ontario M5T 2P3
Telephone: (416) 703-8982 Fax: (416) 703-0826
E-mail: twuc@the-wire.com
Website: www.swifty.com/twuc/publ.htm
For $25 you will receive an excellent package of three publications:
Trade Book Contract
This comprehensive model contract provides reasonable minimum terms for trade book contracts and is a useful comparative tool for evaluating your publisher's contract, complete with a model royalty statement.
Help Yourself to a Better Contract, by Marian Hebb
A checklist of favourable book contract provisions, with advice on what to ask and what to watch for. Designed to aid writers in book contract negotiations with their publishers.
Writers' Guide to Electronic Publishing Rights
A guide to negotiating electronic rights clauses in book contracts, including a checklist of items that should be included in electronic publishing agreements.

Writing Down the Bones: Freeing the Writer Within
Natalie Goldberg
Shambhala Publications, Inc., Horticultural Hall, 300 Massachusetts Avenue, Boston, Massachusetts, USA 02115
A popular book which offers good advice to the creative writer who wants to put pleasure back into the writing process.

The Self-Publishing Manual: How to Write, Print and Sell Your Own Book

Dan Poynter
Para Publishing, PO Box 8206, Santa Barbara, California, USA 93118-8206
www.ParaPublishing.com

Used by thousands of writers and recommended by many writing instructors, *The Self-Publishing Manual* covers everything you need to know about producing and promoting your own book. We can expect the section on electronic publishing to improve in future editions.

CRITICAL JOURNALS

All of these publications offer book reviews, critical essays and literary studies of Canadian poetry and poetics. At least one will be found in any university library.

Ariel

The University of Calgary, Department of English, 2400 University Drive NW, Calgary, Alberta T2N 1N4
www.asc.ucalgary.ca/~ariel

Brick

Linda Spalding, Editor
PO Box 537, Station Q, Toronto, Ontario M4T 2M5

Canadian Literature

University of British Columbia, 167-1855 West Mall, Vancouver, British Columbia V6T 1Z2
www.cdn-lit.ubc.ca

Canadian Poetry: Studies, Documents, Reviews

Department of English, University of Western Ontario, London, Ontario N6A 3K7
www.arts.uwo.ca/canpoetry/journpage.htm

Journal of Canadian Poetry

David Staines, Editor
9 Ashburn Drive, Nepean, Ontario K2E 6N4
www.borealispress.com

Studies in Canadian Literature

University of New Brunswick, PO Box 4400, Fredericton, New Brunswick E3B 5A3
www.unb.ca/scl

5.4 GOVERNMENT RESOURCES

Many writers use government grants to fund periods of writing free from the stress of trying to make a living.

Cuts to most grant programs have resulted in fewer opportunities for emerging writers to receive assistance. However, new programs are announced somewhere in the country every year and it is in your best interest to stay informed of these developments.

It is important to present your grant application in an organized fashion with all supporting documentation requested. Keep a copy of your complete application package for your records. Applications are generally accepted either annually or semi-annually. Travel grants are the exception to this and may be applied for throughout the year as the need arises.

There is heavy competition for funding. You may have to apply a number of times before being successful. Do not apply unless you meet all of the eligibility requirements.

National and provincial arts granting agencies are listed here. There are many regional arts councils, heritage organizations, and municipal cultural affairs departments which might also offer funding.

NATIONAL

The Canada Council for the Arts
350 Albert Street, PO Box 1047, Ottawa, Ontario K1P 5V8
Telephone: (613) 566-4414 ext.5537 Toll free 1-800-263-5588
Contact: Silvie Bernier
E-mail: silvie.bernier@canadacouncil.ca
Website: www.canadacouncil.ca/ccintro.htm

The Canada Council for the Arts offers creative writing grants "to support authors working on new projects in the fields of fiction, poetry, children's literature, comic art/narrative books or literary non-fiction. The program is also open to literary projects that are innovative or founded on technology, and in which the creation of literature is central." Grants vary from $3,000-$20,000. Travel grants are also available. Complete details online or call to request grant application package.

First Peoples' Words: Printed and Spoken grants are available to individuals and publishers. Grants for individuals are a maximum of $5,000. Contact program officer: Paul Seesequasis, at the toll free number above or at the main number, extension 5482.

Department of Foreign Affairs & International Trade
Arts and Cultural Industries Promotion Division, Ottawa, Ontario K1A 0G2
Telephone: (613) 996-2156 Fax: (613) 992-5965
E-mail: tony.advokaat@extott09.x400.gc.ca

"The program objective is the promotion of Canadian interests abroad by increasing public awareness of Canada and Canadian literature through support for the promotion in foreign markets of recently published fiction and works of literary non-fiction."

PROVINCIAL

Alberta Foundation for the Arts
9th Floor, Standard Life Centre, 10405 Jasper Avenue, Edmonton, Alberta T5J 4R7
Telephone: (780) 427-6315 Fax: (780) 422-9132
Contact: Vern Thiessen
E-mail: vthiessen@mcd.gov.ab.ca

Website: www.affta.ab.ca/GrantPrograms/g-lit.html

"Assists qualified writers and other individuals working in the literary arts in Alberta to undertake writing projects and special projects of artistic merit and/or career development value."

Grants to writers are offered in four categories: Junior; Intermediate; Senior; and Special Projects. Amounts vary up to $25,000 maximum for a senior writer.

British Columbia Arts Council

Coordinator of Arts Awards, Cultural Services Branch, Box 9819, Station Provincial Government, Victoria, British Columbia V8W 9W3

Telephone: (250) 356-1718

Website: www.tbc.gov.bc.ca/culture/csb/q-cw.htm

"Assistance is available to professional British Columbia creative writers for specific creative projects." Writers with a minimum of five years experience are invited to apply. Maximum grant is $5,000 in one fiscal year.

Manitoba Arts Council

Writing and Publishing Program, 525-93 Lombard Avenue, Winnipeg, Manitoba R3B 3B1

Telephone: (204) 945-0422 Fax: (204) 945-5925

Contact: Pat Sanders

E-mail: manart1@mts.net

Website: www.infobahn.mb.ca/mac/writpb.htm

The Arts Council supports the work of Manitoba writers who show exceptional promise.

The grant program has four categories and includes support for emerging writers, as well as up to $10,000 for professional writers.

New Brunswick Arts Board

PO Box 6000, Fredericton, New Brunswick E3B 5H1

Telephone: (506) 453-2643

E-mail: charlotte.glencross@gov.nb.ca

Website: www.mch@gov.nb.ca

Offers a variety of grants. Contact for complete details.

New Brunswick Department of Economics

Arts Development Branch, PO Box 6000, Fredericton, New Brunswick E3B 5H1

Telephone: (506) 453-2555 Fax: (506) 453-2416

Contact: Desmond Maillet

Website: www.mch@gov.nb.ca

Offers a variety of grants. Contact for complete details.

Newfoundland and Labrador Arts Council

PO Box 98, St. John's, Newfoundland A1C 5H5

Telephone: (709) 726-2212 Fax: (709) 726-0619

Contact: Ken Murphy, Program Officer

E-mail: nlacmail@newcomm.net

Website: www.nlac.nf.ca/html/grants_qual.htm

The Newfoundland and Labrador Arts Council grants support experienced writers in the development of writing projects by funding "operating, travel and study costs."

The NewTel-Arts Council Cultural Innovation Fund "assists artists in their endeavours to create new content for emerging technologies." Details online or contact the Council.

Northwest Territories Arts Council

Department of Education, Culture and Employment, PO Box 1320, Yellowknife, Northwest Territories X1A 2L9
Telephone: (403) 920-3103 Fax: (403) 873-0205
Grants awarded to professional writers range from $1,000-$10,000.

Nova Scotia Department of Education and Culture

PO Box 578, Halifax, Nova Scotia B3J 2S9
Telephone: (902) 424-5929
Grants offered to both emerging and professional writers. Maximum amount $2,000.

Nunavut

Website: www.com/government/english/resources.htm
Grant programs were not in place at the time of writing. Contact the Nunavut government for more information.

Ontario Arts Council/Conseil Des Arts de L'Ontario

151 Bloor Street West, Toronto, Ontario M5S 1T6
Telephone: (416) 969-7450 or Toll free 1-800-387-0058
E-mail: info@arts.on.ca
Website: www.arts.on.ca
The Works In Progress program "is intended to assist with the completion of book-length works of literary merit in poetry and prose. The sole criterion for funding a project will be the quality of the work." Grant value is $12,000.

The OAC also supports emerging and established writers through the Writers' Reserve grant program which is awarded through the third party recommendation of a publisher. Details available from the council.

Grant programs for franco-ontarians are also available. Contact Lorraine Filyer at (416) 969-7438 or by e-mail at: filyer@arts.on.ca.

Prince Edward Island Council of the Arts

115 Richmond Street, Charlottetown, Prince Edward Island C1A 1H7
Telephone: (902) 368-4410 Fax: (902) 368-4418
Contact: Judy MacDonald, Executive Director
Website: www.peisland.com/arts/grant.htm
Grants are awarded to aid with subsistence for up to four months. Maximum individual grants are $3,000. Individual travel study grants may be approved up to $1,000.

Conseil des arts et des lettres du Québec

79 boulevard René-Lévesque est, bureau 320, Québec, Québec G1R 5N5
Téléphone: (418) 643-1707 ou 1-800-897-1707 sans frais Télécopieur: (418) 643-4558
Liaison: Mme. Marie Lavigne, Présidente-directrice générale
Website: www.mcc.gouv.qc.ca/orgasoc/orgaso.06.htm
Le mission du Conseil est "de soutenir, dans chacune des régions, la création, l'éxpérimen-tation et la production artistique, ainsi que le perfectionnement des artistes." Pour information, téléphonez le numero sans frais.

Saskatchewan Arts Board

Communications and Development, 3rd Floor, 3475 Albert Street, Regina, Saskatchewan S4S 6X6

Telephone: (306) 787-4656 or 1-800-667-7526 Fax: (306) 787-4199
Contact: Ms. Gail Paul Armstrong, Literary Consultant
Website: www.cbsc.org/sask/bis/5854.html
"The creation of art is the primary focus of the Individual Assistance Grant Program."

Graduated levels of funding ranging from $1,500–$20,000 are available within three grant categories: creative grants; professional development grants; and research grants.

Yukon Arts Branch
PO Box 2703, Whitehorse, Yukon Y1A 2C6
Telephone: (867) 667-5264 Fax:(867) 393-6456
Contact: Laurel Parry
E-mail: laurel.parry@gov.yk.ca
Website: www.artsyukon.com/Resources/Lasso/Fundinginformation
Advanced Artists' Awards assist Yukon writers with "innovative projects, travel or educational pursuits that contribute to their personal artistic development and to their community."

Grants are awarded twice a year and may be either $2,500 or $5,000.

SIX: LITERARY AWARDS AND CONTESTS

The contests listed at the end of this section are just some of those found across Canada and around the world. Most are well-established. In many cases, the contests listed have their own websites.

To keep track of the changes in the contest marketplace I suggest you subscribe to E. Russell Smith's CanLit page (www.ncf.carleton.ca/~ab297), the Literary Network News (tplantos@idirect.com) or purchase the annual *Canadian Contest Calendar* published by Mekler & Deahl, Publishers.

Read contest guidelines carefully. Some require specific lengths or types of poetry; some have residency requirements or age limits for entrants. It is up to you to KNOW THE MARKET.

6.1 UNDERSTANDING THE RULES

Entrants who research and follow contest rules give their work its best chance for consideration.

1. Be sure you have the COMPLETE rules for the contest you are about to enter. Do NOT rely on the rules as outlined in this book or any other book, nor on what is noted in general advertising for the contest. Send an SASE to the contest address to obtain complete rules or check their website. Otherwise, you might waste your entry fee.

2. When deciding how much money you need to send to support your entry, read the rules carefully. Some offer you the opportunity to send a limited number of poems (i.e. 1-3 poems) for a single entry fee. Others will ask for an entry fee PER poem.

3. Although as a contest coordinator, I was amused by the poet that faxed in both his entry and his entry FEE (he was disqualified), I was relieved that he was also the only one to do so. NEVER fax in your entry on the assumption that it is acceptable to send the entry fee separately. It is NOT. Your entry fee and entry must arrive together. If you discover you forgot to enclose the cheque, call the contest office to alert them and enclose a note with your cheque to remind the registrar of the error. Remember to note all of your personal information and again list the poem(s) you entered. Thank the registrar for her time.

4. All contests set a deadline date. Where it is not explicitly stated otherwise, this implies a POST-MARKED deadline. If you have your entry prepared and ready to mail ON the deadline date do NOT just drop it in the mailbox. There is no guarantee your entry will pass through the postal system by midnight and you may be disqualified based on a day-late postmark. Instead, take an extra five minutes and have your entry postmarked by the staff at the post office.

5. Check carefully to see to whom you should make your cheque or money order payable. Sometimes this is an individual, magazine or contest name. Where no preference is stated, use the contest name.

6. If you are a Canadian entering a Canadian contest, a personal cheque is almost always acceptable. You may also use a money order. If you are entering a contest outside of Canada it is best to obtain a money order at your bank. Be aware that some contests require entry fees be in American dollars or pounds sterling. Do NOT send the equivalent in Canadian cash.

7. Some contests are nothing more than an attempt to make money off your eagerness to get published. They often offer huge prizes and claim you will be published in an anthology. Once you enter these "free" contests, the company will plaster you with praise and offer you numerous personalized items meant to prey on your ego. These contests are not listed here. They do not care about your talent. They are interested only in stroking your ego long enough to sell you something.

8. Some entry fees may seem extraordinarily high, but most of these will include a one-year subscription to the literary magazine running the contest. If you KNOW THE MARKET you'll realize magazines use the funds raised simply to keep publishing. These contests are legitimate and you will not be told you have won unless your work actually merits it.

9. Generally, entries are NOT returned to the entrant. They are either destroyed or archived. The contest policy will likely be stated in the COMPLETE rules but if it is not stated, you should assume entries will NOT be returned. This is standard and not a reason for concern. If you are uncomfortable with this, you may enclose an SASE for return of your work. However, a copy may be held for contest office records.

10. Can you submit a poem to several contests at once? Yes, unless the complete rules state otherwise. What you CANNOT do is submit previously published work or work under contract. The only exception to this may be chapbook or full-length manuscript contests which allow individual poems within the collection to have been previously published.

11. Send nothing but your best work.

6.2 PREPARING YOUR ENTRY

Just as in manuscript preparation, there are rules to follow when preparing a contest entry.

1. Use plain white letter-sized (8 1/2 X 11") paper only. NEVER use odd-sized paper or coloured paper. Do NOT illustrate your poems unless the contest is for visual poetry.

2. Print on one side of the page only. Never submit an entry in handwriting (though some contests will permit neatly printed entries).

3. Do not use staples. Secure pages with a paper clip.

4. Use a separate letter-size cover sheet and include your name, address, telephone number, fax number or e-mail address if you have one. If you do not have a telephone, provide a number where you can be reached. On the same sheet include the titles of all entries. If your work is untitled, use the first line of the poem.

5. You may include a brief bio below the other information on the cover sheet.

6. On each page of your entry, follow the format requested in the COMPLETE rules. Most contests have blind judging. Do NOT put your name on your entry— even on the back— unless it is requested.

7. If there is a word-count limit or line length limit, respect it. You may include the word count in the upper left hand corner.

8. You cannot revise your entry after it has been submitted. Be sure the copy you

send is free of errors and omissions. Do not send an entry covered in correction tape or fluid.

9. If there is an entry form required be sure you fill it in completely and attach it to your entry with a paper clip.

You're ready. Good luck.

6.3 CANADIAN WRITING CONTESTS AND AWARDS

Acorn-Rukeyser Chapbook Contest
Mekler & Deahl, Publishers, 237 Prospect Street South, Hamilton, Ontario L8M 2Z6
Telephone: (905) 312-1779
E-mail: meklerdeahl@globalserve.net
Prize: $100 US and publication of chapbook
Entry Fee: $10
All poems entered must be in the People's Poetry tradition. Manuscript may contain both published and unpublished work. October deadline.

Alfred G. Bailey Prize
Writers' Federation of New Brunswick, PO Box 37, Station A, Fredericton, New Brunswick E3B 4Y2
Telephone: (506) 459-7228
Website: www.sjfn.nb.ca/Community_Hall/w/Writers_Federation_NB/VIII.htm
Prize: $400
Entry Fee: $15, $10 for members
Open only to residents of New Brunswick. Send unpublished poetry manuscript of at least 48 pages. May include previously published individual poems. Two copies of manuscript required. February deadline.

Atlantic Writing Competition
Writers' Federation of Nova Scotia, 1809 Barrington Street, Suite 901, Halifax, Nova Scotia B3J 3K8
Telephone: (902) 422-0881
E-mail: writers1@fox.nstn.ca
Website: www.chebucto.ns.ca/Culture/WFNS
Prizes: $100-$75-$50 in poetry contest
Entry Fee: $15 for non-members, $10 for members
Open to writers in the Atlantic provinces only. Seven categories: novel, non-fiction book, short story, poetry, writing for children, radio play and short story by youth.

The Amethyst Review Annual Writing Contest

23 Riverside Avenue, Truro, Nova Scotia B2N 4G2
E-mail: amethyst@col.auracom.com
Prizes: 1st-$50; runners-up receive honourable mentions
Entry Fee: $12, includes one year subscription to *Amethyst Review*; entries from US, $14

US; other international entries $24 US.

Winner and other accepted work will be published. Entries may be up to 5,000 words for fiction (can include postcard short stories), or up to 5 poems, up to 200 lines each per entry. Include author's real name and a pseudonym on cover page. Use pseudonym only on each page of entry. No e-mail entries or simultaneous submissions. January deadline.

ARC: Canada's National Poetry Magazine Annual Poem of the Year Contest
PO Box 7368, Ottawa, Ontario K1L 8E4

Prizes: $1,000-$750-$500, plus publication in *ARC*

Entry Fee: $15 for entry of up to four poems, includes year subscription to *Arc*.

Maximum length of each poem is 100 lines. June deadline.

Archibald Lampman Award
ARC, PO Box 7368, Ottawa, Ontario K1L 8E4

Prize: $400

Entry Fee: N/A

Open to residents of the National Capital Region. Awarded for the best book of poems published in the previous calendar year. February deadline.

Asian Canadian Writers' Workshop Emerging Writer Award
ACWW, 311 East 41st Avenue, Vancouver, British Columbia V5W 1N9

Contact: Jim Wong Chu

Website: www.vcn.bc.ca/acww/htm/body_about_the_acww.html

Prizes: Development, publishing and/or promotion of the winning manuscript.

Open to first-time Pacific Rim Asian Canadian writers. Type of work solicited changes each year. Work may have appeared in periodicals and anthologies. Write for application details or see the ACWW website. July deadline.

Backwater Annual Hinterland Award for Poetry
Backwater Review, PO Box 222, Station B, Ottawa, Ontario K1P 6C4

E-mail: backwaters@cybertap.com

Website: www.cybertap.com/backwaters

Prizes: $100, plus publication in *Backwater Review*

Entry Fee: $10, includes one year subscription to *Backwater Review*.

Entry fee covers up to 5 poems. January deadline.

The bpNichol Chapbook Award
316 Dupont Street, Toronto, Ontario M5R 1V9

Prize: $1,000

Given to the author of the best poetry chapbook (10-40 pages) in English published in Canada the previous year. Submit three copies. March deadline.

The Bronwen Wallace Award
The Writers' Development Trust, 24 Ryerson Avenue, Suite 201, Toronto, Ontario M5T 2P3

Telephone: (416) 504-8222

E-mail: writers.trust@sympatico.ca

Prize: $1,000

Alternates between short fiction and poetry. Open to Canadian citizens or landed immigrants, under 35 years of age at the deadline who may have been published in an independent magazine or anthology but are unpublished in book form. An entry is up to 2,500 words of prose fiction. January deadline.

Calgary Writers Association Poetry Contest
c/o PO Box 68083, 7750 Ranchview Drive, North West, Calgary, Alberta T3G 3N8
Telephone: (403) 242-3130
Prizes: $50–$25–$25, plus publication
Entry Fee: $5
Writers may enter only once each year. May include up to three unpublished poems but must not exceed 60 lines total. March deadline. Also offers awards for non-fiction and short fiction.

Canadian Authors Association Awards
PO Box 419, Campbellford, Ontario K0L 1L0
Telephone: (705) 653-0323
E-mail: canauth@redden.on.ca
Website: www.canauthors.org/homepage.html
The Canadian Authors Association offers the following awards each of which has specific entry guidelines: CAA Air Canada Award; CAA Award for Drama/Fiction/Poetry; CAA Lela Common Award; CAA Jubilee Award; CAA Vicky Metcalfe Body of Work Award; CAA Vicky Metcalfe Short Story Award; and the CAA Student Writing Contest. Application required for entry in any category. Deadlines vary— contact the CAA for details.

Canadian Authors Association— Manitoba Branch Poetry Contest
208-63 Albert Street, Winnipeg, Manitoba R3B 1G4
Telephone: (204) 947-0512
Prizes: Varies per category
Entry Fee: Varies per category.
Open to residents of Manitoba. Has two categories: Young Writer and Adult. Send unpublished poetry only. Contact for details.

Canadian Writer's Journal
PO Box 5180, New Liskeard, Ontario P0J 1P0
Telephone: (705) 647-5425 or 1-800-258-5451 Fax: (705) 647-8366
Editor: Deborah Ranchuk
E-mail: cwj@ntl.sympatico.ca
Website: www.nt.net/~cwj/index.htm
Prizes: 30%–25%–15% of total fees in your respective category
Has four categories: free verse, traditional, haiku and sijo. Entries must be original, typed, unpublished and not under consideration elsewhere. You may enter as often as you wish. May deadline. Note: There are specific entry details for this contest; obtain complete rules before entering.

Canadian Literary Awards
CBC-Radio Arts & Entertainment, PO Box 500, Station 'A', Toronto, Ontario M5W 1E6
Telephone: (416) 205-6102
Web: www.cbc.ca
Prize: $10,000 in each category
Entry Fee: $10, cheque or money order payable to: Canadian Literary Awards
Open to all residents of Canada regardless of nationality, and to Canadians citizens living abroad. Neither employees nor long-term contractors to the CBC or any of the sponsoring bodies are eligible to enter. Three categories: Short Story, Personal Essay, Poetry. Editorial

comments are not offered and submissions will not be returned unless accompanied by a self-addressed envelope bearing sufficient postage. Winners receive cash prize, publication in Saturday Night and the works will be produced and broadcast on CBC radio. Blind judging. September deadline (may change).

Cecilia Lamont Literary Contest
c/o White Rock and Surrey Writer's Club, 1334 Johnson Road, White Rock, British Columbia V4B 3Z2
Telephone: (604) 536-8333
Prizes: 1st-$75, plus engraved plaque, 2nd-$50, plus certificate, 3rd-$25, plus certificate
Entry Fee: $6 per piece, $5 each if 4 or more are entered.
Open to residents of British Columbia only. Maximum length of entries is 1,000 words for fiction, creative non-fiction and articles; 36 lines for poetry. October deadline.

The City of Calgary W.O. Mitchell Book Prize
Writers Guild of Alberta, Calgary Office, 305-223-12 Avenue South West, Calgary, Alberta T2R 0G9
Telephone: (403) 269-8844
Prize: $2,000
Entry Fee: N/A
Awarded to a Calgary resident for a literary book published in one of the following areas: poetry, fiction, non-fiction, children's literature or drama. December deadline.

City of Edmonton Book Prize
Writers Guild of Alberta, Percy Page Centre, 3rd Floor, 11759 Groat Road North West, Edmonton, Alberta T5M 3K6
Telephone: (780) 422-8174
Prize: $2,000
Entry Fee: $10
Awarded to an Edmonton resident, or group of residents, over and including the age of 18 for a literary book published in one of the following areas: poetry, fiction, non-fiction, children's literature or drama. All entries must deal in some way with the City of Edmonton. The award is sponsored by Audrey Books in Edmonton. March deadline.

Contemporary Verse 2 Haiku Contest
PO Box 3062, Winnipeg, Manitoba R3C 4E5
Telephone: (204) 943-9066
Prizes: $150-$75-$50, plus payment for publication
Entry Fee: $19, includes one-year subscription.
Traditional haiku of a specific, present event in nature, indicating the season. 17 syllables in three lines— 5,7,5, free of poetic devices. 4 haiku per submission. SASE for notification and/or return of manuscript. November deadline.

Cranberry Tree Poetry Chapbook Contest
5060 Tecumseh Road East, Suite 173, Windsor, Ontario N8T 1C1
E-mail: jeremyd@netcore.ca
Prizes: 1st-publication, plus 100 copies, 2nd-$50, 3rd-$25
Entry Fee: $12
Send 10-20 page titled collection. Include e-mail address on cover page if available. SASE for notification of results. November deadline.

The Dorothy Livesay Poetry Award

West Coast Book Prize Society, 700-1033 Davie Street, Vancouver, British Columbia V6E 1M7

Telephone: (604) 687-2405

Prize: $2,000

Entry Fee: $25

Open to residents of BC or Yukon. Awarded to the author of the best work of poetry. Anthologies and "best of" collections are ineligible. December deadline.

Electric Garden Press/Hook & Ladder Annual Poetry Sampler Award

EGP Poetry Sampler Award, POB 78, Station B, Ottawa, Ontario K1P 6C3

E-mail: martinv@electricgarden.com

Website: www.electricgarden.com/h&l/index.html

Prizes: $500–$250–$125, plus publication in *Hook & Ladder*

Entry Fee: $12 for entry of up to 12 poems, payable to *Hook & Ladder*, includes a two-year subscription.

Maximum length 75 lines. December deadline.

Event Creative Non-fiction Contest

Douglas College, PO Box 2503, New Westminster, British Columbia V3L 5B2

E-mail: event@douglas.bc.ca

Prizes: $500 each to three winners

Entry Fee: $16, includes year subscription to *Event*.

Previously published material or material submitted or accepted for publication elsewhere cannot be considered. Maximum length for submission is 5,000 words, typed, double-spaced. Submissions must include a separate cover sheet with the writer's name, address and telephone number, and the title(s) of the story (or stories). The writer's name must not appear on the manuscript. Include SASE. April deadline.

Fiddlehead Fiction and Poetry Writing Contest

University of New Brunswick, PO Box 4400, Fredericton, New Brunswick E3B 5A3

Prizes: $1,000 for best story; Ralph Gustafson Prize of $1,000 for best poem. Both winners will be published in *The Fiddlehead*.

Entry Fee: $20, includes one year of *The Fiddlehead* (add $8 for USA and overseas).

Max 5 poems or 25 pages of fiction. December deadline.

Gerald Lampert Memorial Award

League of Canadian Poets, 54 Wolseley Street, Toronto, Ontario M5T 1A5

Telephone: (416) 504-1657

E-mail: league@ican.net

Website: www.poets.ca

Prize: $1,000

Entry Fee: $15 per title

Given for the best first book of poetry by a Canadian poet, published in the previous year. Books must meet UNESCO definitions (at least 48 pages). December deadline.

Government of Newfoundland and Labrador Arts and Letters Competition

The Secretary, Arts and Letters Committee, PO Box 1854, St. John's, Newfoundland A1C 5P9

Telephone: (709) 729-5253

Prizes: $600–$200–$100

Open to residents of Newfoundland and Labrador. Two categories: Junior and Senior (over 18). Awards for original work in the following categories: fiction, non-fiction, poetry and drama. A gold medal is reserved for outstanding entries.

Governor General's Awards for Literature

Canada Council, Writing and Publishing Section, 350 Albert Street, PO Box 1047, Ottawa, Ontario K1P 5V8

Telephone: 1-800-263-5588

Website: www.canadacouncil.ca

Prize: $10,000 in each of seven categories

Open to Canadian citizens for best book of fiction, non-fiction, poetry, drama, translation, children's literature and children's illustration in the previous year.

Great Canadian Haiku Contest

c/o Geist Magazine, 103-1014 Horner Street, Vancouver, British Columbia V6B 2W9

E-mail: geist@geist.com

Prizes: Great Canadian Haiku trophy plus other items and some cash

Entry Fee: $5

May enter up to 5 haiku. Entries should have three lines of five, seven, and five syllables each. Reference(s) to winter most appropriate. December deadline.

The Great Canadian Literary Hunt

c/o THIS Magazine, 401 Richmond Street West, Suite 396, Toronto, Ontario M5V 3A8

Website: www.THISmag.org

Prizes: $1,500–$500–$250, plus publication in *THIS Magazine*

Entry Fee: $10 for 2 poems, $10 for one piece of fiction

Send poems of up to 100 lines and short stories of up to 5,000 words. Multiple entries allowed. Each entry must be accompanied by an entry fee. Name, address, telephone number and e-mail address (if available) MUST appear on a separate sheet along with the title(s) of your work. Your name should not appear on the entry itself. July deadline.

Hawthorne Society Poetry Chapbook Contest

1051 Roslyn Road, Victoria, British Columbia V8S 4R4

Telephone: (250) 598-0096

Prize: $500, and publication of chapbook

Entry Fee: $25

Open to all Canadian residents who have not published a book-length (48 pages) collection of verse. Send a titled manuscript of 15–30 previously unpublished, single-spaced poems. April deadline. Runners-up may be published in the *Hawthorne Annual*.

The Heaven Biennial Chapbook Prize

Manitoba Writers Guild, 206-100 Arthur Street, Winnipeg, Manitoba R3B 1H3

Telephone: (204) 942-6134

E-mail: mbwriter@escape.ca

Prize: $250

Entry Fee: N/A

Open to Manitoba writers only. Books published in the two years before each prize year are eligible (i.e. 1998 & 1999 in the year 2000). December deadline.

Herb Barrett Award for Poetry

Mekler & Deahl, Publishers, 237 Prospect Street South, Hamilton, Ontario L8M 2Z6

Telephone: (905) 312-1779

E-mail: meklerdeahl@globalserve.net

Prizes: $75-50-25 US, and publication in anthology

Entry Fee: $10 for 1-2 poems; $15 for 3 or more.

All entries should be written in the haiku tradition. Maximum 4 lines per poem. Please send a short bio regardless of publishing background. All entrants will receive the anthology. November deadline.

The Hope Writers Guild Poetry Contest

PO Box 1683, Hope, British Columbia V0X 1L0

Telephone: (604) 869-9848

Prizes: $200-$100-$50

Entry fee: $5 for one poem, $10 for three poems.

Entries can include up to three poems (see fees) with a total of 100 lines. July deadline.

International People's Haiku Contest.

People's Poetry, Box 31, 2060 Queen Street East, Toronto, Ontario M4E 3V7

Contact: Ted Plantos

E-mail: tplantos@idirect.com

Website: webhome.idirect.com/~tplantos

Prizes: $300 in prizes, and publication in People's Poetry Letter

Entry Fee: $5 for each haiku entered. Send $15 (3 haiku) and get one-year subscription. Ten winners chosen. Entries must include references to people, human nature or the human condition. Accepts traditional or experimental haiku. February deadline.

International 3-Day Novel Contest

Anvil Press, 175 East Broadway, Suite 204A, Vancouver, British Columbia V5T 1W2

Telephone: (604) 876-8710

E-mail: sub-terr@pinc.com

Website: www.anvilpress.com

Prize: A publishing offer from Anvil Press

Entry Fee: $25

Held every year over the three-day Labour Day weekend. Allows for research to be done and for an outline to be prepared in advance. Contact for full details.

Isabel Miller Award

Celebration of Women in the Arts, Box 47075, Edmonton Centre RPO, Edmonton, Alberta T5J 4N1

Prizes: $200-$100-$50

Entry Fee: $20, includes membership in Celebration of Women in the Arts.

Entrants must be Alberta residents. Entrants must adhere to word-count limits. Contest is usually run on a theme. February deadline.

The Jane Jordan Poetry Contest

27 James Street, Ottawa, Ontario K2P 0T7

Telephone: (613) 523-1073

Contact: Jen Gavin

E-mail: tree@maenad.ml.org

Prizes: $250-$150-$100, publication in *BYWORDS*
Entry Fee: $2 per poem, payable to the TREE Reading Series.
Entrants must be residents of the National Capital Region. Any number of poems may be entered, no poem longer than 100 lines. February deadline.

Jewish Book Awards

Diane Uslaner, Director, Cultural Programming, Marketing and Development, Koffler Centre of the Arts, The Bathurst Jewish Centre, 4588 Bathurst Street, Toronto, Ontario M2R 1W6
Telephone: (416) 636-1880, ext.352
Prizes: Certificate and $250-$1,000 to winners in nine categories
Send two copies of the book to be considered. Categories are: poetry, fiction, Holocaust writing, Yiddish/translation from Yiddish, biography/memoir, biblical/rabbinical scholarship, children's/young adult's literature, history, and Canadian Jewish scholarship. Authors must be Canadians or permanent residents of Canada though not necessarily Jewish, and books must be published during the preceding two calendar years. Except in the category of biblical and rabbinical scholarship, the publisher must be Canadian. Books must have a significant Jewish theme or Jewish interest. January deadline.

John Glassco Translation Prize

Glassco Prize Committee, c/o the LTAC, 3492 Laval, Montreal, Québec H2X 3C8
Telephone: (514) 489-9027
Website: www.geocities.com/Athens/Oracle/9070
Prizes: $500
Entry Fee: Nil
Awarded by the Literary Translators' Association of Canada for a translator's first book-length, literary translation into French or English, published in Canada during the previous year. Fiction, non-fiction, poetry, and children's literature are eligible. The translator must be a Canadian citizen or landed immigrant. Submissions can be made by anyone interested, by forwarding three copies of the translated work and one copy of the original to the prize committee. January deadline.

The John Hirsch Award

Manitoba Writers Guild, 206-100 Arthur Street, Winnipeg, Manitoba R3B 1H3
Telephone: (204) 942-6134
E-mail: mbwriter@escape.ca
Prize: $2,500
Entry Fee: N/A
Open to Manitoba writers only. Awarded in recognition of a promising published writer who has not received national or international recognition. Considers writers of work in the following categories: poetry, fiction, creative non-fiction and drama.

Last Poems Contest

sub-TERRAIN Magazine, 204-A, 175 East Broadway, Vancouver, British Columbia V5T 1W2
Telephone: (604) 876-8710
E-mail: subter@pinc.com
Prizes: $250, plus publication in *sub-TERRAIN*
Entry Fee: $15, includes a one-year subscription to *sub-TERRAIN*.
Send a maximum of 4 poems after August 1st on the theme "Poetry that encapsulates

North American experience at the close of the 20th century." Runners-up win book prizes and subsequent publication. SASE for return of manuscript or notification of results. December deadline.

League of Canadian Poets Canadian Poetry Chapbook Competition
54 Wolseley Street, Toronto, Ontario M5T 1A5
Telephone: (416) 504-1657
E-mail: league@ican.net
Website: www.poets.ca
Prizes: 1st–$1,000, plus publication and 10 printed and bound copies
Entry fee: $15 per entry
Entrants must be Canadian citizens or landed immigrants. Send 15 to 24 pages of poetry, one poem per page. Three entrants will receive honourable mention and a copy of the winning chapbook. Winner will supply manuscript on disk and sign a contract. SASE for results. March deadline.

League of Canadian Poets National Poetry Contest
54 Wolseley Street, Toronto, Ontario M5T 1A5
Telephone: (416) 504-1657
E-mail: league@ican.net
Website: www.poets.ca
Prizes: Prizes $1,000-750-500, plus publication in the softcover anthology, *Vintage*, published annually by Quarry Press.
Entry Fee: $6 per poem.
Open to Canadian citizens and landed immigrants. Maximum length of entry is 75 lines. Fifty poems including the three winners will be published in *Vintage* each year. SASE for notification of results only. January deadline.

The League of Canadian Poets Canadian Youth Poetry Competition
54 Wolseley Street, Toronto, Ontario M5T 1A5
Telephone: (416) 504-1657
E-mail: league@ican.net
Website: www.poets.ca
Prizes: $500-$350-$250, plus honourable mentions in each age category
Entry Fee: $5 per poem, or $3/poem for three or more, or $2.50/poem for 30 or more poems (group submission rate), payable to The League of Canadian Poets.
Winning poems will be published in *Vintage* anthology. Two age categories: Junior, grades 7-9 and Senior, grades 10-12 (OAC in Ontario). Length of each poem must not exceed one page. Teachers are encouraged to take advantage of our group submission rate and make the competition a class project. Contest is open to Canadian citizens and landed immigrants. March deadline.

Lina Chartrand Poetry Award
Contemporary Verse 2, PO Box 3062, Winnipeg, Manitoba R3C 4E5
Telephone: (204) 949-1365
Prize: Accrued interest on special award fund
Entry fee: N/A
Award recognizes an emerging writer whose work has been published in *CV2* over the previous year.

Literary Writes

Federation of BC Writers, 1100-1200 West 73rd Avenue, Vancouver British Columbia
V6P 6G5
Telephone: (604) 688-2057
E-mail: fedbcwrt@pinc.com
Website: www.swifty.com/bcwa
Prizes: $1,000–$500–$250
Entry Fee: $20, $15 for members
Annual competition. Entry form required. Short stories to a maximum of 2,500 words.
December deadline.

Malahat Review Long Poem Prize

University of Victoria, PO Box 1700 Victoria, British Columbia, Canada V8W 2Y2
E-mail: malahat@uvic.com
Website: web.uvic.ca/malahat
Prizes: Two prizes of $400 are offered, plus payment for publication at $25 per page.
Entry Fee: $25 per poem, ($25 US for Americans) includes one–year subscription to *Malahat Review*.
Submit a long poem or cycle of poems between five and fifteen pages long. Previously
published work will not be considered. Enclose optional SASE for return of manuscript.
March deadline. Also sponsors novella prize in alternate years.

The Marian Engel Award

The Writers' Development Trust, 24 Ryerson Avenue, Suite 201, Toronto, Ontario M5T
2P3
Telephone: (416) 504-8222
E-mail: writers.trust@sympatico.ca
Prizes: $10,000
Awarded to a female Canadian writer in mid-career in recognition of a body of work and
in hope of future contribution.

Millstone Press Biannual Poetry Chapbook Contest

#305-326 West First Street, Vancouver, British Columbia V7M 1B6
Contact: Kevin Miller
Prizes: 1st–$250, plus five chapbooks, 2nd–$100 and three chapbooks
Entry Fee: $5 per poem, plus SASE
Top 50 entrants will be published and receive a copy of contest anthology. December
deadline. Also runs short story contest.

Milton Acorn People's Poetry Award

People's Poetry, Box 31, 2060 Queen Street East, Toronto, Ontario M4E 3V7
Contact: Ted Plantos
E-mail: tplantos @idirect.com
Website: webhome.idirect.com/~tplantos
Prizes: Medallion plus $250, and announcement in *People's Poetry Letter*
Entry Fee: $25 nomination fee
Awarded to the author of a work in the people's poetry tradition. Details of eligibility and
nomination procedure available for SASE. June deadline.

Milton Acorn Poetry Award

Island Literary Awards, PEI Council of the Arts, 115 Richmond Street, Charlottetown, Prince Edward Island C1A 1H7

Telephone: (902) 368-4410

Prizes: 1st-airfare for two, 2nd-$200, 3rd-$100

Entry Fee: $8 per entry.

Open to residents of Prince Edward Island. Send a maximum of ten pages of unpublished poetry per entry. Multiple entries permitted. January deadline.

NeWest Review Short Story Contest

Box 394, RPO University, Saskatoon, Saskatchewan S7N 4J8

Prizes: $200-$100

Entry Fee: $20 per story

This contest is limited to writers age 40 and over. Stories may be 1,500 words maximum. Deadline not stated.

New Muse Award

Broken Jaw Press/Maritimes Arts Projects Productions, Box 596 Station A, Fredericton, New Brunswick E3B 5A6

Telephone: (506) 454-5127

Contact: Joe Blades

E-mail: jblades@nbnet.nb.ca

Prize: Publication of manuscript by Broken Jaw Press

Entry Fee: $20 or £10

Submit short fiction manuscripts of 100-140 pages double-spaced on letter-size paper (may be accompanied by diskette). Manuscript title and page number (only) must appear on every page. No simultaneous submissions please. Entrants must not have published a first fiction collection or novel (UNESCO minimum of 48 pages literary content). Individual stories may have been published in magazines, anthologies and chapbooks. Include a literary bio on the cover sheet. Send adequate SASE for return of manuscript and/or pre-publication notification of the winner. All entrants will receive a copy of the year's winning book upon publication. February deadline.

The Norma Epstein Award for Creative Writing

University of Toronto, University College, Office of the Registrar, Toronto, Ontario M5S 1A1

Open to students registered at a Canadian university. Send SASE for details.

Okanagan Short Story Award

Box 419, Campbellford, Ontario K0L 1L0

Telephone: (705) 653-0323 Fax: (705) 653-0593

E-mail: canauth@redden.on.ca

Website: www.CanAuthors.org

At the time of writing, this award had been suspended but not eliminated. Check the Canadian Author Association website to update the status of this contest.

Orillia International Poetry Awards

c/o Stephen Leacock Museum, PO Box 625, Orillia, Ontario L3V 6K5

Web: www.transdata.leacock.html

Prizes: $5,000-$1,000-$500, Junior awards: $150-$75-$25, Limericks $1,000-$500-$200.

Entry Fees: $5 per poem, $10 for 3 limericks

NOTE: This contest was undergoing changes in the spring of 1999, including a possible name change, and organizers were unable to confirm details for upcoming contests. However, organizers stated they expected to "maintain the status quo" but could not guarantee this would be the case. Historically, this has been a popular and well-publicized contest and one can expect the same credibility to carry forward. Multiple entries accepted. Put name on the reverse of each page and include your e-mail address if available. All entries must be unpublished. Poems may be up to 50 lines in length. Junior category is for writers who are 16 or under as of December 31 of the year in question. Do NOT send entries by e-mail. Complete details online as available or send SASE. November deadline.

Other Voices Writing Contest
Garneau PO Box 52059, 8210-109 Street, Edmonton, Alberta T6G 2T5
Website: www.ualberta.ca/~kpress/OtherVoices.html
Prizes: $500 in each category which may be divided among winners at the discretion of the judge, plus publication
Entry Fee: $20 for first entry, $5 each additional entry, includes one-year subscription to *Other Voices*.
Two categories: poetry and prose. Poetry entries (up to 3 poems per entry) may be up to 50 lines each. Prose entries (1 story) may be up to 3,500 words each. Send separate sheet with name, address, telephone, fax and e-mail (if available), with short bio. Include SASE. September deadline.

Outlaw Editions Chapbook Competition
2829 Dysart Road, Victoria, British Columbia V9A 2J7
Contact: Jay Ruzesky
E-mail: jruzesky@direct.ca
Prizes: $300, plus publication
Entry Fee: $10 per entry, payable to Jay Ruzesky
Manuscripts of 12 to 32 pages are eligible. We're looking for long poems, poem sequences, short works of biography, creative non-fiction, very short novels, collections of postcard stories or prose poems, and other chapbook-length manuscripts. All entrants will receive a copy of the prize winning chapbook. SASE for notification or return of manuscript. March deadline.

Pat Lowther Memorial Award
54 Wolseley Street, Toronto, Ontario M5T 1A5
Telephone: (416) 504-1657
E-mail: league@ican.net
Website: www.poets.ca
Prizes: $1,000
Entry fee: $15 per entry
Entrant must be a Canadian citizen or landed immigrant. Given for a book (48 pages or more in length) of poetry written by a woman and published in the year of submission. Must contain more than 50 per cent new material. Entries in languages other than English must be accompanied by a translation. December deadline.

People's Poem Contest
People's Poetry Letter, Box 31, 2060 Queen Street East, Toronto, Ontario M4E 3V7
Contact: Ted Plantos

E-mail: tplantos@idirect.com
Website: webhome.idirect.com/~tplantos
Prizes: $200 in cash and poetry book prizes to a winner and a runner-up
Entry Fee: Donation of $15, includes one-year subscription to *People's Poetry Letter*.
Up to two poems of any length may be entered. Include short bio of under 40 words.
Winning poems and authors featured in an issue of *People's Poetry Letter*. December deadline.

People's Political Poem Contests

People's Poetry, Box 31, 2060, Queen Street East, Toronto, Ontario M4E 3V7
Contact: Ted Plantos
E-mail: tplantos @idirect.com
Website: webhome.idirect.com/~tplantos
Prizes: $200 in cash and book prizes, plus publication in *People's Poetry Letter*
Entry Fee: Donation of $15, includes one-year subscription to *People's Poetry Letter*.
For political poems that exhibit a passionate humanity, sensitivity to the human condition, love and moral conviction. Five poems selected in each contest. Up to two poems of any length may be entered. Include a brief biography. Entry form for SASE. Two deadlines: Winter contest March 15th, and Spring Contest, June 15.

Petra Kenney Poetry Prize (In association with *Writer's Forum Magazine*)

38 Langmuir Crescent, Toronto, Ontario M6S 2A7
Telephone: (416) 769-2964
Contact: Molly Yeomans
Prizes: $2,000-$1,000-$500, each also receives Royal Brierly crystal flower vase
Entry Fee: $7 per poem
Entries may be up to 80 lines. Application form required. Include SASE for acknow-ledgement. December deadline.

Poet's Corner Award

Broken Jaw Press, Box 596, Stn A, Fredericton, New Brunswick E3B 5A6
Telephone: (506) 454-5127
Contact: Joe Blades
E-mail: jblades@nbnet.nb.ca
Prizes: Plaque, publication by Broken Jaw Press, 15 copies plus royalties
Entry Fee: $20 entry fee, payable to Broken Jaw Press.
Each entrant receives a copy of the winning poet's book. Awarded to the best poetry manuscript submitted by a Canadian poet. Submit manuscripts of up to 80 pages, manuscript title and page number on every page. Blind judging. Individual poems may have been published in periodicals, anthologies and chapbooks. Include literary bio note on cover page. Entrants must be prepared to supply their manuscript on computer disk. Send SASE for notification of winner's name. One or two Honourable Mentions may be chosen by the judges. December deadline.

Pottersfield Portfolio Compact Fiction/Short Poem Contest

PO Box 40, Station A, Sydney, Nova Scotia B1P 6G9
Prizes: $150
Entry Fee: $20, includes one-year subscription to *Pottersfield Portfolio*.
Maximum of three unpublished poems per entry with a total of 20 lines. Fiction may be up to 1,500 words and include up to 2 stories per entry. February deadline.

Prairie Fire Writing Contests

423-100 Arthur Street, Winnipeg, Manitoba R3B 1H3
Telephone: (204) 943-9066
Prizes: $500–$300–$200, plus paid publication
Entry Fee: $25, includes one-year subscription to *Prairie Fire*.
Long Short Fiction: Send one story of 5,000 to 20,000 words. SASE for return of manuscript or notification of results. November deadline.
Short Fiction: Send one story, maximum 5,000 words. SASE for return of manuscript or notification of results. October deadline.
Poetry Contest: Send a maximum of 3 poems or 150 lines. SASE for return of manuscript or notification of results. June deadline.
Creative Non-Fiction Contest: Send one work, maximum 5,000 words. SASE for return of manuscript or notification of results. December deadline.

PRISM International Earle Birney Prize for Poetry

University of British Columbia, Buchanan E462, 1866 Main Mall, Vancouver, British Columbia V6T 1Z1
Telephone: (604) 822-2514
Prizes: $500 for the best poem or group of poems by an author in each regular volume year of *PRISM International*
Entry Fee: N/A, winners chosen from poets published in *PRISM International*.
Note: *PRISM International* pays $40 per page for poetry.

PRISM International Fiction Contest

Creative Writing Program, University of British Columbia, E462-1866 Main Mall, Vancouver, British Columbia V6T 1Z1
Telephone: (604) 822-2514
Prizes: $2,000, 5 other prizes of $200, plus paid publication in *PRISM International*
Entry Fee: $15 entry fee plus reading fee of $5 per story (outside Canada submit in US dollars please); includes one-year subscription to *PRISM International*.
Stories may be up to 25 pages, double-spaced. Translations are eligible. UBC Creative Writing students are ineligible. December deadline.

QSPELL Literary Awards and First Book Award

1200 Atwater Avenue, Montréal, Québec H3Z 1X4
Telephone: (514) 933-0878
E-mail: qspell@total. net
Website: www.qspell.org
Prize: $2,000 in each of three categories, plus $500 First Book award
Entry Fee: $10 per title.
Open to authors who have lived in Quebec for 3 of the past 5 years and who write in English. Entry form required. Write for details.

Room of One's Own Literary Competition

PO Box 46160, Station D, Vancouver, British Columbia V6J 5G5
Prizes: $300–$150–$75, plus publication in journal
Entry Fee: $10
Open to female writers writing in the first person. Limit poetry entries to no more than 70 lines per poem. May enter 4-5 poems. Include 40-60 word bio on a separate page. Send

SASE for notification of winners. Manuscripts are not returned. Also runs short fiction and creative non-fiction competition. Deadline not stated.

Sandburg-Livesay Anthology Contest

Mekler & Deahl, Publishers, 237 Prospect Street South, Hamilton, Ontario L8M 2Z6
Telephone: (905) 312-1779
E-mail: meklerdeahl@globalserve.net
Prize: $100 US and publication in anthology, $50 US to the runner-up
Entry Fee: $10, payable to Mekler & Deahl, Publishers
All poems entered must be in the People's Poetry tradition as exemplified by Carl Sandburg and Dorothy Livesay. Send up to ten poems per entry. Poems may be published or unpublished and be up to 80 lines each. Author's name, contact information and the list of poems submitted should appear on a separate sheet. All entrants will receive a copy of the anthology. October deadline. International entries in English welcomed.

Saskatchewan Books Awards

PO Box 1921, Regina, Saskatchewan S4P 3E1
Telephone: (306) 569-1585
Prize: $1,000 and a certificate
Entry fee: $15 per title per category
Open to residents of Saskatchewan. Offers a number of awards including: Brenda MacDonald Riches Award for first book; Book of the Year Award (in fiction, non-fiction and children's literature); City of Regina Award; and poetry award. Deadlines vary. Write for details.

Scenes Poetry Contest

PO Box 51531, 2060 Queen Street East, Toronto, Ontario M4E 3V7
Telephone: (416) 690-0917
Prize: $200 and publication in *Scenes*
Entry Fee: $10, $5 for each additional entry
Open to Ontario residents. Send previously unpublished poems of not more than 50 lines. Multiple entries allowed. Entry form required. Spring and summer deadlines. Also runs fiction contest.

Seeds International Poetry Contest

Hidden Brook Press, 412-701 King Street West, Toronto, Ontario M5V 2W7
Telephone: (416) 504-3966
E-mail: writers@pathcom.com
Prizes: $100-$50-$25, plus 3 honourable mentions
Entry Fee: $10 for three poems; US fee is $10 US; all other foreign entrants send $15 US, payable to Hidden Book Press Prize.
Type your name, address and e-mail address on the BACK of each submission. No electronic submissions. All entrants receive a year subscription to *Seeds*. November deadline.

Shaunt Basmajian Chapbook Award

Canadian Poetry Association, PO Box 22571, St. George PO, Toronto, Ontario M5S 1V0
Contact: Jennifer Footman
E-mail: writers@pathcom.com
Website: www.mirror.org/groups/cpa

Prizes: $100, publication and 50 copies
Entry Fee: $15, payable to the Canadian Poetry Association
Honours the founder of the Canadian Poetry Association. Enter 24 single-spaced pages of poetry, published (other than in chapbook or book form) or unpublished, any style or tradition. Simultaneous submissions are acceptable. All entries will be returned if SASE is provided. All entrants will receive a copy of the winning chapbook. March deadline.

Short GRAIN Writing Contest

Box 3092, Saskatoon, Saskatchewan S7K 3S9
Telephone: (306) 244-2828
E-mail: grain.mag@sk.sympatico.ca
Website: www.skwriter.com
Prizes: Short categories: $400-$250-$150; long category: $600-$300-$200, plus all receive paid publication in *GRAIN*
Entry Fee: $22 Can. ($26 US from outside Canada) for 2 entries plus $5 each for each additional entry in the same category. Includes one-year subscription to *GRAIN*.
Specify category and word counts (excluding titles).
Categories as follows:
Short categories, 500 words or less, per entry: (1) dramatic monologue (a self-contained speech given by a single character), (2) postcard story— narrative fiction (3) prose poem— a lyric poem written as prose paragraph(s).
Long category: "Long Grain of Truth"— non-fiction creative prose of up to 5,000 words.
Honourable Mentions may be awarded. Send SASE for notification. January deadline.

Starving Romantics Poetry Competition

93 Charnwood Place, Thornhill, Ontario L3T 5H2
Telephone: (905) 731-8055
Prize: 1st-$125, plus public reading, 2nd-$50, plus public reading, 3rd-$25, plus public reading
Entry Fee: $5 per poem.
Entrants may send up to five poems total ($25). Runners-up will receive one free entry the following year. July deadline.

Stephen G. Stephansson Award for Poetry

Writers' Guild of Alberta, Percy Page Centre, 3rd Floor, 11759 Groat Road North West, Edmonton, Alberta T5M 3K6
Telephone: (780) 422-8174
Prize: $500, and leather bound copy of winning book
Entry Fee: Not stated.
Open to residents of Alberta. All books are eligible regardless of where they were published. December deadline.

Stephen Leacock Medal for Humour

Stephen Leacock Associates, c/o Jean Dickson, 203 Martin Drive, PO Box 854, Orillia, Ontario L3V 3P4
Telephone: (705) 325-6546
Website: www.transdata.leacock.html
Prizes: $5,000, plus medal for best humourous book of the year
Entry Fees: $25

Canadian citizens or landed immigrants eligible. Books in the following genres are eligible: drama, fiction, non-fiction or poetry. Send 10 copies of published book and 5x7 inch b/w photo. Anthologies are not eligible. Send entries September onward. December deadline.

Tickled By Thunder Writing Contests
7385-129 Street, Surrey, British Columbia V8W 7B8
E-mail: Larry_Linder@mindlink.bc.ca
Website: www.home.istar.ca/~thunder
Prize: 50% of all entry fees plus publication in Year's Best Poetry chapbook and video
Entry Fee: See Below.
Subscribers may send three poems free, and $2 for each additional poem. Non-subscribers are welcome to enter; send $5 per poem. Four contests per year; February, May, August and October deadlines. Also runs fiction and article contests.

Very Next Poetry Contest
Canadian Poetry Association York Region Chapter, c/o I.B. Iskov, 31 Marisa Court, Thornhill, Ontario L4J 6H9
Prizes: $100 First Prize, two $50 Second Prizes, plus publication in *POEMATA*
Entry Fee: $5 per poem, payable to Canadian Poetry Association.
Entries may be up to 40 lines each. SASE for results. April deadline.

Windhorse Awards
Samurai Press, RR3, Box 3140, Yarmouth, Nova Scotia B5A 4A7
Prizes: Half of the total entry fees, plus publication on broadsheet.
Entry Fee: $5 per essay.
Essay contest based on a theme. Run by the Warrior-Poet Society and Samurai Press. Twelve essays will be selected for publication as a Windhorse Broadside. Enclose SASE to receive the Broadside. The winning entry on each theme is selected by readers' ballot. March deadline.

Writer's Block Writing Contest
PO Box 32, 9944-33 Avenue, Edmonton, Alberta T6N 1E8
Prize: Cash, books and publication in *Writer's Block Magazine*
Entry Fee: $5
Send only previously unpublished stories or poems in one of the following genres: horror, mystery, sci-fi/fantasy, romance and western. Limit 5,000 words. Send SASE for more details. March and September deadlines.

Writer's Federation of New Brunswick Literary Competition
PO Box 37, Station A, Fredericton, New Brunswick E3B 4Y2
Telephone: (506) 459-7228
Prize: $150-$75-$50
Entry Fee: $15, $10 for members
Open to residents of New Brunswick only. Runs contests in the following categories: poetry, fiction, non-fiction and children's literature. Poetry maximum 100 lines or 5 poems. Children's literature may be poetry or prose. February deadline.

The Writers' Union of Canada Postcard Story Competition
24 Ryerson Avenue, Toronto, Ontario M5T 2P3
Website: www.swifty.com/twuc
Prizes: $500

Entry Fee: $5 per entry

For Canadian citizens or landed immigrants. Up to 250 words, fiction or non-fiction, prose, poetry, or dialogue. Enclose SASE for results only. February deadline.

The Writers' Union of Canada Short Prose Contest
24 Ryerson Avenue, Toronto, Ontario M5T 2P3
Website: www.swifty.com/twuc
Prizes: $2,500–$1,000
Entry Fee: $25
Open to either Canadian citizens or landed immigrants who have not yet been published in book form. Entries must be in English, either non-fiction or fiction, 2,000–2,500 words in length. November deadline.

The Writers' Union of Canada Writing for Children Contest
24 Ryerson Avenue, Toronto, Ontario M5T 2P3
Website: www.swifty.com/twuc
Prizes: $1,500
Entry Fee: $15
Open to either Canadian citizens or landed immigrants who have not yet been published in book form. Entries must be in English and up to 1,500 words in length. April deadline.

Zygote Contest
1474 Wall Street, Winnipeg, Manitoba R3E 2S4
E-mail: tschmidt@mail.escape.ca
Prizes: $75–$50–$25, plus publication in *Zygote*
Entry Fee: $16 per story, includes one-year subscription
Story submissions up to 1,500 words, should have an edge and be rough, tough, bizarre, streetwise, or whodunits. Runners up also considered for publication. December deadline.

OTHER CONTEST INFORMATION

Some publications run contests occasionally; others plan to run a contest in the future but had not finalized details at the time of writing. Send an SASE with a request for details to the addresses below.

filling Station
Box 22135 Banker's Hall, Calgary, Alberta T2P 4J5

In 2 Print
PO Box 102, Port Colborne, Ontario L3K 5V7 (For writers aged 14-21 only.)

The Lazy Writer
Box 977, Station F, 50 Charles Street East, Toronto, Ontario M4Y 2N9

The Plowman
Box 414, Whitby, Ontario L1N 5S4 (monthly contest)

Queen Street Quarterly
Box 311, Station P, 704 Spadina Avenue, Toronto, Ontario M5S 2S8

TickleAce
PO Box 5353, St. John's, Newfoundland A I C 5W2

Trout
PO Box 4017, Station E, Ottawa, Ontario K I S 5B I

6.4 WRITING CONTESTS IN THE US

Named here are some of the larger prizes among the many prizes offered in the US. You will find others noted in the periodical sections of this book.

Follow all the guidelines as set out at the beginning of this section. Contact the publication for COMPLETE contest rules before entering. Many publications post their contest rules online. Never send an entry by fax or e-mail. Entry and entry fee must arrive in the same envelope. All dollar amounts in the following short US list are in US funds. Send only your best work.

Boston Review Poetry Contest
E53-407 Massachusetts Institute of Technology, Cambridge, Massachusetts, USA 02139
Prize: $1,000
Entry Fee: $10
Deadline: April

Boulevard Short Fiction Contest for Emerging Writers
4579 Laclede Avenue, #332, St. Louis, Missouri, USA 63108
Prize: $1,000 and publication in *Boulevard*
Entry: $15 per story
Deadline: November

Field Poetry Prize
Rice Hall, Oberlin College, Oberlin, Ohio, USA 44074
Prize: $1,000, plus publication of winning book-length manuscript
Entry Fee: See website (www.oberlin.edu/~ocpress)
Deadline: December

Ezra Pound Poetry Award
Paintbrush: A Journal of Poetry and Transition, Truman State University, Kirksville, Missouri, USA 63501
Prize: $2,000, and publication of winning book-length manuscript
Entry Fee: $25
Deadline: November

Pig Iron Series: Bi-Annual Kenneth Patchen Competition
26 North Phelps Street, PO Box 237, Youngstown, Ohio, USA 44501
Prize: $500, plus publication and 20 copies
Entry Fee: $10, payable to Pig Iron Press
Deadline: Contact for details.

The Pittsburgh Quarterly
36 Haberman Avenue, Pittsburgh, Pennsylvania, USA 15211-2144
Prize: $200, and publication in *The Pittsburgh Quarterly*

Entry Fee: $12, or $14 Canadian, includes one-year subscription to *The Pittsburgh Quarterly*
Deadline: July

Slipstream Poetry Chapbook Competition
PO Box 2071, Niagara Falls, New York, USA 14301
Prize: $1,000, plus publication of manuscript and 50 copies
Entry Fee: $10
Deadline: December

Sonora Review
English Department, University of Arizona, Tuscon, Arizona, USA 85721
Prize: $500, plus publication in *Sonora Review*
Entry Fee: $10, includes one-year subscription
Deadline: July

6.5 INTERNATIONAL WRITING CONTESTS

Named here are some of the many prizes offered by publications internationally.
You will find others noted in the periodical sections of this book.

Aural Images Open Poetry Competition
5 Hamilton Street, Astley Bridge, Bolton, England BL1 6RJ
Prizes: £100–£75–£050, plus publication in *Lateral Moves Magazine*
Entry Fee: £2 per poem, or £10 for 7 poems
Deadline: September
Also awards a number of smaller prizes. There is a 60-line limit per poem. Send a separate sheet with name, address, and telephone number along with a list of your poems entered. Entry form required. Send SAE with IRCs.

Cardiff International Poetry Competition
PO Box 438, Cardiff, Wales, UK CF1 6YA
Prizes: Total more than £5,000
Entry Fee: £4 per poem
Deadline: October
Each poem must be no more than 50 lines in length. Awarded for unpublished poetry written in English. Entry form required. Requests first publication rights for winning poems. December deadline.

HQ (Formerly the Haiku Quarterly)
39 Exmouth Street, Swindon, Wiltshire, England SN1 3PU
Runs annual haiku contest. Write for details.

James Hackett Award
Blithe Spirit: Journal of the British Haiku Society, Hill House Farm, Knighton, Powys, Wales, UK L07 1NA
Competition for single best haiku. Write for details.

Rhyme International Annual Poetry Competition
199 The Long Shoot, Nuneaton, Warks, UK CV11 6JQ
Prizes: £1,000, divided between categories
Entry Fee: £2.50 per poem, minimum £5

Deadline: September

Has two categories: formal and open. All entries must rhyme.

The Scottish International Open Poetry Competition

Ayrshire Writers' and Artists' Society, 42 Tollerton Drive, Irvine, Ayrshire, Scotland KA12 0QE

Prizes: £100 to winner in UK, The MacDiarmid Trophy to Scottish winners and to the winner of the international section, the International Trophy.

Entry Fee: Stated as "none."

Deadline: December

Open to all poets 16 years and older.

Stand Magazine Biennial Writing Awards

179 Wingrove Road, Newcastle upon Tyne, England NE4 9DA

Prizes: £2,500 total to be distributed among winners in each category

Entry Fee: £3.50 for first poem (Varies for more)

Deadline: June

Entry form required. Offers prizes in two categories: poetry and prose fiction. International competition.

Tsujinaka Fiction Award Contest

The Abiko Quarterly with James Joyce Studios, 8-1-8 Namiko, Abiko-shi, Chiba-ken, 270-1165 Japan

Prize: $1,000 US fiction award.

Entry Fee: $10 US

Deadline: December

Send 2 copies of each story entered.

ABOUT THE EDITOR

Marie Savage has given pragmatic and powerful editorial advice to clients for more than 15 years. She specializes in condensing complicated information into accurate, readable text. Long a supporter of poets and their craft, she edited the limited edition Saltwater chapbooks and is developing a new literary festival to be held in Booktown, Sidney-By-The-Sea, BC. In love with the tactile intimacy of poetry in print but excited by the possibilities of the internet, she has become a webmaster for the new millennium.

LISTINGS INDEX

Canada